Stuart Yeoman

Plate 1 A mixture of pre-grouping and post-grouping locomotives; an LMS built 2P 4-4-0 No. 654 attached to a Bowen-Cooke LNWR 'Prince of Wales' class 4-6-0 coming off shed at Crewe on 7th April 1934.
F.G. Carrier

Overleaf: Plate 2 All out effort from Kirtley rebuilt Johnson single framed Midland 1P No. 84 piloting an LMS built 4F 0-6-0 out of Great Rocks Tunnel on a down freight. No. 84 was a Rowsley engine and would have been attached at Rowsley for the climb to Peak Forest.

No 86
GREAT ROCKS
TUNNEL
161 YARDS

THE BIG FOUR REMEMBERED

by

J.S. WHITELEY and G.W. MORRISON

Oxford Publishing Co.

The LMS Remembered (ISBN 0 86093 030 0)
© J.S. Whiteley, G.W. Morrison and Oxford Publishing Co. 1979 and 1989.

This edition published 1989
Reprinted 1989

A FOULIS-OPC Railway Book

British Library Cataloguing in Publication Data
The Big Four remembered.
1. Great Britain. Steam locomotives, 1922–1968. Illustrations
I. Whiteley, J.S. (John Stuart), *1943*– II. Morrison, G.W. (Gavin Wedderburn), *1936*–
625.2'61'0941
ISBN 0-86093-463-2

Library of Congress catalog card number
88-83558

Published by:
Haynes Publishing Group
Sparkford, Near Yeovil, Somerset. BA22 7JJ

Haynes Publications Inc.
861 Lawrence Drive, Newbury Park, California 91320, USA.

Printed by J.H. Haynes & Co. Ltd.

Plate 3 A Johnson Midland 2P 4-4-0 built 1882-1883 and as subsequently rebuilt by Deeley. No. 338 is seen fitted with a Belpaire firebox and extended smokebox heading a down train between Little Eaton Junction and Peckwash Mill sidings, north of Derby.

F.G. Carrier

ACKNOWLEDGEMENT

The authors would like to express their gratitude and appreciation to all the photographers who have so kindly allowed them to use their work and for the friendly assistance offered by so many during the preparation of this book. Particular thanks are offered to Mike Carrier for allowing inclusion of so many of his Father's hitherto unpublished pictures and to Margaret Morley for her part in typing the manuscript.

Contents

Introduction

On January 1st 1923 the London Midland & Scottish Railway came into being as the largest of the 'Big Four' companies which were created by the grouping of Britain's railways by Act of Parliament. Almost 10,500 locomotives were inherited by the LMS at the grouping and the principal constituents in alphabetical order were the Caledonian Railway, the Furness Railway, the Glasgow & South Western Railway, the Highland Railway, the London and North Western Railway (including the North London Railway which had been worked by the LNWR from 1909), the Midland Railway (including the London Tilbury & Southend Railway which had been absorbed by the MR in 1912) and the North Staffordshire Railway. One notable exception from the above is the Lancashire & Yorkshire Railway which had in fact amalgamated with the LNWR exactly one year before the grouping.

By far the greatest contribution in terms of numbers and also advanced passenger locomotive designs came from the LNWR It is, therefore, easy to understand why there was such bad feeling when the MR became the dominating partner in the London Midland & Scottish group when the best they could offer was a variety of 4-4-0s for express passenger work which were certainly no match for the 'Prince of Wales' and 'Claughton' 4-6-0s of the LNWR.

Things did not improve when Sir Henry Fowler, who had been CME of the MR since 1909, succeeded George Hughes as CME of the LMS in 1925 and perpetuated the MR small engine policy. Only in 1927 did the arrival of the 'Royal Scot' 4-6-0s herald the introduction of some new larger locomotives. The Midland stranglehold on the LMS did not really end until William Stanier (later Sir William Stanier) arrived from Swindon and was appointed CME of the LMS in 1932. This in turn heralded massive withdrawals of pre-grouping locomotives which were being replaced by more efficient modern designs which lasted until steam was withdrawn from BR in 1968.

This book is an attempt to show a balanced selection of locomotive designs, some of which were inherited by the LMS in 1923, the remainder of which were conceived by the LMS during its twenty-five years existence until Britain's railways were Nationalised on January 1st 1948.

J.S. Whiteley
Jan. 1979

Plate 4 Above Kirtley double framed Midland 1P 2-4-0, usually referred to as the '800' class due to the original numbers of the first engines being 800 - 829. Forty-eight of these engines were built 1870-1871 but only twenty-four were in service at the grouping, the last one being withdrawn in 1936. No. 67 is seen here at Nottingham Midland.

F.G. Carrier

Plate 5 Above Johnson Midland 1P 2-4-0 No. 238 heading a down local train from Derby near Little Eaton Junction. Sixty-five of these engines were built 1876-1881 and most were re-built with Belpaire fireboxes from 1926 onwards. One engine survived nationalisation and was withdrawn in 1949.

F.G. Carrier

Plate 6 Left One of the Johnson/ Deeley Somerset & Dorset Joint Railway 2P 4-4-0s built 1903-1914. No. 323 is seen fitted with an exhaust smoke injector and being inspected closely by a young admirer. The five engines in this class were rebuilt by Fowler in 1921 similar to the Midland '483' class and absorbed in LMS stock in 1930. No. 323 is about to leave Cromford on a down train in the early 1930's.

F.G. Carrier

Plate 7 Above Rebuilt Johnson Midland 2P 4-4-0 No. 442 with attractive combined sweeping splashers leaving Derby on an up train, passing London Road Junction. Fifty-five of these 6 ft 6 in engines were built 1893-1900 and all the class was rebuilt by Deeley from 1905. Fowler rebuilt thirty-five from 1914 onwards (excluding No. 442) to conform with his '483' class.

F.G. Carrier

Plate 8 Below Johnson Midland 2P '483' class 4-4-0 No. 443 with bogie brakes, on a most attractive rake of stock overtakes a double-headed freight at Breadsall Crossing whilst heading a down express. These engines were built 1882-1901, rebuilt by Deeley from 1904 and further rebuilt with superheater etc. by Fowler between 1912-1923. They were the final development of the Midland Class 2 4-4-0s.

F.G. Carrier

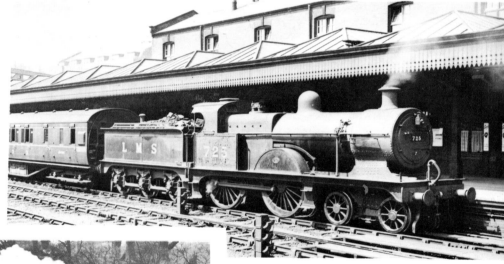

Plate 9 *Above* A BR scene at Stamford Town on 23rd July 1952. Johnson Midland 2P 4-4-0 No. 40543 is seen leaving with the 12.40 Peterborough-Leicester with No. 40559 alongside whilst yard shunting.

P.H. Wells

Plate 10 *Above* Johnson Midland 3P 4-4-0 No. 725 about to depart from Nottingham Midland with a Lincoln train on 23rd May 1939. Eighty of these 6 ft 9 in engines were built between 1900 and 1905 and No. 725 is seen here as rebuilt by Fowler with larger cylinders and superheater.

J.P. Wilson

Plate 11 *Left* Another rebuilt 3P 4-4-0 No. 722 heading a Nottingham-Lincoln train near Colwick Level Crossing in March 1933.

J.P. Wilson

Plate 12 Above One of the two hundred and five Johnson Midland 1P 0-4-4Ts No. 58065 (formerly LMS No. 1367) leaving Southwell with a push and pull train to Rolleston Junction on 29th July 1958. Some of these engines had 5 ft 7 in driving wheels but this is one of the 5 ft 4 in engines as rebuilt from 1925 with Belpaire firebox.

Peter Groom

Plate 13 Right Sister engine 58066 (LMS No. 1368) is seen at Oxenhope with a local train from Keighley about 1955.

W.H. Foster

Plate 14 Left Twenty-eight of these Johnson 0-4-0 Saddletanks were built between 1883 and 1903, some with 13 in x 20 in cylinders and some with 15 in x 20 in cylinders. Twenty-three engines were in service at the grouping, four survived nationalisation and the last was withdrawn from service in 1958. No. 1509 is seen at Derby.

F.G. Carrier

Plate 15 Right Johnson Midland 1F 0-6-0T seen at Skipton in 1950. Two hundred and eighty of these engines were introduced from 1874 and many were rebuilt with Belpaire fireboxes from 1919 onwards. No. 41666, however, is seen with non-Belpaire boiler and safety valve on the dome.

W.H. Foster

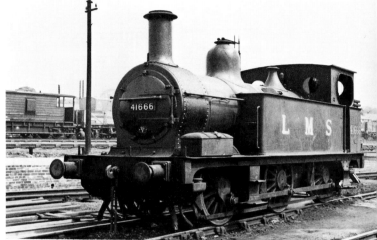

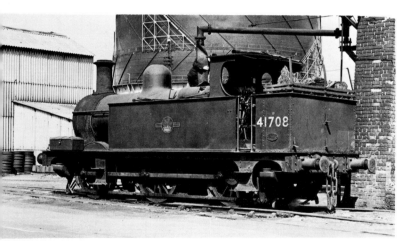

Plate 16 Left No. 41708 of the same class but with a different cab and Belpaire boiler as seen at Staveley on 9th May 1964. This engine has fortunately been preserved.

G.W. Morrison

Plate 17 Right Only eight of these Adams and Hookham North Stafford 0-6-4Ts were built between 1916 and 1919. They were the NSR Class F and No. 2053 is seen at Derby. The last engine was withdrawn from service in 1936.

A.G. Ellis Collection

Plate 18 Right Whitelegg London, Tilbury and Southend 4-4-2T No. 2111 which was actually constructed subsequent to the grouping in 1923 seen on a Southend train.

A.G. Ellis Collection

Plate 19 Below One of the eight Whitelegg London, Tilbury and Southend 'Baltic' tanks at St. Albans in 1930. They were built in 1912 and were the first 4-6-4 tank engines in Britain. This engine was originally numbered 2106 and the last engine in this class was withdrawn in 1934.

A.G. Ellis Collection

Plate 20 Right London, Tilbury and Southend 3P 4-4-2T is seen with a full head of steam on a Fenchurch Street via Upminster train.

A.G. Ellis Collection

Plate 21 *Above* Kirtley Midland double framed 1F 0-6-0
No. 2592 working hard on a down freight near Cromford.
Four hundred and seventy of these engines were built from
1863 and this engine is seen as originally built with Salter
spring balance safety valves on the dome. The last engine
was withdrawn from service in 1951.

F.G. Carrier

Plate 22 *Below* One of the Kirtley Midland double framed
0-6-0s with Class 2 boiler and Ramsbottom safety valves
in place of the original Salter valves.

F.G. Carrier

Plate 23 Right Johnson Midland 2F 0-6-0 with 4 ft 11 in wheels. Nine hundred and thirty-five of these engines were built between 1875 and 1908 and No. 3153 is seen here with Belpaire firebox at Derby.

F.G. Carrier

Plate 24 Above No. 43814 is seen after nationalisation with a freight at Cheadle Heath with a Class 3 Belpaire boiler.

T. Lewis

Plate 25 Right One hundred and ninety-two Fowler Midland 4F 0-6-0s were built between 1911 and 1922 and No. 3951 which was built for the Midland by Armstrong-Whitworth is seen on a down rake of empty wagons near Breadsall Crossing. The housings for tail rods can clearly be seen on the buffer beam and these were later removed and the holes blanked off. The beading on the splashers was a feature of these Midland built 0-6-0s.

F.G. Carrier

Plate 26 *Left* An unidentified Webb LNWR 'Precedent' class 1P 2-4-0 with pre-grouping number is seen just after the grouping on an up train believed to be just south of Tamworth. One hundred and sixty-six of these 6 ft 9 in engines were built between 1874 and 1901.

F.G. Carrier

Plate 28 *Below* Whale LNWR 'Precursor' 4-4-0 No. 25245 *Antaeus* at Shugborough Park on a down local on 11th August 1939. (See also *Plate 240*).

E.G. Ashton

Plate 27 *Above* Webb 'Precedent' No. 5000 *Princess Beatrice* stands at Nottingham Low Level with a Northampton train.
T.G. Hepburn

Plate 29 *Below* Rebuilt 'Precursor' No. 25304 *Greyhound* with superheater and Belpaire firebox stands at Bletchley on an Oxford train in 1938.

C.R.L. Coles

Plate 30 Right Bowen-Cooke 'George the Fifth' class 4-4-0 No. 5343 *Otterhound* which was built in May 1911. This class of ninety engines was a development of the 'Precursor' 4-4-0s and were built at Crewe between 1910 and 1915. Only three engines survived nationalisation, the last one being withdrawn in 1948.

F.G. Carrier

Plate 31 Left Bowen-Cooke 'Prince of Wales' Class 3P 4-6-0 No. 25791 on a very mixed freight at South Kenton. Two hundred and forty-five of these engines were constructed between 1911 and 1921 with one additional engine constructed after the grouping in 1924. 20,000 were added to their numbers in 1934 and many of the latter survivors were rebuilt with Belpaire fireboxes as seen here.

A.G. Ellis Collection

Plate 32 Right Another 'Prince of Wales' rebuilt with a Belpaire firebox, No. 25818 is seen on an up local at Shugborough Park on 11th August 1939.

E.G. Ashton

Plate 33 *Above* The Bowen-Cooke 'Claughton' four cylinder 4-6-0s were surely the pride of LNWR. One hundred and thirty of these fine engines were built at Crewe between 1913 and 1921 and here No. 5984, paired with a Robinson ROD tender is approaching Duffield on a down Manchester express.

F.G. Carrier

Plate 34 *Below* Another 'Claughton' 4-6-0 No. 5903 *Duke of Sutherland* (named after a director of the LNWR) is heading an up express near Tamworth.

F.G. Carrier

Plate 35 Right From 1928 the LMS rebuilt twenty 'Claughtons' with larger boilers. These were later fitted with smoke deflectors and No. 6004 is seen heading a down freight on Dillicar Troughs in 1946. This was the last engine of the Class to remain in service, being formerly named *Princess Louise*. It was finally withdrawn from service in 1948 having outlasted the previous member of the Class by about seven years.

W. Philip Conolly

Plate 36 Left A Webb LNWR 1P 2-4-2T No. 6732 in immaculate condition. One hundred and sixty of these 5 ft 6 in engines were built between 1890 and 1897 and the last one survived until 1955.

A.G. Ellis Collection

Plate 37 Right The slightly heavier 5 ft 0 in Webb LNWR 1P 0-6-2T is seen here. Eighty of these engines were built between 1898 and 1902. Three were withdrawn from service before the grouping and the last was withdrawn in 1953.

F.G. Carrier

Plate 38 *Left* Webb LNWR 'Cauliflower' 0-6-0 No. 8589 on a local near Keswick. Three hundred and ten of these engines were built between 1880 and 1902 and this was one of the latter survivors, being rebuilt with a Belpaire firebox.

E.E. Smith

Plate 39 *Right* Another rebuilt 'Cauliflower' No. 8422 is seen on a three coach train near Keswick. Sixty-nine of these engines survived until nationalisation.

E.E. Smith

Plate 40 *Below* A Whale '19 in Goods' Class 4F 4-6-0 No. 8843 heading a down train has just emerged from Milford Tunnel shortly after leaving Duffield. One hundred and seventy of these engines were built between 1906 and 1909 many being fitted with Belpaire fireboxes in later years. Only three survived nationalisation, the last one being withdrawn in 1950.

F.G. Carrier

Plate 41 *Above* Bowen-Cooke LNWR 7F Class 'G2a' No. 49340 climbing Grayrigg Bank with a down freight in April 1954.

W.H. Foster

Plate 42 *Below* Only four of these Pettigrew Furness 6 ft 6 in 4-4-0s were built between 1900 and 1901, the last engine being withdrawn in 1931. No. 10144 is seen leaving Carlisle believed to be on a Maryport train.

A.G. Ellis Collection

Plate 43 *Above* An Aspinall 2P 4-4-2 (L & YR Class L1) in full cry seen in its final form with wide chimney and circular smoke box on saddle. Forty of these 'high flyer' Atlantics were built between 1899 and 1902 with massive 7 ft 3 in driving wheels. All were in service at the grouping and the last one was withdrawn in 1934.
A.G. Ellis Collection

Plate 44 *Right* Sister engine No. 10307 picks up water on Salwick troughs in August 1930 with a Blackpool Central-Skipton train. These engines were never superheated and were the only inside cylinder Atlantics in Britain with the exception of one unique GWR 4-4-2.
F. Dean

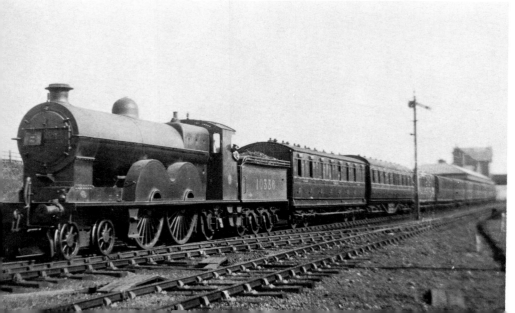

Plate 45 *Left* Another 7 ft 3 in Atlantic No. 10336 is seen leaving Ansdell in October 1926 with an afternoon Liverpool Exchange-Blackpool Central train.
F. Dean

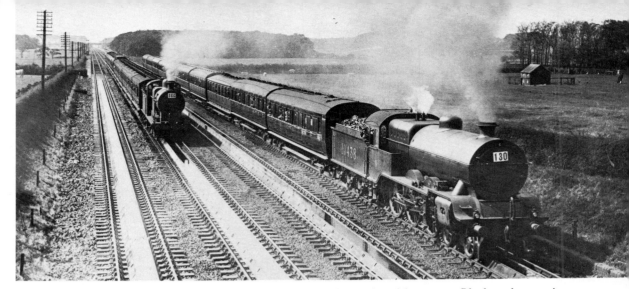

Plate 46 *Above* Hughes L & YR 5P 4-6-0 No. 10438 on Lea Road troughs with a return Blackpool excursion overtaking a 4F 0-6-0 also on a return excursion. No. 10438 was one of the engines which entered service early in 1923, the first engines of this class appearing in 1921 (see also *Plate 248*).

A.G. Ellis Collection

Plate 47 *Above* Only one of these Hughes 4-6-0s survived long enough to carry its BR number and it is seen here as No. 50455 passing Burton Salmon on a Blackpool-York special on 1st July 1951.

P.H. Wells

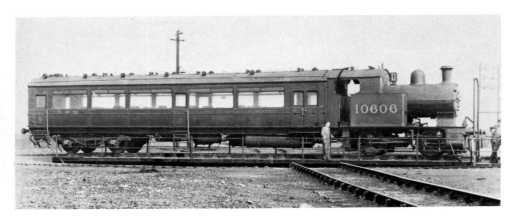

Plate 48 *Left* Hughes L & YR Rail Motor No. 10606 at Agecroft. Eighteen of these were built between 1906 and 1911, the last unit being withdrawn shortly after nationalisation in 1948.

A.G. Ellis Collection

Plate 49 Right Aspinall L & YR 2-4-2T No. 10869 passes Holbeck with a down local. These were the L & YR Class K2 engines, 309 of which were built between 1889 and 1910.

A.G. Ellis Collection

Plate 50 Below Late in its life No. 50646 is seen running into Bamford with the 09.00 Hope—Sheffield local on 28th September 1955.

R.E. Vincent

Plate 51 Right On 26th May 1956 No. 50865 fitted with extended bunker is seen heading a Calder Valley local passing Heaton Lodge Junction, Mirfield.

B.R. Goodlad

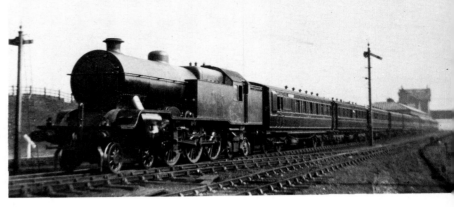

Plate 52 Right Hughes L & YR 4-6-4T, No 11113 leaving Ansdell in July 1927 with a Manchester Victoria-Blackpool Central train. These engines were not built until 1924 but were essentially a Lancashire and Yorkshire design being Class P1. These were the tank engine version of the Hughes 4-6-0 and all ten were withdrawn between 1938 and 1942.

F. Dean

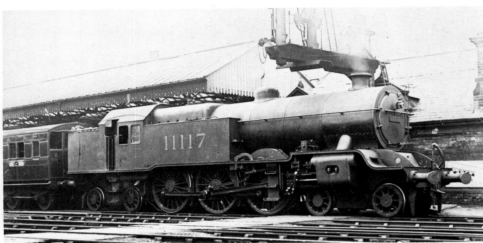

Plate 53 Left The massive proportions of these 6 ft 3 in four cylinder 'Baltic' tanks can be seen in this side view of No. 11117.

A.G. Ellis Collection

Plate 54 Below The Aspinall L & YR 2F 0-6-0s were a Class of 448 being built between 1889 and 1917 (L & YR Class F19). Some of these engines were later rebuilt with Belpaire fireboxes but No. 52362 is seen as originally built heading a special goods near Leyland in 1949.

W.H. Foster

Plate 55 *Above* McIntosh Caledonian 'Dunalastair IV' with non-superheated boiler. Nineteen of these engines were built between 1904 and 1910 the last one surviving until 1948.

A.G. Ellis Collection

Plate 56 *Right* Drummond built twenty 'Small Ben' Class 2P 4-4-0s for the Highland Railway between 1898 and 1906. No. 14401 *Ben Vrackie* is seen still with smokebox wingplates shunting at Inverness on 22nd August 1928.

E.G. Ashton

Plate 57 *Below* The smokebox wingplates have been removed in this picture of Nos. 14402 *Ben Armin* and 14408 *Ben Hope* seen leaving Keith.

A.G. Ellis Collection

Plate 58 Left The 'Large Ben' 2P 4-4-0s were built by Drummond for the Highland Railway between 1908 and 1909. Only six of these engines were built and No. 14417 *Ben na Caillach* is seen fitted with extended smokebox at Aviemore on 15th April 1933.
F.G. Carrier

Plate 59 Right Pickersgill Caledonian 3P 4-4-0 is seen here with its BR No. 54494 at Perth with a train from Dundee. These were the Pickersgill '72' class.

T.G. Hepburn

Plate 60 Left Sister engine No. 14501 in LMS days at Perth on 21st May 1933. All forty-eight of these engines carried their BR numbers 54461-54508, the first one being withdrawn in 1953 and the last one ten years later.

F.G. Carrier

Plate 61 Left Ten of these McIntosh Caledonian '908' Class 4P 4-6-0s were built in 1906, mainly for use on the Clyde coast line. Nos. 14610 and 14612 were originally named *Sir James King* and *Barochan* but these names were removed shortly after the grouping. No. 14616 is seen here on a northbound freight shortly after leaving Perth in the early 1930's .

A.G. Ellis Collection

Plate 62 Above The Drummond Highland Railway 3P 'Castle' 4-6-0s were built between 1900 and 1917 in three separate batches by Dübs & Co and NBL. A total of nineteen were built, sixteen with 5 ft 9 in driving wheels and the last three, Nos. 14691/3 with 6 ft 0 in driving wheels. Here we see one of the three 6 ft 0 in engines No. 14692 *Darnaway Castle* leaving Inverness.

A.G. Ellis Collection

Plate 63 Left 'River' class 4-6-0 No. 14757, formerly HR No. 71 *River Spey*, standing at Perth shed. Six of these engines were designed by Smith for the HR in 1915 but after they were found to be too heavy for the lines of the HR they were sold to the Caledonian Railway and subsequently proved to be probably their best 4-6-0s.

T.G. Hepburn

Plate 64 Right 'River' class 4-6-0 No. 14761 seen leaving Carlisle on a northbound freight.

A.G. Ellis Collection

Plate 65 Left McIntosh Caledonian 2P 0-4-4T No. 55204 shunting on the docks of Oban in the summer of 1961. There were sixty-eight of these CR '439' class engines built between 1900 and 1914, the majority survived to Nationalisation, the last one being withdrawn in 1962. In later years many were fitted with these ugly stove pipe chimneys.

J.S. Whiteley

Plate 66 Right One of the twelve Pickersgill Caledonian '944' class 4P 4-6-2Ts No. 15351 seen on a Glasgow suburban train. They were built in 1917 and the last engines of the class ended their days as banking engines at Beattock.

A.G. Ellis Collection

Plate 67 Left Whitelegg G & SWR 5P 4-6-4T No. 15402 leaving Glasgow St. Enoch on a suburban train of six wheelers. Only six of these splendid engines were built just prior to the grouping, in 1922, and the last one was withdrawn in 1935.

A.G. Ellis Collection

LMS DESIGNS

Plate 68 Above A Fowler 2-6-2T No. 40060 fitted for push and pull working leaving Kensal Green Tunnel on a down empty stock train on 20th June 1959. Seventy of these engines were built between 1930 and 1932 nineteen of which were fitted with condensing apparatus for working to Moorgate.

Peter Groom

Plate 69 Above No. 40061 of the same class and also fitted with push and pull apparatus seen between duties.

Author's Collection

Plate 70 Left These engines were not a particularly good design and after the War most of the Class were fitted with a larger blast-pipe and chimney and outside steampipes in an attempt to improve their performance. No. 40047 is seen as modified on 21st March 1954 on empty stock at Willesden.

P.H. Wells

Plate 71 Above In 1935 the Stanier development of the 1930 Fowler design was introduced with a taper boiler with the same basic dimensions. A total of 139 were built at Derby and Crewe between 1935 and 1938 and here No. 40082 is seen fitted with a larger diameter chimney used in conjunction with the 'Adams Vortex' blastpipe. It is seen in July 1959 near Altofts on a Leeds-Sheffield train.

N. Stead

Plate 72 Below Class 2P 4-4-0 No. 40666 leaving Saltcoates near Ardrossan on 27th July 1959. One hundred and thirty-eight of these engines were built between 1928 and 1932 and were a development of the Midland design with modified dimensions and boiler mountings. All these engines had left-hand drive and they operated over most parts of the LMS System.

G.W. Morrison

Plate 73 *Above* Three-cylinder compound 4P 4-4-0 No. 40929 heading a Nottingham-Aintree Grand National special near Hazel Grove on 7th April 1951. One hundred and ninety-five of these engines were built between 1924 and 1932 and they were a Fowler post-grouping development of the Midland design.

T. Lewis

Plate 74 *Left* A down Morecambe train as seen in 1937 near Bell Busk behind 4P 4-4-0 No. 931 which was built by the Vulcan Foundry in 1927.

W.H. Foster

Plate 75 *Above* Three Compounds for the price of one at Sheffield Midland on August Bank Holiday Saturday 1952. No. 41191 is standing on the platform whilst No. 41119 piloting 41181 pass on the centre road.

B.R. Goodlad

Plate 76 *Below* Holbeck Compound No. 41137 makes an impressive departure from Bradford Forster Square for Leeds.

L. Overend

Plate 77 Above Stanier 2P 0-4-4T No. 41900 is seen standing at Ashchurch.

J.D. Edwards

Plate 78 Below What a difference a chimney can make: No. 6408 (BR re-numbered 41908) is seen on a Watford - St. Albans train. Ten engines of this class were introduced in 1932 and credited to Stanier simply because it was a coincidence that they were constructed shortly after Stanier had taken up office, although designed previously by E.G.H. Lemon.

F.G. Carrier

Plate 79 Right A picture taken at St. Pancras in 1936 showing on the left a Fowler 2-6-4T No. 2341 which was Derby built in 1929 and on the right a Fowler 2-6-2T No. 28 which was also built at Derby in 1931 and fitted with condensing apparatus for working to Moorgate.
W. Philip Conolly

Plate 80 Below Fowler 2-6-4T No. 42393 stands at Chester Northgate on 18th May 1959. The last of this class was withdrawn from service in 1966.
S.D. Wainwright

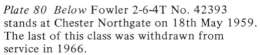

Plate 81 Below Fowler 2-6-4T No. 42339 accelerating from Melton Mowbray (Town) with the 13.45 local to Nottingham in April 1957.
Peter Groom

Plate 82 *Above* Fowler 2-6-4T No. 42398 on an up local drifting into Heaton Norris alongside LNW G2a Class 0-8-0 No. 49355.

T. Lewis

Plate 84 *Below* One of the Fairburn 2-6-4Ts introduced in 1945. No. 42680 is seen leaving Mill Hill and Broadway with the 16.40 St. Pancras-St. Albans stopper in May 1957.

B. Morrison

Plate 83 *Below* Thirty-seven of these three cylinder 2-6-4Ts were built at Derby in 1934 for use on the Southend line. No. 42534 is seen on a down Tilbury Line suburban between Purfleet and Grays on 6th April 1957.

R.E. Vincent

Plate 85 *Above* Hughes/Fowler mixed traffic 2-6-0s Nos. 13103 and 13101 north of Dunkeld heading the 15.45 Inverness-Glasgow express early in the 1930's. Two hundred and forty-five of these engines were built between 1926 and 1932, ten of which were allocated to the Highland section early in their working lives.

F.G. Carrier

Plate 86 *Right* These engines were nick-named 'Crabs' and No. 42920 is seen at Nottingham Victoria on 9th May 1964 shunting stock on transfer to the Midland route.

T. Boustead

Plate 90 Above Only forty of these Stanier 2-6-0s were built between 1933 and 1934 at Crewe and No. 42959 is climbing past Thrimby Grange on an early morning up freight on 21st August 1964.

J.S. Whiteley

Plate 91 Left Another member of the Class, No. 42964 is on a Leeds—Manchester local passing Farnley Junction MPD on 17th May 1960.

G.W. Morrison

Plate 92 Above LMS built 4F No. 4153 which was one of the first batches built with right-hand drive, is seen on down mixed freight soon after leaving Derby. These engines were a development of the Midland design and 575 were built by the LMS between 1924 and 1928.

F.G. Carrier

Plate 93 Below 4F No. 44335 heads a down coal train past Wortley Junction, Leeds, on 18th December 1962.

J.S. Whiteley

Plate 94 Above The 4Fs were often seen on passenger workings and here No. 44273 makes a somewhat smokey departure from Kings Lynn in July 1959 with a Hunstanton train.

N. Stead

Plate 95 Below The Stanier Class 5 4-6-0s were possibly the most successful of Stanier's designs with as many as 842 being built between 1935 and 1947. Here No. 45444 with banking assistance climbs past Shap Wells with a mixed freight on 7th October 1967.

J.S. Whiteley

Plate 96 Above Crewe South Class 5 No. 45067 thunders through Bangor with the relief 'Irish Mail' in summer 1963.
B. Wynne

Plate 97 Below A bird's eye view of Bangor on 27th June 1956 with three Class 5s in evidence. The MPD is in the centre of the picture and the goods depot can be seen on the right hand side.
R.E. Vincent

Plate 98 Above Simultaneous departures from Bradford Exchange at 08.20 on Saturday 22nd July 1963, No. 44662 on the right hand side is on a Skegness train and No. 44694 on the left is heading a Bridlington train.

D.J. Wood

Plate 99 Left The Stanier Class 5s wandered far and wide and No. 44836 is seen leaving Bristol Temple Meads on a holiday extra to Weston-super-Mare on 2nd June 1963.

J.S. Whiteley

Plate 100 Right Class 5s or 'Black Fives' as they were often referred to were regularly to be seen on freight duties and early one stormy morning No. 45025 slows at Tebay for banking assistance to Shap Summit on a down mixed freight.

W. Philip Conolly

Plate 101 Above In 1930 two four-cylinder re-boilered 'Claughtons', Nos. 5902 and 5971, were rebuilt at Derby to a design similar to the three-cylinder 'Royal Scot' class 4-6-0s, but with a lower axle loading. In fact very little of the 'Claughtons' was retained and they were quickly nicknamed 'Baby Scots'. No. 5971, as yet un-named, was the first of these two engines to appear and it is seen here near Bingley on an up express before being fitted with smoke deflectors. This engine was renumbered 5500 in 1934 and given the name *Patriot* in 1937 from a withdrawn 'Claughton', the whole class being subsequently officially described as the 'Patriot' class.

W.H. Foster

Plate 102 Below A further forty 'rebuilds' appeared in 1932 and 1933 from Crewe and Derby although it is very doubt-ful if any of the original 'Claughton' parts were retained. One of these engines as BR renumbered 45511 *Isle of Man* is passing through Penrith heading an up freight.

W. Philip Conolly

Plate 103 *Above* The last regular passenger workings of the 'Patriots' were between Leeds and Carnforth and No. 45543 *Home Guard* of Carnforth MPD is leaving Leeds on 6th June 1962 on the 13.54 to Carnforth.

G.W. Morrison

Plate 104 *Right* An interesting scene at Chester General on 4th March 1961. No. 45547, one of the 'Patriots' never to receive a name, is seen coupled up to 'Hall' class 4-6-0 No. 6922 *Burton Hall* waiting to proceed to 6A shed. Pacific No. 46209 *Princess Beatrice* is seen in the background heading a Holyhead-London meat train.

S.D. Wainwright

Plate 105 *Above* Eighteen of the class of fifty-two 'Patriots' were rebuilt from 1946 with the same Crewe 2A boiler which had been fitted to the converted 'Royal Scots' (see *Plates 121-4*). They were also fitted with a new Stanier cab and 4000 gallon, nine ton high curved tender. Despite a slightly lower tractive effort these rebuilt 'Patriots' were considered equal to the converted 'Royal Scots' and No. 45530 *Sir Frank Ree* is heading an up Manchester express near Adlington.

T. Lewis

Plate 106 *Below* No. 45530 *Sir Frank Ree* is leaving Euston during rebuilding of the terminal on 20th May 1964 with the 17.27 semi-fast to Rugby. This was the last of the rebuilt 'Patriots' to be withdrawn in January 1966.

M. Welch

Plate 107 Right Between 1934 and 1936 one hundred and ninety-one three-cylinder 'Jubilee' Class 4-6-0s were built by Stanier for intermediate main line passenger work. They were essentially a taper-boiler development of the Fowler parallel-boilered 'Patriots', and here No. 5614 *Leeward Islands* of Kentish Town is standing at St. Pancras in 1937 paired with the high sided version of the narrow Fowler tender.

F.G. Carrier

Plate 108 Right In 1949 No. 45675 *Hardy* fitted with a Stanier tender is leaving Elstree Tunnel with a down express.

J.G. Dewing

Plate 109 *Left* No. 45601 *British Guiana* of Camden, with a 2-6-4T banking, starts the two mile climb at 1 in 100 at Macclesfield with the midday Manchester–Euston express in 1957.

M. Welch

Plate 110 *Below* On the evening of 8th June 1964 No. 45653 *Barham* takes the West Coast main line out of Preston with a down express.

D.I. Wood

Plate 111 *Above* No. 45606 *Falkland Islands* accelerating away from Bingley towards Keighley on a Leeds—Morecambe train.

W.H. Foster

Plate 112 *Below* The 'Jubilees' ended their day working from Holbeck MPD, Leeds and No. 45593 *Kolhapur* seen here was one of the last engines to be withdrawn from service, and subsequently preserved. On 12th August 1967 during its Indian summer it is seen nearing Gargrave with the afternoon relief to the down 'Thames-Clyde Express'.

J.S. Whiteley

Plate 113 *Above* The introduction of the Fowler three-cylinder 'Royal Scot' class 4-6-0s in 1927 made a vast improvement to the express passenger power of the LMSR. The first batch of fifty were all built by North British in 1927 and they proved so successful that a further twenty were built at Derby in 1930. No. 6110 *Grenadier Guardsman,* fitted with bogie brakes which were removed by Stanier, leaves Rugby with a Euston–Glasgow train.

T.G. Hepburn

Plate 114 *Left* By 1932 all the 'Royal Scots' had been fitted with smoke deflectors and No. 6151 *The Royal Horse Guardsman* is seen fitted with the first type of vertical deflectors at Lancaster Castle but still paired with the original Fowler tender.

W.H. Foster

Plate 115 *Below* Stanier was responsible for substituting new high sided curved top tenders for the original Fowler tenders and No. 6109 *Royal Engineer* is seen at Tring in 1939, so fitted, heading a down Manchester express. It has also been fitted with angled top smoke deflectors.

C.R.L. Coles

Plate 116 Above No. 46165 *The Ranger (12th London Regt.)* rushes through Watford Junction on a down express.
N. Stead

Plate 117 Below No. 46156 *The South Wales Borderer* in early BR lined black livery is heading a Fleetwood-London fish train near Farrington in the early 1950s.
W. H. Foster

Plate 118 *Left* Twenty-eight of the 'Royal Scots' were still running with Fowler parallel boilers when the railways were nationalised in 1948 and No. 46165 *The Ranger (12th London Regt.)* is seen in BR days near Colwyn Bay.

N. Stead

Plate 119 *Right* No. 6119 *Lancashire Fusilier* passing Carpenders Park in 1933 on an up working of the Royal Train on the occasion of a Royal visit to Liverpool to open the Mersey Tunnel.

C.R.L. Coles

Plate 120 *Left* The up 'Irish Mail' passing Tring Summit in 1938 behind No. 6127 *Old Contemptibles*.

C.R.L. Coles

Plate 121 *Above* In 1943 the first of the 'Royal Scots' was fitted by Stanier with the new 2A taper boiler and double chimney. These engines were known officially as 'Converted Royal Scots', although bearing in mind very little of the Fowler engine remained 'Rebuilt Scot' is more appropriate. No. 46144 *Honourable Artillery Company* is seen passing Hatch End on a down Liverpool express in 1949.

C.R.L. Coles

Plate 122 *Below* No. 46105 *Cameron Highlander* makes a fine sight at Scout Green on the climb to Shap Summit heading a down express.

W. Philip Conolly

Plate 123 *Above* Smoke deflectors were not fitted immediately after rebuilding but problems with drifting exhaust caused small curved smoke deflectors to be fitted to the entire class from 1947 with the exception of No. 46106 which received straight sided deflectors. No. 46118 *Royal Welch Fusilier* is seen at Hatch End in 1950 on a down Liverpool express.

C.R.L. Coles

Plate 124 *Below* Converted 'Scots' were extremely successful locomotives and in later years often deputised at short notice for Pacifics. Here the heavy afternoon Euston-Perth, usually Pacific-hauled, is seen on 18th August 1959 leaving Rugby behind No. 46141 *The North Staffordshire Regiment*.

Peter Groom

Plate 125 *Above* The first of Stanier's Pacifics appeared from Crewe in July 1933, just seventeen months after he had taken office as CME of the LMSR. These supremely handsome four-cylinder engines were designed to replace 'Royal Scots' on the heavy Euston-Glasgow services and a further locomotive was also introduced in 1933, the remaining ten in the class not being delivered until 1935. Here No. 6201 *Princess Elizabeth* nears Carlisle on an up express with its original domeless boiler but with a 4000 gallon, ten ton capacity high curved side tender which was fitted to all twelve of the class late 1936/early 1937.

F.G. Carrier

Plate 126 *Below* No. 46205 *Princess Victoria* pounding past Harrisons sidings on the climb to Shap Summit with the morning Glasgow-Birmingham train on 19th May 1959.

G.W. Morrison

Plate 127 Left In 1938 No. 6205 *Princess Victoria* is seen heading the up 'Merseyside Express' passing King's Langley. A modified valve motion was fitted to this locomotive in 1937 and the modified bracket can clearly be seen in both this picture and also the picture of No. 46205 on the previous page.

C.R.L. Coles

Plate 128 Right Edge Hill 'Princess Royal' No. 46203 *Princess Margaret Rose* in blue livery heads north past Wembley in 1951 on the down 'Merseyside Express'.

C.R.L. Coles

Plate 129 Below A fine picture of No. 46207 *Princess Arthur of Connaught,* one of the four engines of this class to receive Crimson Lake livery in 1958, leaving Euston on 31st August 1961 heading the down 'Midday Scot'. The entire class had been put into store by early 1961 but some, including No. 46207 were returned to traffic during the summer, only to be put into store again in the autumn. Six engines were rather surprisingly returned to traffic in January 1962 and were finally withdrawn from service in the autumn of 1962.

Peter Groom

Plate 130 Above In June 1935 the sole non-condensing turbine engine was built at Crewe, the Turbomotive as it became known. Although basically similar in many respects to the 'Princess Royal' class, the principle of turbine drive was totally different. There were two turbines at the front of the engine, the large one on the left hand side for forward running and a smaller one on the right hand side for reverse running. During the majority of its life it was employed on Euston-Liverpool services and it is seen here on an up express south of Crewe with its second boiler with steam dome and separate top feed.

F.G. Carrier

Plate 131 Below Although the Turbomotive was given the No. 6202 it was never officially named. It is seen here on 13th August 1949 as BR No. 46202 passing Watford Junction with the 08.30 Euston-Liverpool, having been fitted with smoke deflectors in 1939. When the locomotive required extensive renewals it was decided to rebuild it as a conventional Pacific and she emerged from Crewe in August 1952 as BR No. 46202 *Princess Anne* (see *Plate 267*). Tragically it was damaged beyond economic repair in the Harrow disaster of October 1952.

H.C. Casserley

Plate 132 *Above* In 1937 five of Stanier's streamlined Pacifics Nos. 6220-6224 were delivered in striking blue livery with silver lining and No. 6223 *Princess Alice* is seen heading the up 'Coronation Scot' near Tamworth. The performance of these outstanding engines was improved still further when they were later fitted with double blast-pipes and chimneys.

F.G. Carrier

Plate 133 *Below* No. 6231 *Duchess of Atholl* was turned out in 1938 non-streamlined in maroon and gilt livery and it is seen passing Tring Summit on the down 'Midday Scot' shortly after being delivered. This first batch of non-stream-lined engines comprised Nos. 6230-6234 and altogether twenty-four engines were constructed in streamlined condition and fourteen engines non-streamlined between 1937 and 1948.

C.R.L. Coles

Plate 134 Right In blue and silver livery the 'Coronation Scot' passing Headstone Lane in 1937 behind No. 6221 *Queen Elizabeth*.
        A.G. Ellis Collection

Plate 135 Above No. 6227 *Duchess of Devonshire* was one of the second batch of streamlined engines built in 1938 and is seen in maroon and gold livery coming off the water troughs at Hest Bank on the up 'Royal Scot' in July 1939.
        W.H. Foster

Plate 136 Right Maintenance problems aggravated by many inaccessible parts prompted the decision to be taken to remove the streamlined casings from all the locomotives so fitted from 1946. Front end modifications were necessary but the original smokeboxes were retained until they became life expired. As a result the angled smokebox which can be seen in this picture was for sometime a feature of de-streamlined engines. No. 46240 *City of Coventry* recovers from a signal check at Bletchley on the down 'Royal Scot'.
        W. Philip Conolly

Plate 137 *Above* The 'Coronation' Pacifics were all fitted with smoke deflectors after the war and de-streamlined No. 46242 *City of Glasgow* is passing Bay Horse in 1952 on an up express.

W. H. Foster

Plate 138 *Below* By 1958 de-streamlined No. 46241 *City of Edinburgh* had obtained a new smokebox and it is seen climbing towards Shap Summit at Scout Green on the down 'Royal Scot' on 26th May 1958.

G.W. Morrison

Plate 139 Right No. 46223 *Princess Alice* is still seen with an angled smokebox on 7th May 1950 passing Polmadie on an up express.

J.L. Stevenson

Plate 140 Above No. 46250 *City of Lichfield* was one of the non-streamlined engines built in 1944 and here it is seen leaving Lancaster Castle with a down express. Note the continuation of the footplating at the front end which was a feature of the non-streamlined engines.

British Rail/Oxford Publishing Co.

Plate 141 Right On 12th August 1960 No. 46244 *King George VI* is ready to leave Glasgow Central on the up 'Midday Scot'. It is hard to understand why the last nineteen engines of this fine class, precisely half the entire class of thirty-eight, were so unceremoniously withdrawn in September 1964, only to be replaced by very mediocre diesels, when some of the 'Coronation' Pacifics were reputed to be in such extremely good mechanical condition.

G.W. Morrison

Plate 142 Above The Fowler post-grouping development of the Johnson Midland design was the standard LMS shunting engine. 422 of these 0-6-0Ts were built between 1924 and 1930 and several examples have been preserved. These 3F 0-6-0Ts were nick-named 'Jinties' in later years and No. 47662 is on station pilot duties at Lancaster Castle on 13th May 1964.

M. Welch

Plate 143 Below Class 3F 0-6-0T No. 47410 climbs from the Quay at Holyhead with a train of cattle bound for the cattle dock on the left hand side of the picture on 2nd September 1965.

S.D. Wainwright

Plate 144 *Above* Thirty-three of these 2-6-0: 0-6-2 Garratts were delivered by Beyer Peacock, the three prototypes in 1927 and the remaining thirty in 1930. No. 4999 was one of the prototypes, Nos. 4997-9, and these first three were the only ones to be fitted with vacuum brakes. They were also fitted with rigid rectangular coal bunkers and No. 4999 worked a test train from Derby to St. Pancras in 1936 with a Dynamometer car next to the engine. It is seen after leaving Derby near Borrowash just before it ran hot and had to be removed from the train.

F.G. Carrier

Plate 145 *Below* In December 1954 BR No. 47987 is nearing Melton Mowbray with an up freight. The Beyer Peacock patent steam driven rotary coal bunker as fitted in 1932/3 to all but two engines is clearly seen. BR Nos. 47998 and 47999 retained their rigid bunkers and the last of the class, No. 47994 was withdrawn in 1958.

Peter Groom

Plate 146 Above The Stanier 8F 2-8-0 became the standard heavy freight engine of the LMS, 852 being built between 1935 and 1945, many going overseas during World War II. Unusually No. 48553 is seen on passenger duty heading a return excursion from Cleethorpes in May 1959.

N. Stead

Plate 147 Below In 1962 No. 48294 on more customary freight duty is passing Heaton Lodge Junction, Mirfield heading an eastbound fitted freight.

D.I. Wood

Plate 148 Above On 15th February 1962 No. 48532 struggles past Peak Forest summit with a heavy mixed freight from the Manchester area to Buxton. Several of these efficient engines lasted until steam was eliminated from British Rail in 1968 and a few examples have been preserved.

J.S. Whiteley

Plate 149 Below One hundred and seventy-five of these Fowler 7F 0-8-0s were introduced between 1929 and 1932 but were superseded by Stanier's taper-boilered 8Fs. Often referred to as 'Austin Sevens' No. 49578 is leaving Standedge Tunnel near Marsden in 1957 with a train of coal and coke empties. The last member of the class was withdrawn in 1962.

G.W. Morrison

A GLIMPSE AT THE SOMERSET AND DORSET

Plate 150 Left The Somerset and Dorset Joint Railway ran from Bath Junction to Broadstone connecting Bath and Bournemouth via a very scenic line which ran over the Mendip Hills with a summit of 811 feet above sea level at Masbury. The MPD at Bath was not far from the terminus, Bath, Green Park and on shed on Sunday 7th June 1964 are to be seen two classes of engines which gave stirling service to the line. On the left is S & D Class 7F 2-8-0 No. 53807 and on the right Class 4F 0-6-0 No. 44558.

G.W. Morrison

Plate 151 Above On 28th July 1962 S & D 7F 2-8-0 No. 53808 near Wellow on a Nottingham-Birmingham train.

G.W. Morrison

Plate 152 Left A summer Saturdays only Birmingham-Bournemouth train behind 2P 4-4-0 No. 40700 and BR standard Class 5 4-6-0 No. 73087 on 12th August 1961. They are leaving Chilcompton Tunnel working hard on the severe climb from Radstock to Masbury Summit.

G.W. Morrison

Plate 153 Right The severe climb to Masbury Summit started at Evercreech Junction and many northbound trains were assisted from here for the climb over the Mendips. Class 2P 4-4-0 No. 40564 and 7F 2-8-0 No. 53806 are leaving Evercreech Junction on 9th September 1961 on a Bournemouth-Nottingham train. The mechanical tablet catching apparatus for single line working can be seen behind the cab of the 2P.

G.W. Morrison

Plate 154 Below Nos. 40564 and 53806 are seen again on the same train working hard on the 1 in 50 gradient at the approach to Winsor Hill Tunnel about two miles from Masbury Summit.

G.W. Morrison

TITLED TRAINS

Plate 155 Left The name 'Royal Scot'
was given to the 10.00 departures
from Euston and Glasgow Central in
1927 and during its career has incorporated stops at Rugby, Crewe,
Preston, Carlisle and Symington with
additional stops during part of the
War. In this 1955 picture 'Coronation'
4-6-2 No. 46238 *City of Carlisle* makes
an impressive sight restarting from
Carlisle on the up train.

I.S. Carr

Plate 156 Below De-streamlined
Pacific No. 46220 *Coronation* is
passing through Crewe, also on the up
train.

T. Lewis

Plate 157 Above Prior to 1927 the 'Mid-Day Scot' was known as 'The Corridor' as it was one of the first LNWR expresses to be formed of entirely corridor stock. On 21st May 1956 the 'Mid-Day Scot' is seen leaving Euston at 13.15 on its eight hour and twenty minutes journey to Glasgow Central behind 'Coronation' Pacific No. 46233 *Duchess of Sutherland*.

Peter Groom

Plate 158 Below The down train is seen again, this time behind 'Princess Royal' Pacific No. 46212 *Duchess of Kent*, restarting from its Rugby stop on 24th July 1958.

Peter Groom

Plate 159 Left The 'Coronation Scot' began running in summer 1937 between Euston and Glasgow with one intermediate stop at Carlisle, leaving both Euston and Glasgow Central at 13.30. No. 6220 *Coronation* is heading the up train near Tamworth.

F.G. Carrier

Plate 160 Above The 'Caledonian' was only introduced in 1959 and 'Coronation' Pacific No. 46240 *City of Coventry* is seen leaving Glasgow Central on 21st July 1959 at 08.30 on the up train. In 1962 both the up and down trains were retimed including additional stops and the title disappeared in Autumn 1964.

G.W. Morrison

Plate 161 *Above* When the 'Comet' first received its name in 1932 it left Manchester London Road station at 17.40 and Euston at 11.50. Over the years various alterations were made and in summer 1954 it had been retimed to leave Euston at 09.45, with stops at Stoke-on-Trent, Macclesfield and Stockport, and to leave Manchester at 17.50 with an arrival of 21.20 at Euston. Here the down train is seen on 26th November 1951 passing Heaton Norris behind converted 'Scot' No. 46160 *Queen Victoria's Rifleman*.
T. Lewis

Plate 162 *Right* The 'Mancunian' also ran between Euston and Manchester London Road and the up train is seen near Cheadle Hulme behind Stanier Class 5 4-6-0 No. 44750 fitted with Caprotti valve gear.
T. Lewis

Plate 163 Above In the late 1950's the up 'Mancunian' is running into Euston past the customary collection of spotters behind Longsight 'Scot' No. 46160 *Queen Victoria's Rifleman.*

M. Welch

Plate 164 Below The 'Palatine' ran between St. Pancras and Manchester Central via the Midland route and the name was revived in 1957. Here Kentish Town converted 'Scot' is about to leave St. Pancras at 07.55 on the down train on 9th April 1958.

J.D. Edwards

Plate 165 *Above* The 'Red Rose' began running in 1951 as the 12.05 ex Euston and the 17.25 ex Liverpool Lime Street. Later in 1951 it was retimed to 12.30 ex Euston with a three and three quarter hour non-stop run to Lime Street. Here 'Princess Royal' pacific No. 46204 *Princess Louise* passes a crowd of spotters at Crewe on 28th March 1959 on the down train.

S.D. Wainwright

Plate 166 *Right* In 1951 the down 'Merseyside Express' which left Euston for Liverpool Lime Street at 18.05 is seen tearing through Harrow and Wealdstone behind Edge Hill Pacific No. 46200 *The Princess Royal*. The only intermediate stop was at Edge Hill to detach the Southport portion and Lime Street was reached at 21.50.

C.R.L. Coles

Plate 167 Above In 1954 the 16.30 Euston-Liverpool Lime Street was retimed to depart Euston at 16.55 and given the name the 'Shamrock'. It is seen here at Euston on 14th June 1954 about to leave on its inaugural non-stop run behind converted 'Scot' No. 46153 *The Royal Dragoon*, arriving at Lime Street at 20.22.

B. Morrison

Plate 168 Left The up 'Shamrock' left Liverpool Lime Street at 08.10, and with only one intermediate stop at Bletchley was due into Euston at 11.45. However, during the electrification period there were several timetable alterations and it is seen at 12.34 after arrival at Euston behind a rather dirty 'Princess Royal' Pacific No. 46211 *Queen Maud*.

W. Philip Conolly

Plate 169 Right In 1957 the title of the 'Waverley' was given to the 09.15 St. Pancras-Edinburgh Waverley replacing the title of the 'Thames-Forth Express' which the train had carried from 1927 until the outbreak of war. The train ran via Nottingham, Leeds, Carlisle and via the Waverley route to Edinburgh and it is seen ready to leave St. Pancras in 1959 with Midland 2P 4-4-0 No. 40421 piloting an unidentified 'Jubilee' 4-6-0.

M. Welch

Plate 170 Left The morning train in each direction between St. Pancras and Glasgow was given the title the 'Thames-Clyde Express' in 1927, regaining it after the War in 1949. The route was via Leicester, Leeds, Carlisle and the Glasgow and South Western Line to Glasgow St. Enoch. On 21st February 1960 Holbeck 'Jubilee' No. 45564 *New South Wales* is preparing to leave Leeds City, after reversal, on the down train.

G.W. Morrison

FREIGHT TRAFFIC

Plate 171 Above Kirtley Midland double framed 1F 0-6-0 No. 2498 on a down rake of empties near Peckwash Mill Sidings, between Derby and Duffield.

F.G. Carrier

Plate 172 Left One of the ten Maryport and Carlisle 2F 0-6-0s No. 12488 leaving Carlisle northbound on a mixed freight in the late 1920s. The last of these 5 ft 1½ in engines was withdrawn in 1930.

A.G. Ellis Collection

Plate 173 *Above* Pride of the LNWR express passenger engines on a class 'A' freight. Reboilered 'Claughton' No. 6017 *Breadalbane* heading a Camden-Walsall freight passing Headstone Lane in 1938.
C.R.L. Coles

Plate 174 *Left* The London Tilbury and Southend Railway only possessed two 0-6-0s which were built in 1899. No. 2898 which was withdrawn in 1933 heads an up freight.
A.G. Ellis Collection

Plate 175 *Right* On 8th October 1930 Hughes L & YR 6F 0-8-0 No. 12826 leaves Agecroft for Gorton towing Beyer-Peacock Garratt No. 4972 which had not yet been officially handed over to the LMS from the builders, Beyer-Peacock. Representatives of the big four railways had been displayed at Wavertree playing fields, Liverpool, on the occasion of the Liverpool & Manchester Railway Centenary and then stabled at Agecroft before being dispersed.
A.G. Ellis Collection

Plate 178 Above On 15th March 1959 Class 3F 0-6-0T No. 47297 is shunting in the yard at Chester, adjacent to Chester General station.

S.D. Wainwright

Plate 179 Below Class 8F 2-8-0 No. 48448 struggles up the last few yards to Copy Pit Summit between Burnley and Todmorden on 6th April 1968 heading a Wyre Dock-Healey Mills coal empties.

J.S. Whiteley

Plate 180 *Above* Unrebuilt 'Patriots' were frequently seen on both freight and parcels traffic and No. 45506 *The Royal Pioneer Corps* is leaving the picturesque station of Colwyn Bay on 1st September 1953 heading an up parcels.

R.E. Vincent

Plate 181 *Below* Only in their latter years were the rebuilt 'Patriots' to be seen regularly on freight workings and on a stormy August day in 1964 No. 45531 *Sir Frederick Harrison* is climbing Shap with banking assistance on a down freight.

M. Welch

Plate 182 Right Class 7F 0-8-0 of LNW design No. 49078 is seen in West London passing Kensington Olympia on 18th June 1955.

A.G. Ellis Collection

Plate 183 Left Freight of a slightly different kind, to be more precise, the Horwich works shunter on 9th August 1953. Eight of these 18 in gauge 0-4-0STs were built 1887/1901 for shunting at the L & YR works. *Wren* was the last working locomotive of the class surviving until 1962 and can now be seen preserved at the York National Railway Museum.

A.G. Ellis Collection

Plate 184 Right Jack of all trades; Class 5 4-6-0 No. 45024 recovering from a cruel signal check on the climb to Shap Summit near Thrimby Grange on 13th April 1963 heading a heavy southbound freight.

J.S. Whiteley

Plate 185 Above 'Jubilee' class 4-6-0 No. 45581 *Bihar and Orissa* heading a short westbound parcels passes Class 3F 0-6-0T No. 47379 on shunting duties just outside Batley. 18th July 1962.

D.I. Wood

Plate 186 Below Many of the last surviving 8F 2-8-0s ended their days in the Buxton area and on 15th February 1968 No. 48191 passes Peak Forest Summit with a local freight from Buxton.

J.S. Whiteley

DOUBLE-HEADED TRAINS

Plate 187 Above Two 4-4-0s passing non-stop through Duffield make a superb sight heading a down express. Midland 6 ft 9 in 2P No. 338 is piloting LMS 6 ft 9 in Compound No. 1050.

F.G. Carrier

Plate 188 Below A 'Claughton' 4-6-0 and a 2P 4-4-0 are double-heading a down train near Breadsall Crossing in the mid 1930s.

F.G. Carrier

Plate 189 *Above* Two Kirtley Midland double-framed 1F 0-6-0s, the leading one No. 2430, both with Salter spring balance safety valves, head a down mixed freight near Peckwash Mill sidings.

F.G. Carrier

Plate 190 *Below* In August 1934 Johnson Midland 1P 2-4-0 No. 213 is piloting an unidentified Midland 4F near Bell Busk on a Skipton-Carnforth train.

W.H. Foster

Plate 191 *Left* On the Highland main line a 'Small Ben' 4-4-0 is piloting a 'Castle' 4-6-0 on a southbound train in the mid 1930s.

F.G. Carrier

Plate 192 *Below* Double-heading north-bound from Carlisle was often the order of the day before the 4-6-0s were introduced and in this picture 'Dunalastair IV' 4-4-0 No. 14358 is piloting LMS built three cylinder compound No. 1066 on a down express leaving Carlisle.

A.G. Ellis Collection

Plate 193 *Left* An unusual pairing at Mill Hill in 1923; Whitelegg London Tilbury & Southend 'Baltic' tank No. 2106 paired with Midland '483' class 4-4-0 No. 555 provide super power for a down St. Albans train.

A.G. Ellis Collection

Plate 194 Above On 21st May 1955 Midland 2P 4-4-0 No. 40556 is piloting BR standard Class 2 2-6-0 No. 78023 away from Dore and Totley on an up Sheffield local.

B.R. Goodlad

Plate 195 Below An impressive combination of LNWR and LMS engines on an up express near Tamworth. A 'Prince of Wales' 4-6-0 is coupled in front of a 'Royal Scot' 4-6-0 which has been fitted with the first type of straight sided smoke deflectors.

F. G. Carrier

Plate 196 *Above* A fine picture of Rugby 6 ft 9 in 'Precedent' class 2-4-0 No. 5011 *Director* piloting a reboilered 'Claughton' near Tamworth on a down express.

F.G. Carrier

Plate 197 *Right* Whale LNWR 'Precursor' 4-4-0 No. 5295 *Scorpion* is picking up on Brock troughs, between Preston and Lancaster, whilst piloting a 'Claughton' 4-6-0 on a heavy down express.

A.G. Ellis Collection

Plate 198 Left LNWR 'George the Fifth' class 4-4-0 with its 1934 number 25393 *Loyalty* is restarting a down Bletchley train from Harrow and Wealdstone whilst piloting an LMS 2-6-4T in the mid 1930s.
C.R.L. Coles

Plate 199 Above In the autumn of 1938, Midland 2P 4-4-0 No. 489 is piloting 'Jubilee' class 4-6-0 No. 5621 *Northern Rhodesia* near Cotehill, on an up express, attached for the severe climb to Ais Gill Summit on its journey to Leeds and the south.
E.E. Smith

Plate 200 Left It was very unusual to see a 4-4-0 piloting a Pacific but on 7th August 1958 2P No. 40679 was paired at Crewe with 'Coronation' No. 46228 *Duchess of Rutland* on the nineteen coach down 'Mid-Day Scot'. In all probability the Pacific would be pushing the 4-4-0 as well as pulling the train for most of the journey!
S.D. Wainwright

Plate 201 *Above* Double-heading was common between Manchester and Leeds for the climb over the Pennines with the summit at Standedge Tunnel. On 12th May 1956 LMS 2P 4-4-0 No. 40587 and 'Jubilee' 4-6-0 No. 45646 *Napier* are passing Heaton Lodge Junction, Mirfield on the morning Liverpool-Newcastle.

B.R. Goodlad

Plate 202 *Below* The Euston-Perth trains were often worked by Pacifics but on 9th August 1960 Stanier Class 5 4-6-0 No. 45174 and 'Jubilee' class 4-6-0 No. 45729 *Furious* double-head the down morning train out of Carlisle near Kingmoor MPD.

G.W. Morrison

Plate 203 Above LMS and LNER motive power combined on the Heaton-Manchester Red Bank empty vans passing York MPD on 22nd August 1959. Class 4F 0-6-0 No. 44207 is piloting LNER Class J39 0-6-0 No. 64824.

N. Stead

Plate 204 Below Another picture of the Heaton-Red Bank vans, this time in the Calder Valley on Luddendenfoot troughs. Hughes/Fowler 'Crab' 2-6-0 No. 42701 is piloting a Stanier Class 5 4-6-0, both picking up water before the westbound climb to Summit Tunnel followed by the long descent to Manchester.

G.W. Morrison

Plate 205 Right The peace of the desolate fells near Shap Summit is disturbed by Fairburn 2-6-4T No. 42198 and Stanier Class 5 4-6-0 No. 45218 battling up the last mile of 1 in 75 heading the Sunday 13.05 Manchester and Liverpool-Glasgow and Edinburgh on 28th June 1964.

J.S. Whiteley

Plate 206 Left Between intermittent snow showers on a bitterly cold day in April 1964 Fairburn 2-6-4T No. 42110 pilots 'Royal Scot' No. 46162 *Queen's Westminster Rifleman* on a Crewe-Carlisle parcels. The tank engine was attached at Oxenholme and will pilot the 'Scot' to Shap Summit. The pair are seen on Dillicar Troughs, Tebay, taking a run at the climb from Tebay to Shap Summit.

J. S. Whiteley

Plate 207 Right On 12th July 1964 Stanier 2-6-4T No. 42449 and rebuilt 'Patriot' 4-6-0 No. 45512 *Bunsen* are nearing Shap Summit on the Sunday 09.30 Manchester-Glasgow and Edinburgh. On Sundays at this period, Tebay shed was closed and any train wanting assistance took a pilot from Oxenholme.

J.S. Whiteley

Plate 208 Above A pair of Stanier Class 5s, Nos. 44956 and 44973 are leaving Arrochar on 13th August 1960 heading the 06.30 Mallaig-Glasgow Queen Street.

G.W. Morrison

Plate 209 Below Stanier Class 5 4-6-0s Nos. 44973 and 44975 are climbing the 1 in 45 from Glasgow Queen Street to Cowlairs on the 10.15 to Fort William on 12th August 1960.

G.W. Morrison

SHED SCENES

Plate 210 Right Holbeck, Leeds on 17th March 1963. One of the roundhouses can be seen on the left and the Manchester line on the viaduct in the background.
J.S. Whiteley

Plate 211 Below Inside Holbeck in July 1967.
J.S. Whiteley

Plate 212 Above In the yard at Carlisle Upperby on 22nd May 1961. 'Jubilee' No. 45700 *Amethyst* and 'Coronation' No. 46248 *City of Leeds* are in the foreground.

G.W. Morrison

Plate 213 Below Super power inside Crewe North on 26th February 1961 in the shape of three 'Coronation' Pacifics and Polmadie 'Royal Scot'.

S.D. Wainwright

Plate 214 *Left* A mixture of Midland and Lancashire & Yorkshire designs at Manningham on 23rd March 1952.
B.R. Goodlad

Plate 215 *Left* Four of the total class of ten L & YR 'Baltic' tanks, at Agecroft.
A.G. Ellis Collection

Plate 216 *Below* In the yard at Springs Branch (Wigan) on 26th August 1955. Aspinall L & YR Class F19 0-6-0 as BR No. 52341 appears to have recently had a new smokebox fitted.
B. Morrison

Plate 217 Above Both these locomotives have just had their smokeboxes cleaned out at Camden on 5th June 1960.

Peter Groom

Plate 218 Below An unusual visitor to St. Rollox in the shape of a 'Coronation' Pacific, there because of diversions from Glasgow Central on 12th April 1959.

G.W. Morrison

Plate 219 Top Shap bankers at Tebay on 16th August 1958.
  G.W. Morrison

Plate 220 Centre Beattock shed on 20th May 1961.
  G.W. Morrison

Plate 221 Right Some of the last Stanier 8F 2-8-0s at Rose Grove on 17th February 1968, only a few months before BR withdrew the last steam locomotives from service.
  G.W. Morrison

SHAP

Plate 223 Below Having taken a run at the final 1 in 75 through the Lune Gorge from Grayrigg, 'Coronation' Pacific No. 46225 *Duchess of Gloucester* roars past Greenholme just north of Tebay on a lightweight down express on 29th April 1963.

J.S. Whiteley

Plate 222 Above Shap Summit at 914 feet above sea level on the West Coast main line is the culmination of almost thirty-two miles of steady climbing for northbound trains from Carnforth which is only just above sea level. Heavy down trains often took banking assistance from Tebay for the final five and three quarter miles to the summit which is mainly at 1 in 75. Southbound trains are also faced with about thirty-two miles of uphill work, from Carlisle, but the final climb to Shap Summit is not quite as severe as for northbound trains. On 17th July 1965 Class 8F 2-8-0 No. 48730 is seen passing Shap Wells on a down freight with a Fowler 2-6-4T working equally hard at the rear.

J.S. Whiteley

Plate 224 Above On Whit Sunday, 10th June 1962 No. 46252 *City of Leicester* makes a splendid sight climbing through the woods near Little Strickland heading the up 'Royal Scot' combined with the relief, probably because of engine failure, a fifteen coach train.

J.S. Whiteley

Plate 225 Below For up trains the final thirteen miles from Penrith to the summit is predominantly at 1 in 125 and No. 46243 *City of Lancaster* is nearing Shap village on 29th August 1959 on the up 'Royal Scot'.

G.W. Morrison

THE LICKEY INCLINE

Plate 226 Left On the Midland line from Gloucester to Birmingham northbound trains are faced with slightly more than two miles at 1 in 37¾ from Bromsgrove to Blackwell. Most trains took banking assistance and on 7th July 1956 Midland 2P 4-4-0 No. 40486 comes slowly up the gradient with a Gloucester-Birmingham stopping train.

G.W. Morrison

BEATTOCK

Plate 227 Right The other notorious climb on the West Coast main line is between Carlisle and Glasgow and Beattock Summit at 1015 feet above sea level is almost exactly half way between the two cities. The northbound climb is the most severe with virtually ten miles between 1 in 88 and 1 in 69 from Beattock station to the summit. Most northbound trains took banking assistance for the climb and Stanier Class 5 4-6-0 No. 45485 is nearing Greskine on 23rd April 1962 with a down freight.

J.S. Whiteley

Plate 228 *Above* 'Royal Scot' class 4-6-0 No. 46107 *Argyll and Sutherland Highlander* is working hard with a full head of steam on the 09.30 Manchester-Glasgow passing Harthope on 23rd April 1962.

J.S. Whiteley

Plate 229 *Below* 'Jubilee' class 4-6-0 No. 45602 *British Honduras* is also seen near Harthope on the last lap of the climb to the summit on the morning Liverpool-Glasgow on 23rd April 1962.

J.S. Whiteley

CAMDEN BANK

Plate 230 Above The southbound climb to Beattock Summit is far more leisurely with just a gentle climb up the Clyde Valley from Carstairs to Crawford and a final two and a quarter miles at 1 in 99 from Elvanfoot to the summit. Pacific No. 46256 *Sir William A. Stanier, F.R.S.* is near Crawford on the 09.00 Perth-Euston on 15th April 1963.

J.S. Whiteley

Plate 231 Below Just out of Euston, down trains face a sharp climb of almost one mile at between 1 in 70 and 1 in 112 to Camden No. 1. This often proved tricky for cold engines and rebuilt 'Royal Scot' 4-6-0 No. 46157 *The Royal Artilleryman* is seen with sanders on heading an afternoon Liverpool express in October 1956.

Peter Groom

Plate 232 Above En route from Carnforth to Shap Summit, between Crewe and Carlisle, the first prolonged stiff climb facing northbound trains is the thirteen miles from near Milnthorpe to the intermediate summit at Grayrigg. The last seven miles from Oxenholme steepen to between 1 in 104 and 1 in 131 and converted 'Royal Scot' No. 46107 *Argyll and Sutherland Highlander* with the help of banking assistance from Oxenholme is heading a Manchester-Glasgow in April 1954.

W.H. Foster

GRAYRIGG

Plate 233 Below Earlier in the day, at the same location near Lambrigg Crossing, Carlisle Kingmoor unrebuilt 'Patriot' 4-6-0 No. 45549 climbs towards Grayrigg with a Crewe-Carlisle parcels.

W.H. Foster

AIS GILL AND BLEA MOOR

Plate 234 Above Without doubt one of the most spectacular railway lines in Britain is the Settle and Carlisle section of the Midland route from Leeds to Carlisle. It crosses the backbone of England in a most breathtaking manner with the help of some superb feats of railway engineering which claimed many lives during construction between 1869 and 1875. The summit of the line is at Ais Gill, 1169 feet above sea level in bleak and windswept Fells, about sixty-four miles from Leeds and forty-eight miles from Carlisle. 'Jubilee class 4-6-0 No. 45597 *Barbados* is crossing the 440 yard long Batty Moss viaduct at Ribblehead heading the down 'Waverley' on 3rd October 1959, nearing the top of the fourteen and a half mile climb at mainly 1 in 100 from Settle Junction to Blea Moor Tunnel.

G.W. Morrison

Plate 235 Above Between Blea Moor and Ais Gill the railway hugs the 1150 feet contour for about eleven miles and Class 5 4-6-0 No. 45254 approaches the summit at Ais Gill on a southbourn freight, having almost completed the fifteen and a half mile climb at mainly 1 in 100 from Ormside viaduct, just south of Appleby on 30th April 1966.

J.S. Whiteley

MIDLAND

Plate 236 Left Kirtley double framed 1P 2-4-0 No. 20012 as renumbered in 1934. Twenty-nine of these engines were built between 1866 and 1874, the last one being withdrawn in 1947.

F.G. Carrier

Plate 237 Right Johnson '483' class 4-4-0 as fitted with bogie brakes.

F.G. Carrier

Plate 238 Left Johnson 3P 4-4-0 as rebuilt by Fowler.

F.G. Carrier

Plate 239 Right Johnson 3F 0-6-0 No. 3826. The beaded splashers can clearly be seen in this picture.

F.G. Carrier

LONDON AND NORTH WESTERN

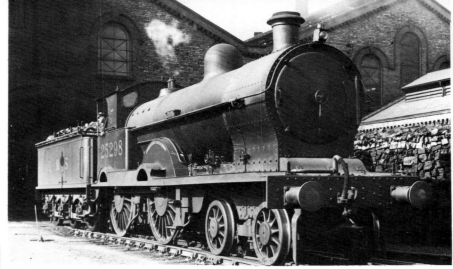

Plate 240 Right Whale rebuilt 'Precursor' No. 25298
Dragon at Peterborough on 29th August 1936.
One hundred and thirty of these 4-4-0s were built
between 1904 and 1907 but only one survived
nationalisation and was withdrawn later in 1948.
A.G. Ellis Collection

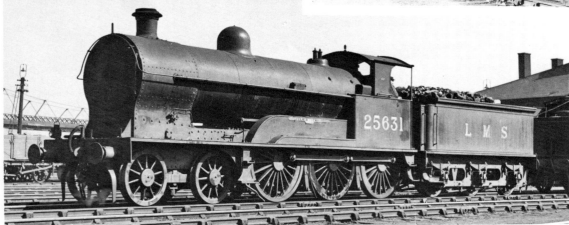

Plate 241 Left Bowen-
Cooke 'Prince of Wales'
Class 3P No. 25631
Felicia Hemans.
F.G. Carrier

NORTH LONDON

Plate 242 Right Sharp
Stewart crane engine built
in 1858 as 0-4-0ST but
rebuilt as 0-4-2ST in 1872
and crane fitted. It was BR
No. 58865 and was with-
drawn in 1951 after being a
permanent shunter at Bow
Works.

F.G. Carrier

Plate 243 Left J.C. Park 1F 0-6-0T No. 58857 at
Poplar Dock on 5th May 1956. Thirty of these were
built between 1887 and 1905 and this engine was
formerly NLR No. 18, LNWR No. 2878 and LMS No.
7517.

R.E. Vincent

LONDON AND NORTH WESTERN

Plate 244 Left BR No. 58926 at Crewe Works in May 1959, the last surviving Webb 'coal tank'. Three hundred of these engines were built between 1881 and 1896.

N. Stead

Plate 245 Right Beames 5F 0-8-4T No. 7953. Thirty of these engines were built but were not delivered until after the grouping, between 1923 and 1924.

A.G. Ellis Collection

FURNESS

Plate 246 Left Rutherford 3P 4-6-4T No.11103. Only five of these massive engines were built in 1921 and lasted until 1940.

A.G. Ellis Collection

Plate 247 Right Pettigrew 3F 0-6-0 seen as BR No. 52494. Nineteen of these engines were built between 1913 and 1920, six survived nationalisation, the last one being withdrawn in 1957.

N. Stead

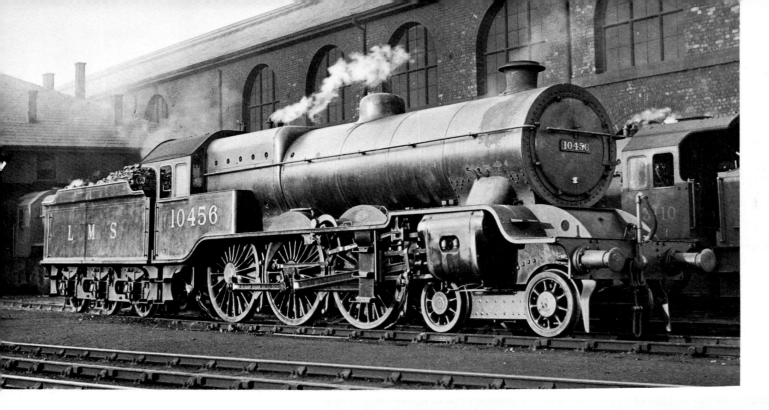

LANCASHIRE & YORKSHIRE

Plate 248 Above Hughes 5P 4-6-0 No. 10456 as rebuilt as a compound in 1926. It is seen at Upperby shed on 16th July 1933. A total of seventy of these superheated four cylinder 'Lanky Bombers' were built between 1921 and 1925 (L & YR class N1), fifteen of which were rebuilt from the original saturated design of 1908.

F.G. Carrier

Plate 249 Right Aspinall 6F 0-8-0 No. 12753 which was built at Horwich in 1907 and withdrawn in March 1939.

N. Stead

HIGHLAND

Plate 250 Left Jones 'Loch' 2P 4-4-0 No. 14379 *Loch Insh* built in 1896. Eighteen of these engines were built, fifteen in 1896 and three in 1917. No. 14379 was one of several rebuilt with larger CR type boilers as seen here at Aviemore in 1948.

F.G. Carrier

Plate 251 *Left* Drummond 'Small Ben' 2P 4-4-0 as BR No. 54398 *Ben Alder*. Twenty 'Small Bens' were built between 1898 and 1906, all eventually acquiring CR type boilers.

N. Stead

Plate 252 *Right* Smith 'River' Class 4P 4-6-0 No. 14761 at Perth MPD. This was one of six engines built for the Highland but subsequently sold to the CR after being found too heavy for the lines of the HR.

T.G. Hepburn

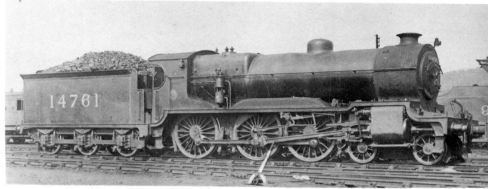

CALEDONIAN

Plate 253 *Left* The sole 7ft 0in Neilson & Co. 1P 4-2-2 built in 1886. This engine has been restored as original CR No. 123 but is seen on 17th April 1933 at Perth.

F.G. Carrier

Plate 254 *Right* McIntosh 'Dunalastair II Rebuilt' 3P 4-4-0 No. 14432 at Stirling. Only four of this class were built in 1898 and were rebuilt in 1914 with superheated boiler.

T.G. Hepbur

Plate 255 Left McIntosh '139' class 3P 4-4-0 No. 14443 at Kingmoor. Twenty-two of these 6 ft 6 in engines were built between 1910-14, the last one surviving until 1957.

T.G. Hepburn

Plate 256 Right One of the two D. Drummond unclassified 'Killin Tanks' built at St. Rollox in 1885. These engines worked the Killin branch until 1895 when they were replaced by 0-4-4Ts. No. 15001 is at Inverness on 16th April 1933.

F.G. Carrier

Plate 257 Left McIntosh '34' class 3F 2-6-0 No. 17801 at Perth on 21st May 1934. Only five of these were built in 1912 and they were withdrawn between 1935 and 1937.

F.G. Carrier

Plate 258 Right Eleven of these handsome McIntosh '179' class 4-6-0s were built between 1913-14, the last one surviving until 1946. No. 17913 is at Perth on 21st May 1934.

F.G. Carrier

LONDON MIDLAND
AND SCOTTISH

Plate 259 Right Fowler 2P 4-4-0 No. 653 built at Crewe in 1931. This engine together with No. 633 was fitted with Dabeg feed water heater in 1933 as seen here.

F.G. Carrier

Plate 260 Above Compound 4-4-0 No. 40931 at Derby on 13th December 1956. This engine was built at the Vulcan Foundry in 1927 and has left hand drive.

Peter Groom

Plate 261 Right Ivatt 2-6-2T No. 1205 at Hellifield MPD in 1946 during turns on the Ingleton Branch. This class was introduced in 1946 shortly before nationalisation.

W.H. Foster

Plate 262 Left No. 13245 was the first of forty of Stanier's mixed traffic 2-6-0s to emerge from Crewe in October 1933 and it is seen here at Crewe South on 7th April 1934. The first ten engines had the safety valves combined with the top feed on the boilers as here.

F.G. Carrier

Plate 263 Right 'Baby Scot' 4-6-0 No. 5954 which was 'rebuilt' from a 'Claughton' at Derby in 1933. It was renumbered 5520 in 1934 and named *Llandudno* in 1937. It is seen at Derby on 25th March 1933 shortly after emerging from the Works.

F.G. Carrier

Plate 264 Left Fowler 'Royal Scot' class 4-6-0 No. 6106 *Gordon Highlander* at Crewe. It is still fitted with bogie brakes and has not yet received smoke deflectors which were fitted to all the class by early 1932.

T.G. Hepburn

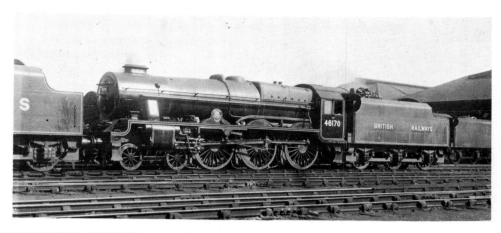

Plate 265 Right The unique three cylinder 6P 4-6-0 No. 46170 *British Legion* which was for convenience included in the 'Royal Scot' class. This engine was rebuilt at Crewe in 1935 from the ill-fated high-pressure compound 4-6-0 No. 6399 *Fury* which was originally built in 1929 by North British Locomotive Co. It was withdrawn from service in December 1962.

A.G. Ellis Collection

Plate 266 Left Another unique locomotive, the Turbomotive which was introduced in 1935. It is seen here as BR No. 46202 after the fitting of smoke deflectors in 1939.

A.G. Ellis Collection

Plate 267 Right When the Turbomotive needed extensive renewals, including a new main turbine, it was decided to rebuild it as a conventional Pacific. In August 1952 it emerged from Crewe and was named *Princess Anne*. Tragically the locomotive was damaged beyond economic repair in the Harrow disaster of October 1952 after only running 11,443 miles.

A.G. Ellis Collection

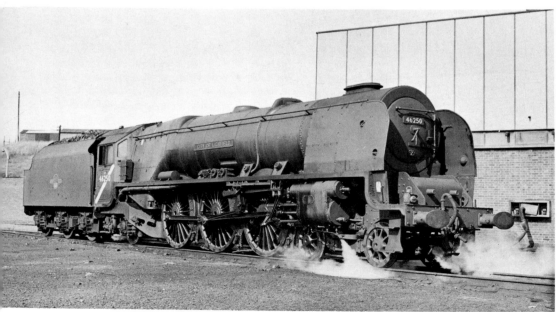

Plate 268 Left The 'Coronation' Pacifics were often referred to as 'Duchesses', ten members of the class being named after Duchesses. No. 46250 *City of Lichfield* is on shed at Carlisle Upperby on 10th August 1964, only a few weeks before being withdrawn.

J.S. Whiteley

Plate 269 *Above* One of the first batch of 3F 0-6-0Ts built at Vulcan Foundry in 1924 as No. 7117 and renumbered 7277 in 1934.

F.G. Carrier

Plate 270 *Right* Only the first twenty of these 128 Ivatt 2F 2-6-0s introduced in 1946 ever carried LMS livery, Nos. 6400-6419. No. 6418 was built at Crewe in 1947 and was photographed at Manchester Victoria on station pilot duty immediately before Nationalisation.

A.G. Ellis Collection

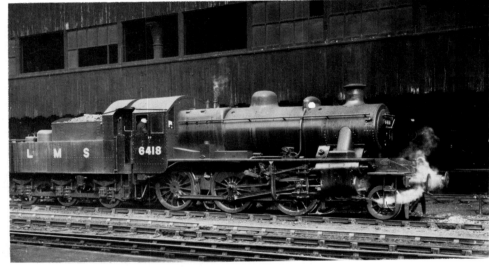

Plate 271 *Left* Fittingly two of Stanier's Class 5s were the last steam locomotives to be used on a BR operated train on Sunday, 11th August 1968 — tribute to a fine design. No. 45312 in mint condition is at Eastfield on 27th March 1964. Fortunately, several of these locomotives have been preserved.

G.W. Morrison

THE LNER REMEMBERED

Plate A One of the very handsome Ivatt GNR class C1 4-4-2s No. 4421 at Grantham. This locomotive was built at Doncaster in 1907 as a four-cylinder compound but rebuilt as a standard two-cylinder locomotive in 1920.

F.G. Carrier

Plate B A Gresley class A1 Pacific which was built after the grouping. No. 2548 *Galtee More* is climbing Stoke Bank from Grantham with an up express.

F.G. Carrier

THE

LNER

REMEMBERED

by

J.S. WHITELEY and G.W. MORRISON

Oxford Publishing Co.

ISBN 0 86093 069 6

Plate C Ivatt GNR class D2 4-4-0 No. 4323 soon after leaving
Peascliffe Tunnel, north of Grantham, heading a Grantham —
Doncaster stopping train.

F.G. Carrier

Contents

Introduction

The London and North Eastern Railway came into being on 1st January, 1923 as the second largest of the "Big Four" companies formed under the Railways Act, 1921 and this book has been prepared as a companion volume to "The LMS Remembered", previously published.

The LNER inherited an extremely varied collection of locomotives from seven major constituent companies, the Great Central Railway, the Great Eastern Railway, the Great Northern Railway, the Great North of Scotland Railway, the Hull and Barnsley Railway (which had amalgamated with the North Eastern Railway from 1st April, 1922), the North British Railway and the North Eastern Railway.

The oldest and largest of the constituent companies was the North Eastern Railway which alone contributed well over 2000 locomotives. It was, however, the former Great Northern Railway which came to dominate the partnership, due largely to the fact that Nigel Gresley, (later Sir Nigel Gresley) who was the Locomotive Engineer of the GNR, became Chief Mechanical Engineer of the newly formed London and North Eastern Railway. He was to hold that office for just over 18 years, being succeeded after he died in office in April 1941 by Edward Thompson, who in turn was succeeded by Arthur Henry Peppercorn in June 1946 for the short period until nationalisation.

Although both Thompson and Peppercorn made valuable contributions to the locomotive policy and construction of the LNER, it was Gresley who will be remembered as the outstanding locomotive designer responsible for the big engine policy which was so much a feature of the LNER. It was Gresley's Pacifics of class A1 (subsequently reboilered A3) and later his 'A4s' which were to be seen at the head of express passenger trains of the East Coast route from the early years of the LNER until steam was replaced by diesel traction in the early 1960s as part of the modernisation plan of British Railways. It is, therefore, a fitting tribute to his design capabilities that one of his magnificent class A4 Pacifics holds the world speed record for steam traction.

Included in this book are pictures of pre-grouping classes seen after the formation of the LNER, together with pictures of classes of locomotives which were designed by the LNER during its 25 years existence.

We would like to express our gratitude to all the photographers who have allowed inclusion of their pictures and to the many enthusiasts who have so kindly offered advice and assistance. Lastly, thanks again to Margaret Morley for typing the manuscript.

J.S. Whiteley.
January 1979

Plate 1 Left Only two Gresley class A1 Pacifics entered service in 1922 just before the grouping, Nos. 1470 *Great Northern* and 1471 *Sir Frederick Banbury. Great Northern* as renumbered 1470N is passing Ganwick shortly after the grouping heading a down express.
W.B. Yeadon Collection

Plate 2 Below Ten more class A1 Pacifics were built at Doncaster in 1923, Nos. 1472-1481 (renumbered 4472-4481 from February 1924). One of these engines, No. 4473 *Solario* which entered service in March 1923, is leaving Stoke Tunnel with a down express. Both pictures on this page clearly show the large GNR chimney and high cab roof fitted to these early 'A1s'.
F.G. Carrier

Plate 3 Above A further forty class A1s were ordered late in 1923 and entered service between June 1924 and July 1925, twenty being built at Doncaster and twenty by the North British Locomotive Co. These engines were numbered 2543-2582 and here Doncaster built No. 2555 *Centenary* is climbing Stoke Bank with an up express including postal vans.

F.G. Carrier

Plate 4 Below The first of this batch of forty engines, No. 2543 *Melton* also built at Doncaster, is leaving Peascliffe Tunnel on a down afternoon express.

F.G. Carrier

Plate 5 Left The other two Pacifics inherited by the LNER at the grouping were the Raven NER class A2s, Nos. 2400 and 2401, (named *City of Newcastle* and *City of Kingston upon Hull* respectively in 1924), both built in December 1922. Three more Raven Pacifics were built at Darlington in 1924, but after trials had taken place between the Gresley and Raven designs the Gresley engines were chosen for future construction and no further Raven Pacifics were built. The pioneer Raven class A2 No. 2400 *City of Newcastle* is seen bringing empty stock through Princes St Gardens, Edinburgh for an up departure from Waverley station on 1st August, 1931.
H.C. Casserley

Plate 6 Right One of the 1924 built locomotives, No. 2403 *City of Durham* is seen standing at York MPD in the early 1930s. The first of these five huge locomotives was withdrawn in July 1936 and the last one in May of the following year.
T.G. Hepburn

Plate 7 Left In September 1929 Raven class A2 No. 2404 *City of Ripon* was rebuilt by Gresley with a modified Doncaster 'A1' boiler, firebox and cab. It is seen paired with a Gresley eight wheel tender on 11th July, 1936 running into York with a Newcastle — Kings Cross express.
J.P. Wilson

Plate 8 Right Only two of these Robinson GCR class B1 4-6-0s were built in 1903-4 (GCR class 8C) by Beyer Peacock & Co, Nos. 5195 and 5196. Both engines were withdrawn in 1947 having been reclassified B18 in April 1943 to make way for Thompson's new 4-6-0s. No. 5195 is standing on shed, thought to be Immingham.

E.E. Smith

Plate 9 Left No. 5196 as reclassified B18 is seen about 1945 near Ruddington heading a Nottingham — Leicester local.

T.G. Hepburn

Plate 10 Below Robinson GCR "Sir Sam Fay" class B2 4-6-0 No. 5424 *City of Lincoln* leaving Sheffield Victoria on a Manchester — London express. Six of these 6'9" engines were built at Gorton Works 1912-13 (GCR Class 1) but were soon replaced by the more successful class D10 "Director" 4-4-0s on the principal expresses. In August 1945 the five surviving engines were reclassified B19 to make way for Thompson's rebuilt "Sandringham" 2-cylinder 4-6-0s and the last of the class was withdrawn in November 1947.

A.G. Ellis Collection

Plate 11 Above Two-cylinder Class B2 4-6-0 No. 5426 *City of Chester* makes a fine sight passing Bagthorpe Jn soon after leaving Nottingham Victoria heading a Leicester — Cleethorpes express about 1939.

T.G. Hepburn

Plate 12 Right Robinson's largest passenger locomotive was the 4-cylinder "Lord Faringdon" class B3 4-6-0 (GCR class 9P). Six were built at Gorton 1917-20 and No. 6164 *Earl Beatty* pauses at Retford heading an up express during August Bank Holiday, 1937. The last engine of the class was withdrawn in 1949.

S. Dewsbery

Plate 13 Left The Robinson GCR "Immingham" class B4 2-cylinder 4-6-0s were essentially the same as the earlier class B1s, the main difference being a slightly smaller diameter driving wheel as they were designed for working fast goods and fish trains. Ten were built in 1906 by Beyer Peacock & Co. (GCR class 8F) and they were soon to be seen on passenger workings. No. 6095 is on a return Leicester — Cleethorpes excursion at Nottingham Victoria on 21st August, 1938.

J.P. Wilson

Plate 14 Above Class B4 No. 6099 is displaying a generous exhaust in this picture but neither the train nor the location has been able to be identified.
F.G. Carrier

Plate 15 Right The class B5 was the first of Robinson's 4-6-0 designs for the Great Central (GCR class 8) and fourteen of these 6′ 1″ engines were built 1902-4, six by Neilson and Co. and eight by Beyer Peacock & Co. They were designed for working fast fish trains from Grimsby and although in later years they were often used on passenger trains they were nicknamed "fish engines". No. 5184 is on a Cleethorpes — Nottingham passenger and fish at Bagthorpe Jn about 1938.
T.G. Hepburn

Plate 16 Right Class B5 No. 5185 is leaving Sheffield Victoria with a Retford train on 2nd July, 1939. With the exception of one engine, No. 6070, they all survived the Second World War, seven engines survived nationalisation and the last one, No. 5183, was withdrawn in June 1950.
J.P. Wilson

Plate 17 Left Three Robinson GCR class B6 4-6-0s were built at Gorton 1918-21 (GCR class 8N). Thee 5′8″ mixed traffic engines gained an excellent reputation and although a small class were not withdrawn until late 1947. No. 5416 is seen crossing the River Trent at Nottingham heading the 10.00 Bradford — Marylebone express on 18th May, 1937 whilst allocated to Sheffield.

J.P. Wilson

Plate 18 Right the last of the nine classes of 4-6-0s designed by Robinson were the mixed traffic class B7s (GCR class 9Q). Twenty-eight were built 1921-22 and a further ten were built after the grouping in 1923-24. No. 5461 was one of the 1921 engines built at Vulcan Foundry and is seen on the GN main line at Barnby Moor north of Retford heading a down freight.

A.G. Ellis Collection

Plate 19 Left Holden GER class B12 4-6-0 No. 8517, fitfed with 'ACF1' feed-water heater, about 1929. Seventy-one of these 6′6″ engines were built before the grouping between 1911 and 1921 (GER Class S69) and a further ten were built after the grouping, in 1928. Many of these engines were rebuilt by Gresley with round-topped boiler and other modifications and reclassified (see plate 250).

A.G. Ellis Collection

Plate 20 Right Worsdell NER class B13 4-6-0 (NER class S) No. 761. Forty of these 6′1¼″ engines were built 1899-1909 at Gateshead, initially for working main line passenger trains between Newcastle and Edinburgh. With the exception of the engine seen here, all the class were withdrawn between 1928 and 1938 but No. 761 survived until 1951.

F.G. Carrier

Plate 21 Left Twenty Raven NER class B15 4-6-0s were built at Darlington 1911-13 (NER Class S2) for mixed traffic duties and in a lot of respects were similar to the earlier Worsdell class B13s. After the grouping they were often seen on the former GC and No. 820 is heading a down troop special at Nottingham Victoria on 30th May, 1937. None of these engines survived nationalisation.

J.P. Wilson

Plate 22 Below The class B16s were a more numerous class of Raven 4-6-0 totalling seventy engines, all built at Darlington (NER Class S3). Thirty-eight of these 3-cylinder engines were built before the grouping between 1919 and 1922 and thirty-two after the grouping until 1924. No. 925 is leaving York with a Leeds express about 1924 and was the ill-fated engine suffering bomb damage in the war and withdrawn in June 1942.

A.G. Ellis Collection

Plate 23 Above BR No. 61436 was the last class B16 to be built before the grouping (1923 No. 2365) and is heading an up stock train through Grantham on 27th August, 1958. Many of these engines were rebuilt by Gresley and Thompson but No. 61436 was an unrebuilt engine and classified B16/1.

Peter Groom

Plate 24 Below Regarded by many as the most handsome LNER locomotives, the large boilered Ivatt class C1 Atlantics were built at Doncaster between 1902 and 1910 for the GNR. Ninety-four of these fine engines were built and formed the largest class of express passenger engines inherited by the LNER at the grouping. No. 4450 is climbing to Stoke Tunnel heading an up Pullman.

F.G. Carrier

Plate 25 Above GNR class C1 4-4-2 No. 1442 was the Royal engine and carried the Company's coat of arms on its rear splasher. It is seen on 3rd July, 1939 as renumbered 4442, still carrying the coat of arms, passing Grantham on a return race special.

J.P. Wilson

Plate 26 Left No. 3279 was rebuilt by Gresley in 1915 (GNR No. 279) with four cylinders, but after proving costly on maintenance was converted back to two cylinders in 1938 and withdrawn in February 1948. It is seen here at Grantham on 5th June, 1933.

F.G. Carrier

Plate 27 Right Immediately after the grouping No. 4419 was fitted with a booster engine on its trailing axle by Gresley. It was also fitted with a Pacific type cab and it is seen passing Marshmoor in 1930 heading a Pullman. The booster was removed in 1935.

A.G. Ellis Collection

Plate 28 Left Only twenty-two of Ivatt's earlier small boilered class C2 Atlantics were built at Doncaster between 1898 and 1903. The first engine in the class, LNER No. 3990 *Henry Oakley* was the first Atlantic type locomotive to run in Britain and is now preserved at the National Railway Museum, York. No. 3258 seen here was one of the last class C2s to be built and was withdrawn in April 1937. *F.G. Carrier*

Plate 29 Right Class C2 4-4-2 No. 3949 is heading a down 'local' near Potters Bar on 6th August, 1938, shortly before being withdrawn. *S. Dewsbery*

Plate 30 Below The class C2s were often referred to as "Klondykes" and No. 3259 is accelerating hard away from Potters Bar on an up 'stopper'. The first of these engines was withdrawn in 1935 and the last in 1946. *E.E. Smith*

Plate 31 Above Atlantics were outnumbered by 4-6-0s on the GC but 27 class C4 4-4-2s were built by Robinson from 1903-1906 (GCR classes 8B and 8J) and handled top main line work. On 15th May, 1943 No. 6087, in rather run down wartime condition is heading a Leicester Central-Woodford slow near Braunstone and Willoughby, a few miles south of Rugby. Twenty of these engines survived nationalisation and the last one was withdrawn in 1950.

E.E. Smith

Plate 32 Above The graceful lines of these engines can be seen in this side view of No. 6091 at Immingham.

E.E. Smith

Plate 33 Right Class C4 4-4-2 No. 6085 is accelerating northwards away from Nottingham Victoria at Bagthorpe Jn in 1935 heading a Bournemouth-Newcastle express.

T.G. Hepburn

Plate 34 Above One of the twenty Worsdell NER class C6 Atlantics, No. 696 leaving Newcastle in the 1930s on a southbound express. These engines were built in two batches, ten at Gateshead 1903-4 (NER class V) and ten at Darlington in 1910 (NER class V1). Only two survived nationalisation but were withdrawn later in 1948.

Authors' collection

Plate 35 Below Raven introduced his very fine three-cylinder NER class C7 Atlantics in 1911, shortly after taking office as CME. Fifty were built 1911-18 (NER class Z) and were handling the majority of NER express workings at the grouping. No. 2202 is leaving York on a down express in the late 1920s.

A.G. Ellis Collection

Plate 36 Right Ivatt GNR class C12 4-4-2T No. 4505 rests at New England on 21st May, 1938. Sixty of these Atlantic tanks were built at Doncaster 1898-1907 (GNR class C2) and the last one was not withdrawn until 1958.

E.E. Smith

Plate 37 Left Class C12 4-4-2T No. 4513 is seen with shorter chimney at Nottingham Victoria on 24th May, 1938 awaiting departure on a Mansfield train.

J.P. Wilson

Plate 38 Right In Spring 1956 BR No. 67357 is nearing the end of its life and is seen heading the 07.30 to Essendine away from Stamford East which closed the following year.

P.H. Wells

Plate 39 Left The GCR had two classes of Atlantic tanks, the Robinson class C13 (GCR class 9K) and Robinson class C14 (GCR class 9L). Class C13 is seen as BR No. 67401 leaving Guide Bridge sidings on a local train. Forty of these engines were built from 1903-05, all survived nationalisation and the last one was withdrawn in 1960.
T. Lewi.

Plate 40 Right The class C14s were the later version, twelve being built in 1907. The dimensions were similar to the earlier engines although they were slightly heavier and No. 6126 is seen on the Metropolitan and GC joint near Chorley Wood heading an Aylesbury — Baker Street train.
E.E. Smith

Plate 41 Below The same engine is between duties at Nottingham Victoria on 5th June, 1933. Like the class C13s, all the class survived nationalisation and the last was withdrawn in 1960.
F.G. Carrier

Plate 42 Above On 12th February, 1933 Ivatt GNR class D2 4-4-0 No. 3044 makes a superb sight heading the 11.30 Derby Friargate — Nottingham Victoria composed of articulated stock seen near Breadsall. Seventy of these engines were built from 1898-1909 (GNR class D1) and the last was withdrawn in 1951.

F.G. Carrier

Plate 43 Right Class D3 4-4-0 No. 4075 standing at Grantham on 10th April, 1939 heading a Peterborough slow train. Fifty-one of these engines were built by Ivatt between 1896 and 1899 (GNR class D2) but were rebuilt by Gresley between 1912 and 1928 (GNR class D3). Towards the end of the war No. 4075 underwent further changes as can be seen in plate 44 overleaf.

J.P. Wilson

Plate 44 *Above* In September 1944 class D3 No. 4075 was fitted with a new cab and repainted green for working officers' saloons. When it first emerged from Doncaster late in September it was painted shop grey and numbered 1, but within a few days it was repainted green. It was renumbered 2000 which was the starting number for 4-4-0s in the LNER block renumbering scheme prepared in 1943 but not actually implemented until January 1946. This locomotive was one of only two ever to carry the LNER official coat of arms (the other being class A1 Pacific No. 4472 *Flying Scotsman* for the British Empire Exhibitions at Wembley 1924-25) and it can be seen between the initials 'N' 'E' on the tender. It is leaving Grantham on a Lincoln train on 24th April, 1948.

J.P. Wilson

Plate 45 *Below* Ivatt class D2 4-4-0 No. 4339 is heading a Hitchin — Kings Cross train approaching Potters Bar in Winter 1938.

E.E. Smith

Plate 46 Right Ten Robinson GCR "Director" class D10 4-4-0s were built at Gorton in 1913 (GCR class 11E). No. 5432 *Sir Edward Fraser* is seen at Doncaster standing in front of a Gresley class A1 Pacific. All ten engines of the class were withdrawn between 1953 and 1955.

F.G. Carrier

Plate 47 Above Eleven Robinson GCR "Improved Director" class D11 4-4-0s were built 1919-22 (GCR class 11F) which were slightly heavier than the 'D10s' and had a higher pitched boiler. They were reclassified D11/1 when a further 24 engines were introduced in 1924 with reduced boiler mounting for NB gauge in Scotland. These 1924 engines were classified D11/2. Class D11/1 No. 5508 *Prince of Wales* is taking water at Nottingham Victoria on 1st April, 1939 heading a Cleethorpes — Leicester train.

J.P. Wilson

Plate 48 Right On 8th June, 1957 class D11/1 No. 62667 *Somme* (LNER No. 5503) is leaving Bulwell Common on a Sheffield Victoria — Nottingham Victoria 'slow'.

J.P. Wilson

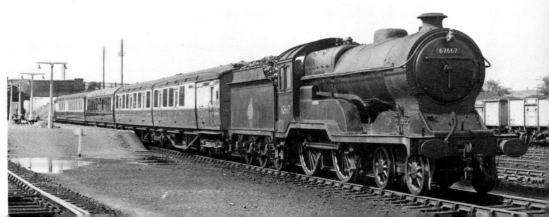

Plate 49 Left Worsdell NER class D17/2 No. 1880, still lettered 'L & NER' on the tender, is leaving Carlisle with a Newcastle train formed of eight wheel clerestory coaches. Twenty of the heavier class D17/1s were built from 1892-94 (NER Class M) and thirty class D17/2s from 1896-97 (NER class Q).

A.G. Ellis collection

Plate 50 Right Sixty of these very successful Worsdell NER class D20 4-4-0s (NER class R) were built between 1899 and 1907 and the last one survived until November 1957 as BR No. 62395. No. 2106 is seen at York MPD.

F.G. Carrier

Plate 51 Below After the success of his class R, Worsdell introduced his NER class R1 4-4-0 in 1908 but only ten were built at Darlington 1908-09. These were the last 4-4-0s built for the NER and No. 1240 as LNER class D21 is leaving Newcastle on an up express.

Authors' Collection

Plate 52 Below Class D21 4-4-0 No. 1239 is being prepared for its next duty at Gateshead. None of these engines lasted until nationalisation and the last one (No. 1245) was withdrawn in February 1946.

Authors' Collection

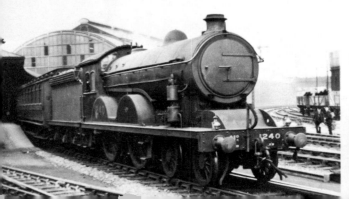

Plate 53 Right One of the twelve Holmes NBR class D26 4-4-0s No. 9325 at Portobello on an Edinburgh — Galashiels train about 1924. These 6′6″ engines were built in 1903 (NBR class K) but did not last very long. Nine of the class were in service at the grouping and No. 9325 was the last to be withdrawn in July 1926.

A.G. Ellis Collection

Plate 54 Above Reid NBR "Scott" class D30/2 No. 62418 *The Pirate* at Thornton in September 1959. Twenty-seven of these engines were built at Cowlairs 1912-20 (NBR class J). The first two engines were built in 1912 and classified D30/1, the remaining twenty-five, which were modified and slightly heavier, were built 1914-20 and classified D30/2.

N. Stead

Plate 55 Left Reid NBR "Glen" class D34 4-4-0 No. 62488 *Glen Aladale* standing at Carlisle on 3rd September, 1960 prior to working an evening train to Riccarton. Thirty-two of these engines were built at Cowlairs 1913-20 (NBR class K) and the last one, No. 62496 *Glen Loy* was withdrawn in November 1961.

I.S. Carr

Plate 56 Left One of the twenty-one Pickersgill GNSR class D40 4-4-0s No. 62260 at Fraserburgh on 17th June, 1949 on an Aberdeen train. These engines were built 1899-1920 (GNSR class V and F) and many were later superheated by Heywood.

H.C. Casserley

Plate 57 Below Heywood GNSR class D40 No. 62275 *Sir David Steward* leaving Ballater on an Aberdeen train.

J.G. Dewing

Plate 58 Left Johnson GNSR class D41 4-4-0 No. 6901 at Ferryhill Jn, shortly after leaving Aberdeen on a Ballater train, just after the grouping. Thirty-two of these engines were built between 1893 and 1898 (GNSR classes S and T) and were very similar to the saturated class D40s.

A.G. Ellis Collection

Plate 59 *Right* Raven NER class H1 4-4-4T No. 1524. These locomotives were the NER class D and were the only 4-4-4Ts inherited by the LNER at the grouping. Forty-five were built 1913-21 and they were all rebuilt at Darlington between 1933 and 1936 to 4-6-2Ts of class A8.
F.G. Carrier

Plate 60 *Left* In November 1937 the LNER took over eight 4-4-4Ts from London Transport. These had been introduced in 1920 by Jones and were classified H2 by the LNER. London Transport 4-4-4T No. 110 is heading an Aylesbury train near Chalfont Latimer in Spring 1937.
E.E. Smith

Plate 61 *Below* LNER class H2 4-4-4T No. 6416 is leaving Nottingham Victoria on a Mansfield train on 18th June, 1946. The last engine of this class was withdrawn in November 1947.
J.P. Wilson

Plate 62 Above An attractive winter scene at Melton Mowbray (North) in February 1955 with Ivatt GNR class J5 0-6-0 No. 65498 shunting the yard. A total of 20 of these engines were built 1909-10 (GNR class J22), all surviving nationalisation.

Peter Groom

Plate 63 Left The later Ivatt GNR class J6 0-6-0s were slightly heavier and were a far more numerous class, a total of 110 being built between 1911 and 1922 (GNR class J22), the first fifteen to Ivatt's design and the remainder to a design which was slightly modified by Gresley after he became CME of the GNR in 1911. The last of this very useful class of engines was withdrawn in 1962 and in this picture No. 64232 is seen on the down slow line adjacent to Werrington troughs, north of Peterborough, on 15th July, 1954, heading a freight bound for the Doncaster area.

P.H. Wells

Plate 64 Right The class J6 0-6-0s were very versatile engines and No. 64235 is heading a Nottingham Victoria — Derby Friargate train about 1950 near Derby.

E.E. Smith

Plate 65 Below A total of 289 T.W. Worsdell GER class J15 0-6-0s were built between 1883-1913 (GER class Y14) and these were withdrawn over a period of 42 years!, 272 surviving the grouping and the last one being withdrawn in 1962. On 11th April, 1955 No. 65390 is standing at Kettering on a Cambridge train.

Lance Brown

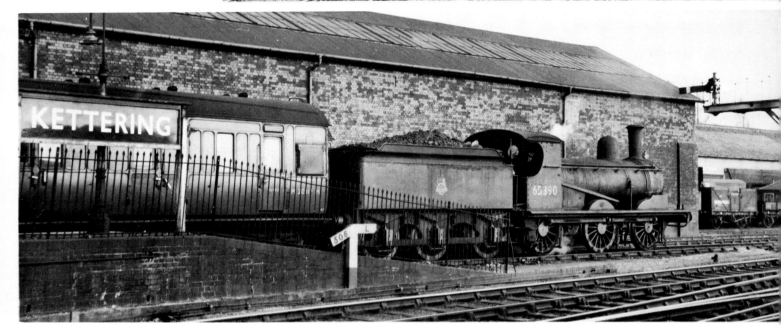

Plate 66 Right The year after T.W. Worsdell became CME of the NER in 1885, he introduced the class J21 0-6-0s. A total of 201 were built from 1886-1894, (NER class C1), the majority of which were initially compounds and converted to simples from 1901. No. 65089 is leaving Kirkby Stephen in May 1952 heading the 16.09 Penrith — Darlington. The last engine of the class survived until 1961.

E.E. Smith

Plate 67 Above The class J23 0-6-0 was a Stirling design for the Hull and Barnsley Railway introduced in 1889 (H & BR class B). A total of 55 were built 1889-1908 and although they all survived the grouping the last one was withdrawn in 1938. No. 2518 is heading a down freight near Barnby Moor on 27th June, 1936.

A.G. Ellis Collection

Plate 68 Below A most attractive scene at Whitby on 30th July, 1955 with W. Worsdell NER class J25 0-6-0 No. 65685 in the foreground and Gresley 'V3' 2-6-2T No. 67638 of Middlesbrough between duties in the background. One hundred and twenty of these 0-6-0s were built 1898-1902, (NER class P1), the last one being withdrawn in 1962.

Lance Brown

Plate 69 Above The W. Worsdell class J27 0-6-0s were a familiar sight in the North East until steam was eliminated from that area in September 1967. In 1964 No. 65814 is passing West Slekburn with coal for Blyth Power Station. A total of 105 of these engines were built before the grouping from 1906 (NER class P3) and a further ten engines were built in 1923, all 115 surviving nationalisation.

P.J. Robinson

Plate 70 Below One of the NBR 0-6-0 designs inherited at the grouping was the Reid class J35, seventy-six of which were built 1906-13 (NBR class B), and here No. 64507 is seen at Dunfermline Lower.

N. Stead

Plate 71 Left The class J67 0-6-0T was a Holden GER design (GER class R24) and fifty-one were built between 1890 and 1901 with some subsequently rebuilt from and to class J69. This scene at Galashiels on 10th July, 1950 shows class J67/1 No. 68511 coupled to a 'J37' tender and class J67/2 No. 68492 coupled to a 'J36' tender. Because of weight restrictions on the Lauder and other Border branches they ran with the engine side tanks empty utilising the 0-6-0 tenders.

A.G. Ellis collection

Plate 72 Above The class J72 0-6-0T was introduced by W. Worsdell in 1898, seventy-five being built until 1921 (NER class E1). Ten more engines were built in 1925 and the design was perpetuated when another twenty-nine were built by BR 1949-51. No. 68680 is seen shunting stock at Newcastle Central.

F.G. Carrier

Plate 73 Left On 27th August, 1956 Holmes NBR class J83 0-6-0T No. 68481 is on familiar duties acting as No. 1 station pilot at Edinburgh Waverley. Forty of these engines were built 1900-1901 (NBR class D) and all but one survived nationalisation, the last engine being withdrawn in December 1962.

G.W. Morrison

Plate 74 Above Sixty-five Gresley GNR class K2 2-6-0s were built 1913-21 (GNR class H3) and ten of his earlier small-boilered class K1 2-6-0s were subsequently rebuilt to class K2. Some of these engines were later transferred to Scotland and thirteen of the class were named after Scottish Lochs. On 19th April, 1954 No. 61779 as BR classification K2/2 is leaving Aberdeen with a Deeside train.

G.H. Robin

Plate 75 Above One of the named 'K2s', No. 61788 Loch Rannoch is standing at Fort William shed on 1st September, 1958.

G.W. Morrison

Plate 76 Right On 23rd February, 1959 class K2/2 No. 61763 of Colwick is climbing away from Saxby on the through Birmingham — East Coast "Express" on the last week of the M & GN, with the Midland main line on the left. This 'K2' had been drafted in from Colwick specially for the last week, evoking memories of earlier days when this class worked the service.

Peter Groom

Plate 77 Above In the mid 1950s Ivatt class N1 0-6-2T No. 69471 is climbing out of Bradford at Laisterdyke on the Bradford portion of the up "Yorkshire Pullman". Fifty-six of these engines were built 1906-12 as the GNR class N1, all but one surviving nationalisation, and the last one was withdrawn in April 1959.

L. Overend

Plate 78 Below The class N5 0-6-2Ts were built 1891-1901 by Thomas Parker for the MS & LR, later becoming GCR classes 9C and 9F. One hundred and twenty-nine were built for the MS & LR and two more were subsequently acquired by the GCR in 1905 from the Wrexham, Mold & Connahs Quay Railway. No. 69293 is seen on station pilot duties at Peterborough North on 16th August, 1958.

Peter Groom

Plate 79 Right W. Worsdell NER class Q5 0-8-0 with its post war number, 3314, as reclassified Q5/1 at Port Clarence on 13th August, 1951. This was one of the last survivors of the class, ninety being built 1901-11 as NER classes T and T1.

P.H. Wells

Plate 80 Below Vincent Raven built the first of his NER 0-8-0s in 1913, 120 being built as class T2 between 1913 and 1921. No. 63407 as BR class Q6 is heading a coal train to Hartlepool Docks passing Cemetery North Jn, Hartlepool in 1966.

N. Stead

Plate 81 Right Only five of Raven's more powerful three-cylinder 0-8-0s were built in 1919 (NER class T3) but ten more were built in 1924. All fifteen engines survived until 1961 and No. 63471 as BR class Q7 is seen near Washington about 1960 on a Tyne Dock — Consett train.

E.E. Smith

Plate 82 Left Hill GER class Y4 0-4-0T No. 68129 shunting at Stratford Works on 19th February, 1951. Five of these 3′ 10″ engines were built between 1913-20 (GER class B74) the last one being withdrawn in 1963.

R.E. Vincent

Plate 83 Below The Holmes NBR class Y9 0-4-0ST was introduced in 1882 and thirty-eight were subsequently built until 1899 as NBR class G. Several ran in later years permanently attached to a wooden tender and No. 68118 is seen so fitted at Bathgate.

N. Stead

Plate 84 Left On 23rd September, 1955 Manning, Wardle GNSR class Z5 0-4-2T No. 68193 is shunting at Aberdeen Docks. Four of these engines were built in 1915 (GNSR classes X and Y) specifically for this work and they were all withdrawn between 1956 and 1960.

P.H. Wells

Plate 85 Above Peppercorn class A1 4-6-2 No. 60117 *Bois Roussel* leaving Leeds Central on 25th April, 1964 with the 17.10 to Doncaster. This design appeared a few months after nationalisation and was a 6′8″ version of this class A2 Pacific. A total of forty-nine class A1s were built at Doncaster and Darlington in 16 months, entering service from August 1948.

J.S. Whiteley

Plate 86 Below Class A1 Pacific No. 60149 *Amadis* is climbing past Holloway South Down signal box heading the 10.10 Kings Cross — Leeds on 20th September, 1953. This engine was built at Darlington in May 1949 and withdrawn in June 1964, a very short life for such a reliable and efficient class of engine.

R.E. Vincent

Plate 87 *Above* The up "Yorkshire Pullman" is accelerated away from Retford by class A1 Pacific No. 60141 *Abbotsford* in Summer 1958.

D. Penney

Plate 88 *Left* No. 60147 *North Eastern* is being coaled at York on 11th April, 1964. Four class A1s were named after constituent companies of the LNER and these nameplates incorporated the appropriate coat of arms as can be seen in this picture.

G.W. Morrison

SIR VINCENT RAVEN

Plate 89 *Above* Nameplate of class A1 No. 60126 which was named at Darlington on 3rd August, 1950.

J.S. Whiteley

WILSON WORSDELL

Plate 90 *Above* No. 60127 was also named after a NER Chief Mechanical Engineer and was given the name at a ceremony at Newcastle Central Station on 30th October, 1950.

J.S. Whiteley

Plate 91 Above Class A2/2 No. 60504 *Mons Meg* on a down express at Potters Bar in Autumn 1959. Six class A2/2 Pacifics were rebuilt from Gresley class P2 2-8-2s (see plates 140 and 141) by Edward Thompson in 1943 and 1944.

D. Cross

Plate 92 Above No. 60505 *Thane of Fife* was the first of the class P2s to be rebuilt by Thompson, appearing as a Pacific in January 1943. The 'A2/2s' had 6'2" driving wheels and the leading bogie positioned in front of the outside cylinders, all in all not a particularly attractive design and not enhanced in this instance by the unlipped chimney. It is seen at Grantham on 9th July, 1958.

Peter Groom

Plate 93 Right Class A2/3 No. 60520 *Owen Tudor* at Oakleigh Park in September 1960 heading an up parcels train.

D. Cross

Plate 94 Above Thompson class A2/3 No. 60500 *Edward Thompson* is heading a Kings Cross — Newcastle express at Oakleigh Park in September 1960. These 6′2″ engines were a development of the class A2/2s and a total of fifteen were built in 1946/47. This locomotive was named after the retiring CME at Marylebone station on 31st May, 1946 and the other fourteen were all given the names of racehorses.

D. Cross

A.H. PEPPERCORN

Plate 95 Above Nameplate of class A2 Pacific No. 60525, the name having been given to the engine at a ceremony at Marylebone station on 18th December, 1947. This engine was the first Peppercorn Pacific and the only one to appear before nationalisation on 1st January, 1948.

J.S. Whiteley

Plate 96 Below The Peppercorn class A2 Pacifics were also a development of the 'A2/2s' with 6′2″ driving wheels but a shorter wheelbase. Fifteen were built, one before nationalisation and the remaining fourteen in 1948. They were a far more attractive design than the Thompson engines having the outside cylinders astride the front bogie. Surprisingly only six engines were fitted with double chimneys and No. 60535 *Hornets Beauty* is seen with single chimney, near Mauchline heading an Ayr — Carlisle Mail.

D. Cross

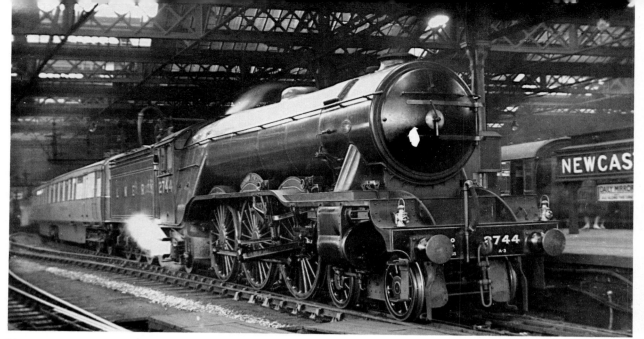

Plate 97 Above In 1927 two of the Gresley class A1 Pacifics were fitted with new 220 lb sq. in. boilers replacing the original 180 lb sq. in. boilers. These reboilered engines became class A3 and between 1927 and 1948 all but one of the fifty-two class A1s were converted to class A3, the exception being No. 4470 *Great Northern* which was rebuilt by Thompson in 1945 (see plate 240). Twenty-seven engines were built to class A3 at Doncaster between 1928 and 1938 and one of these engines, No. 2744 *Grand Parade* is seen at Newcastle on the down "Coronation".

Authors' Collection

Plate 98 Below Another one of the engines originally built to class A3, No. 60039 *Sandwich*, leaving High Wycombe on 28th February, 1957 on the 12.15 Marylebone — Manchester.

J.D. Edwards

Plate 99 Above Gresley class A3 4-6-2 No. 60055
Woolwinder was built at Doncaster in 1924 as class A1 and
reboilered to class A3 in 1942. It is seen heading a down
Hull train at Potters Bar on 29th July, 1949, still with right
hand drive.

R.W. Beaton

Plate 100 Above Nameplate of class A3 No. 60060
photographed at Darlington on 17th May, 1952.

R.E. Vincent

Plate 101 Left Between 1958 and 1960
all the 'A3s' were fitted with double
chimneys (No. 60097 *Humorist* had
been fitted with one in 1937 and had
been the subject of smoke deflection
experiments) and No. 60062 *Minora* is
seen in this condition on 20th May,
1961 leaving Leeds near Copley Hill on
the up "Yorkshire Pullman". The
fitting of double blastpipes and
chimneys to the class A3s produced a
marked improvement in their
performance but did cause problems
with the softer exhaust obscuring
vision from the footplate.

J.S. Whiteley

Plate 102 Above After unsuccessful trials with very small wing type deflectors fitted at each side of the chimney, it was decided to fit the class A3s with German style trough smoke deflectors which proved most effective, but some would suggest at the cost of the appearance of these beautifully proportioned engines. Fifty-five of the seventy-nine class A3s were fitted with trough deflectors from 1961 and No. 60044 *Melton* is seen in this condition passing through Cleckheaton on 8th October, 1961 on the 10.25 Kings Cross — Leeds, diverted via Low Moor because of engineering work between Wakefield and Leeds.

J.S. Whiteley

Plate 103 Below On 19th August, 1961 No. 60100 *Spearmint* fitted with new type non-corridor tender, is leaving Peterborough North on a down express.

P.H. Wells

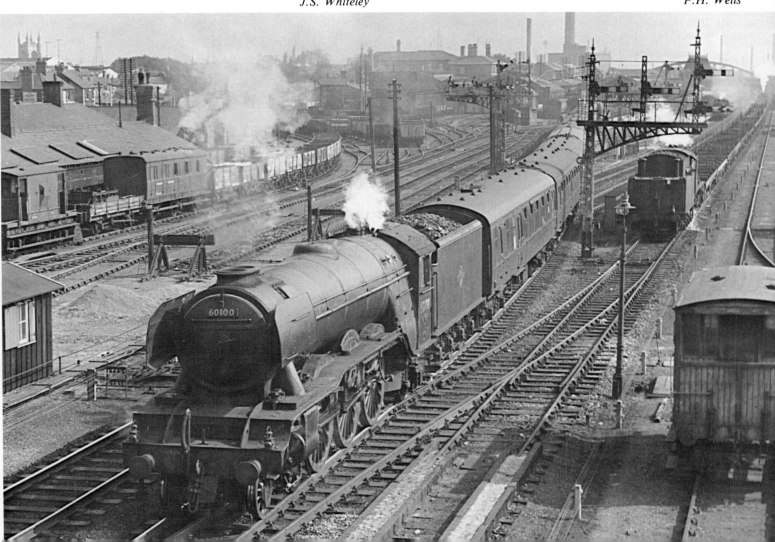

Plate 104 Above In 1935 Gresley built four three-cylinder class A4 streamlined Pacifics for working the "Silver Jubilee" express, and another thirty-one of these magnificent locomotives were built from 1936-38. No. 4496 *Golden Shuttle* (re-named *Dwight D. Eisenhower* in September 1945) is seen in garter blue livery passing Hornsey on a down express in the late 1930s.

N. Stead

Plate 105 Right No. 4469 *Gadwall* (renamed *Sir Ralph Wedgwood* in March 1939) was built in March 1938 and tragically scrapped in June 1942 as a result of bomb damage at York on 29th April, 1942. It is seen climbing to Potters Bar on a down express in Summer 1938.

E.E. Smith

Plate 106 Left A light task for the locomotive which had secured the world record of 126 mph for steam traction in the previous year. No. 4468 *Mallard* is heading an up local near Tuxford on 22 July, 1939. This was one of the four 'A4s' fitted with a double blastpipe and chimney when first built in 1938.

S. Dewsbery

Plate 107 Above The down "Flying Scotsman" is nearing the end of its journey on 13th July, 1938 as it approaches Portobello behind class A4 No. 4489 *Dominion of Canada*. This engine was originally named *Woodcock* but was renamed in June 1937 and was fitted with a Canadian railway type bell on 11th March, 1938, having been presented with it by the Canadian Pacific Railway Company.

J.P. Wilson

Plate 108 Right In striking silver-grey livery, one of the four original class A4s No. 2512 *Silver Fox*, with the name painted on the side of the boiler, speeds past Barnby Moor in 1936 on the up "Silver Jubilee".

A.G. Ellis Collection

Plate 109 Below Right During 1941 and 1942 the skirting both in front of and behind the outside cylinders was removed from all the A4s to facilitate easier maintenance. No. 60022 *Mallard* is coming off an up express at Newcastle Central in the mid 1950s.

E.E. Smith

Plate 110 Above Plaques commemorating the record of *Mallard* were fitted to the locomotive by BR in 1948 and one can be seen on the side of the boiler in the picture on the right.

J.S. Whiteley

Plate 111 Above In BR green livery No. 60017 *Silver Fox* is near Finsbury Park on the down 16.30 from Kings Cross on 14th June, 1962. The class A4s not fitted with double chimneys when built were all so fitted in 1957 and 1958. No. 60017 was the last 'A4' to work a normal service train out of Kings Cross on 29th October, 1963; shortly afterwards it was withdrawn.

Peter Groom

Plate 112 Below Towards the end of 1963 the class A4s remaining on the Eastern Region were transferred to Scotland, together with four from Gateshead. The remaining members of the class ended their days in fine style working the 3 hour Glasgow — Aberdeen expresses and No. 60019 *Bittern* is leaving Stirling on 20th April, 1965 with the up "Bon Accord".

J.S. Whiteley

Plate 113 Above Class A8 4-6-2T No. 69872 crossing the Monkwearmouth Bridge with a South Shields — Sunderland stopping train in October 1957. These engines were introduced in 1931 by Gresley being a rebuild of the Raven class H1 4-4-4Ts (see plate 59).

S.E. Teasdale

Plate 114 Right Thompson class B1 4-6-0 No. 61032 *Stembok* crossing Relly Mill Viaduct with the 12.07 Darlington — Newcastle, via Bishop Auckland, on 23rd July, 1960. Four hundred and ten of these versatile 6'2" engines were built 1942-52 but only fifty-nine were named, the majority being given "antelope" names.

I.S. Carr

Plate 115 Above Shortly before its withdrawal, in September 1967, class B1 4-6-0 No. 61306 stands inside Bradford Exchange with an evening parcels train.

J.M. Rayner

Plate 116 Below Class B12/3 4-6-0 No. 61553 hurries down from Stoke Summit with an up 'local' from Grantham on 23rd April, 1956 during the few years these engines were shedded at Grantham. The 'B12/3s' were rebuilt by Gresley with larger round topped boilers from Holden's GER design of 1911. A total of fifty-four engines were rebuilt to class B12/3 between 1932 and 1944 and the last one was withdrawn in 1961.

Peter Groom

Plate 117 Right Class B16/3 4-6-0 No. 61454 is climbing to Speeton Summit on 15th August, 1959 with a Newcastle — Filey Camp train. Seventeen of these engines were rebuilt by Thompson between 1944 and 1949 from Raven's NER class S3 design of 1919, incorporating three sets of Walschaerts valve gear.

N. Stead

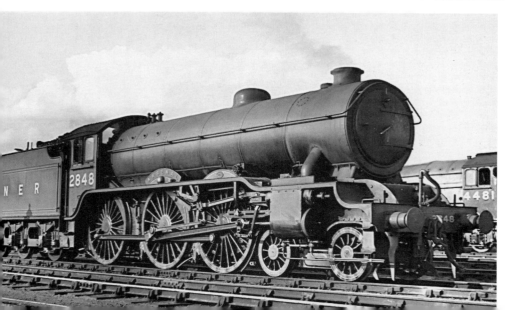

Plate 118 Above Between 1928 and 1937 a total of seventy-three class B17 three-cylinder 4-6-0s were built by the North British Locomotive Co., Darlington and R. Stephenson & Co. The third engine to be delivered on 7th December, 1928 was numbered 2800, given the name *Sandringham* and headed the class. The first forty-eight engines were named after English country houses and the following 25 after Football clubs, although some name changes were later made. No. 61625 *Raby Castle* as 'B17/1' is heading a Kings Cross — Cambridge near Potters Bar with GER type tender as fitted to the first forty-seven engines.

N. Stead

Plate 119 Left The first of the "footballers", class B17/4 No. 2848 *Arsenal*, built at Darlington in 1936, is seen at Doncaster.

F.G. Carrier

Plate 120 Above The last twenty-five engines of the class were fitted with the larger LNER 4200 gallon tender and on 14th April, 1952 BR No. 61652 *Darlington*, as rebuilt to class B17/6 with B1-type boiler, is approaching Welwyn viaduct on a down Cambridge train.

R.E. Vincent

Plate 121 Right In September 1937 Nos. 2859 and 2870 were streamlined for working the "East Anglian" service between Norwich and Liverpool Street, became class B17/5 and were renamed *East Anglian* and *City of London* respectively (see plate 243). In April 1951 the streamlining was removed, and as reclassified B17/6 No. 61659 *East Anglian* is seen at Manchester London Road in May 1951.

T. Lewis

Plate 122 Below Left Shortly after Edward Thompson succeeded Gresley, standardisation proposals were produced to reduce the large number of classes then in existence. Amongst several classes selected for rebuilding were Gresley's B17s, but in the event only nine class B17/1s and one class B17/4 were rebuilt between 1945 and 1949 with two cylinders and the Diagram 100A boiler used on the Thompson B1 class. The first of these engines rebuilt to class B2 at Darlington was No.2871 *Manchester City* which emerged in August 1945 with its original 4200 gallon tender. In April 1946 it was renamed *Royal Sovereign* for working the Royal trains to and from Wolferton station for Sandringham, and it is seen on 16th May, 1952 as BR No. 61671 heading an up Cambridge train at Greenwood.

R.W. Beaton

Plate 123 Right "Super Claud" class D16/2 4-4-0 No. 8787 nears Potters Bar on 6th August, 1938 with a Cambridge — Kings Cross train. These engines had been rebuilt with extended smokeboxes from 'D16s' built in 1923, and this particular engine was one of two Cambridge Royal "Clauds" kept in immaculate green livery for working the Royal trains. Both these Royal "Clauds" were, however, replaced on this duty by the B2 seen in the previous picture.

S. Dewsbery

Plate 124 Below From 1933 until 1948 104 Claud Hamilton 4-4-0s of classes D14, D15 and D16 were rebuilt with 5'1″ boiler with round top firebox replacing the Belpaire firebox, and became class D16/3. On 10th October, 1951 class D16/3 No. 62566 is approaching East Suffolk Jn, Ipswich heading the 14.22 Ipswich — Cambridge stopping train. This engine had been rebuilt by Gresley from a class D15 and has modified footplating.

R.E. Vincent

Plate 125 Above The Gresley three-cylinder class D49 4-4-0s were introduced late in 1927, and in all seventy-six were built at Darlington. Thirty-four "Shire" class D49/1s eventually had piston valves and the forty-two "Hunt" class D49/2s had Lentz rotary cam poppet valves. On 7th August, 1956 "Hunt" class D49/2 No. 62774 *The Staintondale* finishes watering at Leeds City. The last engine of the class was withdrawn in 1961 but fortunately one has been preserved.

G.W. Morrison

Plate 126 Left Class D49/2 No. 62763 *The Fitzwilliam* is near Hammerton on a York — Harrogate train about 1956. Only one member of the class was ever substantially rebuilt, BR No. 62768 *The Morpeth*. This engine was altered from three cylinders to two inside cylinders by Thompson in 1942 and remained so until withdrawal in 1952 after damage sustained in a collision.

E.E. Smith

Plate 127 Above Nameplate of "Hunt" class D49/2.

J.S. Whiteley

Plate 128 Above Nameplate of "Shire" class D49/1.

J.S. Whiteley

Plate 129 Above One hundred and seventy-four Robinson class J11 0-6-0s were built from 1901-10 (GCR class 9J), many subsequently being rebuilt and superheated. Class J11/3 No. 64450 was one of the engines rebuilt from 1942 by Thompson with long-travel piston valves and higher-pitched boiler, and it is seen leaving Guide Bridge.

T. Lewis

Plate 130 Below Class J39 0-6-0 No. 64812 at Alston on a Sunday excursion from Newcastle Central. Two hundred and eighty-nine of these engines were built between 1926 and 1941 to Gresley's design and they became extinct late in 1962.

E.E. Smith

Plate 131 *Above* Ten class K3 2-6-0s were built by Gresley before the grouping and a further 183 were built between 1924 and 1937 to LNER loading gauge, being a development of the GNR design. Class K3/2 Mogul No. 61896 is leaving Basford North, Nottingham, with an excursion to Skegness on 17th August, 1958.

T. Boustead

Plate 132 *Below* Class K3/2 No. 61839 is leaving the Waleswood branch at Killamarsh on 9th October, 1956 with an up fish train.

B.R. Goodlad

Plate 133 Right Only one of Thompson's class L1 2-6-4Ts was built before nationalisation but a further ninety-nine were built between 1948 and 1950. BR No. 67756 was one of the 1948 engines built by the North British Locomotive Co. and it is seen on 27th April, 1958 at Annesley. The entire class was withdrawn from service by December 1962 with the mass introduction of diesel multiple units for use on local passenger services.

G.W. Morrison

Plate 134 Below Early on the morning of 7th July, 1954 class N2/4 No. 69589 is lifting empty stock from Kings Cross to Finsbury Park carriage sidings. This was one of the forty-seven post-grouping engines which were all built with left hand drive unlike the sixty pre-grouping engines. The class N2/4s were all built with condensing apparatus although the remainder of the LNER built class N2s were not.

B. Morrison

Plate 135 Above Thompson class O1 2-8-0 No. 63712 heading a Tyne Dock — Consett ore train with banking assistance, seen near West Stanley about 1958. Just over fifty of these engines were **rebuilt from Robinson class O4s with new cylinders and diagram 100A boiler.**

E.E. Smith

Plate 136 Below Class O1 2-8-0 No. 63571 was rebuilt by BR from a Robinson class O4/1 of 1911 and it is passing Brighouse on 26th May, 1962 with a westbound coal train.

J.S. Whiteley

Plate 137 Above The class O2 2-8-0s were introduced by Gresley in 1918 and No. 63932 as class O2/4 is at Doncaster on 4th May, 1958. These engines had also been rebuilt by Thompson with 100A B1 type boilers.

G.W. Morrison

Plate 138 Below Thompson class O4/8 2-8-0 No. 63853 with 100A B1 type boiler, but retaining original cylinders, is labouring past Godley East Junction on the climb to Woodhead with eastbound empties on 8th March, 1952.

T. Lewis

Plate 139 Above Two class P1 2-8-2s were built by Gresley in 1925 specifically for working heavy coal trains between New England and Hornsey. In 1930 No. 2393 with booster engine is near Marshmoor.
A.G. Ellis Collection

Plate 140 Right Class P2/2 2-8-2 No. 2002 *Earl Marischal* in August 1935 on the up "Aberdonian". Two of these three-cylinder engines were introduced in 1934 for use between Edinburgh and Aberdeen, and the first one, Class P2/1 No. 2001 *Cock o' the North* was fitted with 'ACFI' feed water heater, unlike No. 2002.
A.G. Ellis Collection

Plate 141 Left Four more 'P2s' were built in 1936, Nos. 2003-6. These were mechanically similar to No. 2002 but had the streamlined appearance of the 'A4' Pacifics and No. 2004 *Mons Meg* is seen at Grantham. Both the earlier class P2s were rebuilt as Nos. 2003-6 by 1938, but all six were subsequently rebuilt as Pacifics by Thompson in 1943-4 (see plates 91 and 92).

Plate 142 Above The Gresley class V2 three-cylinder 2-6-2 was designed as a mixed traffic locomotive for working fast freight traffic and 184 were built, twenty-five at Doncaster and the remainder at Darlington, between 1936 and 1944. They were equally at home on express passenger duties and No. 858, with a liberal coating of post-war grime, roars past Hitchin on an up express.

W. Philip Conolly

Plate 143 Below Whilst the majority of the class V2's work was done on the East Coast main line, they were to be found at work throughout the length and breadth of the system, and on 16th September, 1958 No. 60842 is seen on former GC and GW joint metals near Beaconsfield heading the midday Manchester express.

G.W. Morrison

Plate 144 Above So successful was the design of these versatile engines that no major modification was made throughout their working life. A few were, however, fitted with double chimneys late in their lives, but ironically these were largely the engines which suffered early withdrawal on the Eastern Region. The only other variation occurred when several engines were latterly fitted with outside steam pipes when the original monobloc cylinder casting was replaced by three separate cylinders. No. 60961 is heading an up express at Low Fell about 1950.

E.E. Smith

Plate 145 Below Class V2 Prairie No. 60943 is climbing away from Grantham on 26th July, 1958 on the up "Northumbrian". The last V2 was withdrawn from service late in 1966, but fortunately the prototype is beautifully preserved in working order (see plate 266).

Peter Groom

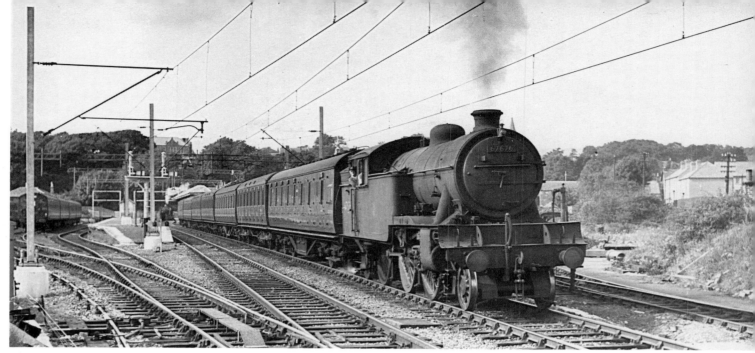

Plate 146 *Above* In 1930 the first Gresley class V1 three-cylinder 2-6-2Ts appeared and eighty-two were built until 1938, primarily for use on suburban services in the Edinburgh, Glasgow and Newcastle districts. In 1939 and 1940 ten further engines were built with a 200lb/sq.in. boiler and classed V3. Many of the earlier 'V1s' fitted with 180lb/sq.in. boilers were altered to 'V3', one of them being No. 67676 seen on 23rd July, 1959 as class V1 leaving Milngavie with a Bridgeton train.

G.W. Morrison

Plate 147 *Below* The three-cylinder class V4 2-6-2 was the last steam locomotive design of Gresley and only two were built in 1941 for the West Highland. These were lightweight versions of the class V2 and No. 61701 is at the head of the 06.25 local freight for Laurencekirk in Aberdeen Yards on 26th June, 1957. This was the last of the two to be withdrawn, only five months after this picture was taken.

B. Morrison

Plate 148 Left In 1930 Gresley's experimental class W1 4-6-4 high pressure compound appeared, the "hush-hush" as it was nicknamed. It was built at Darlington and fitted with a Yarrow 450lb/sq.in. water tube boiler which subsequently proved troublesome to maintain. In October 1930 it was displayed at Wavertree on the occasion of the centenary of the Liverpool & Manchester Railway and it is seen in front of GWR No. 6029 *King Stephen*, later renamed.

F.G. Carrier

Plate 149 Right In 1937 Gresley rebuilt his W1 as a three-cylinder engine similar in appearance to his A4s, but with larger cylinders and retaining the unique 4-6-4 wheel arrangement. It is heading a down express past Potters Bar in 1938. The engine was renumbered 60700 by BR and eventually withdrawn from service in June 1959.

S. Dewsbery

Plate 150 Left No. 10000 is on shed at Doncaster in the late 1930s, and in this view the baltic wheel arrangement can clearly be seen.

F.G. Carrier

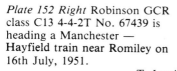

Plate 151 Above Gresley class V3 2-6-2T No. 67638 is at Whitby Town on 30th July, 1955 on a Whitby — Middlesbrough (via Battersby) train. This engine was built as a class V1 in 1935 and reboilered to class V3 earlier in 1955.

Lance Brown

Plate 152 Right Robinson GCR class C13 4-4-2T No. 67439 is heading a Manchester — Hayfield train near Romiley on 16th July, 1951.

T. Lewis

Plate 153 *Above* Raven NER class A7 4-6-2T (NER class Y) No. 1180 emerging from Bramhope Tunnel on a local freight from Leeds. Twenty of these heavy 4'7¼" tank engines were built at Darlington in 1910-11, all survived nationalisation and the last one was withdrawn in 1957.

A.G. Ellis Collection

Plate 154 *Right* On 20th April, 1957 Worsdell class J72 0-6-0T No. 68700 is seen at Keith, formerly GN of SR metals.

R.E. Vincent

Plate 155 *Left* Ten of these 2-4-2Ts were built in 1896 by Pollitt for the MS&LR subsequently becoming GCR class 9G. On 8th September, 1947 No. 7105 (1946 number) as class F2 is leaving Bulwell Common heading the Annesley "Dido", the staff train which operated between Annesley and Bulwell. All the class F2s were fitted with push and pull gear between 1936 and 1943 and the last engine was withdrawn from service late in 1950.

J.P. Wilson

Plate 156 Above Between 1904 and 1910 three of these M & GN class A 4-4-2Ts were built at Melton Constable Works to a design of W. Marriott. In October 1936 these engines were taken over by the LNER but not classified C17 until July 1942. No. 09 was the last of these three engines to be withdrawn from service in July 1944 and is seen at Melton Constable.

S. Dewsbery

Plate 157 Right Reid NBR class N15/1 0-6-2T No. 69186 (NBR class A). Ninety-nine of these engines were built between 1910 and 1924, based on the six Reid class N14 engines which were built in 1909. The N15 class was divided into parts 1 and 2, class N15/1 having either steam or steam and vacuum brakes and the six class N15/2s having Westinghouse brakes.

N. Stead

Plate 158 Left Holden GER class F5 2-4-2T No. 67209 at Palace Gates on 10th April, 1954 with a North Woolwich train. Thirty class F5s were built 1903-9 at Stratford and all were withdrawn between 1955 and 1958.

B. Morrison

Plate 159 Above A total of 100 Thompson class L1 2-6-4 tank engines were built, but only one appeared before nationalisation, in 1945, and the remainder after nationalisation, between 1948 and 1950. They were built at Doncaster, Darlington and by the NB Loco. Co. and R. Stephenson & Hawthorns. No. 67754 is crossing Staithes viaduct on 3rd May, 1958 heading a Middlesbrough — Scarborough train.

Lance Brown

Plate 160 Below Gresley class N2/2 No. 69529 rushes up Holloway Bank on 31st August, 1961 with the Kings Cross breakdown train.

Peter Groom

DOUBLE-HEADED TRAINS

Plate 161 Above Double-heading of the "Flying Scotsman" north of Newcastle was not uncommon during the winter timetable as the relief did not run, and on 15th September, 1938 the up train is seen at Plessey behind class D49/1 No. 264 *Stirlingshire* and A4 Pacific No. 4493 *Woodcock*.

E.E. Smith

Plate 162 Below Until the Gresley Pacifics took over the expresses on the GN main line, 4-4-0s and Atlantics often double-headed. In 1926 Ivatt class D2 4-4-0 No. 4336 pilots Ivatt class C1 Atlantic No. 4410 near Potters Bar on a down train.

A.G. Ellis Collection

Plate 163 Left Reid NBR class D34 4-4-0s Nos. 9281 *Glen Murran* and 9256 *Glen Douglas* are lifting a heavy train up the 1 in 45 of Cowlairs Bank about 1929.

A.G. Ellis Collection

Plate 164 Right Reid NBR class C11 Atlantic No. 9875 *Midlothian* is piloting one of the fifteen Ivatt GNR class D1 4-4-0s which had all been transferred to Scotland in the mid 1920s. The pair are seen passing Haymarket on an Aberdeen — Edinburgh Waverley train.

T.G. Hepburn

Plate 165 Below On Royal Train duties at Monkseaton about 1958 are Gresley class V3 2-6-2Ts No. 67689 and 67653.

E.E. Smith

Plate 166 Left On 8th August, 1936 Gresley class K2/2 No. 4641 is piloting Robinson class B5 4-6-0 No. 6068 near Bulwell Common on a down relief Manchester express.

J.P. Wilson

Plate 167 Below A pair of Robinson class B4 "Immingham" 4-6-0s Nos. 6100 and 6098 are heading a Sheffield — Skegness special near Firsby Junction, a few miles from their destination.

T.G. Hepburn

Plate 168 Below In the late 1950s double-heading was fairly rare on the southern section of the GN main line, although one such working was the 16.12 Kings Cross — Hitchin semi-fast seen here on 13th June, 1957. Thompson class B1 4-6-0 No. 61139 is piloting bunker first class L1 2-6-4T No. 67749 through New Southgate.

Peter Groom

Plate 169 Above Robinson GCR class O4/1 2-8-0 No. 63797 is heading a southbound freight away from
Sheffield on the former GC line near Beighton on 12th September, 1953.

B.R. Goodlad

Plate 170 Left Unrebuilt
Raven class B16 4-6-0
seen as BR class B16/1
No. 61424 on 1st May,
1954 heading a
northbound freight near
Killamarsh.

B.R. Goodlad

Plate 171 Above Road, rail and sea transport meet in this picture taken on the quay at Newcastle about 1950. An unidentified class J72 0-6-0T is shunting on the quayside.

E.E. Smith

Plate 172 Below Early on the morning of 15th March, 1952 Ivatt class C12 4-4-2T No. 67368 is crossing from former MR metals (Leicester-Peterborough) to former GN metals (Essendine branch) with a transfer freight.

P.H. Wells

Plate 173 Above Class O4/8 2-8-0 No. 63644 is emerging from Sherwood Rise Tunnel, New Basford, on 8th June, 1963 with a northbound coal train.

T. Boustead

Plate 174 Below The first of Robinson's class J11 0-6-0s (nicknamed 'Pom-Poms') seen as BR No. 64280 in the late 1950s at the head of a westbound freight from South Humberside, near Brigg.

N. Stead

Plate 175 Above Gresley class K2/2 2-6-0 No. 61768 speeds through Essendine on 16th June, 1951 heading a down freight.

P.H. Wells

Plate 176 Below Gresley's heavier Mogul, class K3 2-6-0 seen on 4th October, 1962 in the shape of 'K3/2' No. 61973, climbing out of Leeds at Copley Hill with an up express freight.

G.W. Morrison

Two eras of crack LNER express passenger locomotives demoted to mundane freight duties; *Plate 177 Left* Ivatt class C1 4-4-2 No. 4455 is passing Barnby Moor on an up mixed freight.

A.G. Ellis Collection

Plate 178 Below Gresley A4 Pacific No. 60019 *Bittern* is passing Essendine on 3rd June, 1951 at the head of a down rake of empties.

P.H. Wells

Plate 179 Left Not too taxing a load for Worsdell class J25 0-6-0 No. 65645 at Low Fell about 1950.

E.E. Smith

Plate 180 Above Former GC line freight leaving Barnston Tunnel, between Nottingham and Loughborough, behind Thompson class O1 2-8-0 No. 63591 on an up mixed freight. 4th September, 1959.

Peter Groom

Plate 181 Below Gresley class V2 2-6-2 No. 60854 on a duty for which it was primarily designed; it is pulling out the loop at Stoke Summit on a down express freight on 21st July, 1962.

G.W. Morrison

TITLED TRAINS

Plate 182 Above A selection of headboards on display at the National Railway Museum, York.

J.S. Whiteley

Plate 183 Below The name "Northumbrian" was conferred in summer 1949 to a train connecting Newcastle Central and Kings Cross. A mid-morning departure was made from Newcastle and a lunchtime departure from Kings Cross. A4 Pacific No. 60022 *Mallard* is accelerating away from Retford early in 1957 on a 14 coach up train.

D. Penney

Plate 184 Above Gleaming Kings Cross Pacific No. 60028 *Walter K. Whigham* awaits the "right away" from Edinburgh Waverley on its scheduled non-stop run to Kings Cross on 17th July, 1961. The 09.30 and 09.45 departures from Kings Cross and Edinburgh Waverley respectively were given the name "Capitals Limited" in 1949 but in 1953, in honour of the Coronation of Queen Elizabeth II, the name was changed to "Elizabethan".

J.S. Whiteley

Plate 185 Right The "Elizabethan" was one of the most exacting duties ever required of a steam locomotive and was entrusted to the 'A4s'. On 4th September, 1954 No. 60009 *Union of South Africa* suffers the indignity of a signal check at Peterborough North on the up train.

P.H. Wells

Plate 186 Above Towards the end of steam haulage on the "Thames-Clyde Express", Gresley class A3 Pacifics were transferred to Holbeck, Leeds, to work between Leeds and Glasgow. On 13th July, 1960 No. 60077 *The White Knight* enters Carlisle on the up train.

T. Boustead

Plate 187 Left When the "East Anglian" was introduced in 1937 between Liverpool Street and Norwich Thorpe, two class B17 4-6-0s, Nos. 2859 and 2870, were specially streamlined and given the names *East Anglian* and *City of London* respectively. With an intermediate stop at Ipswich the journey time of 2¼ hours was not especially sparkling. On 28th July, 1949 class B17/5, as BR numbered 61659 *East Anglian* arrives at Liverpool Street on the up train. Both *East Anglian* and *City of London* had their stream-lining removed in 1951 and reclassified B17/6 (see plate 121).

R.E. Vincent

Plate 188 Above The "South Yorkshireman" ran over the Great Central main line and was first named in 1948. It ran between Marylebone and Bradford Exchange via Leicester, Nottingham and Sheffield. Here class B1 4-6-0 No. 61182 has just taken over from a Stanier class 5 on the up train at Sheffield Victoria about 1950.

E.E. Smith

Plate 189 Below Shortly after the grouping a through train was introduced from Kings Cross to Scarborough with a non-stop run to York, normally behind Pacifics. On 2nd August, 1952 class A3 No. 60039 *Sandwich* emerges from Hadley Wood North Tunnel on the down train.

R.W. Beaton

Plate 190 Above The "White Rose" ran between Kings Cross and Leeds Central, the name being conferred in 1949 on the 09.18 down train and 17.15 up train. A4 Pacific No. 60013 *Dominion of New Zealand* nears Ganwick on the down train on 2nd August, 1952. The title "White Rose" was transferred in Summer 1964, to the Pullman train serving Harrogate when the title "Queen of Scots" was dropped after this train ceased running north from Harrogate. Just prior to disappearing in March 1967 the "White Rose" left Kings Cross at 11.25 and Harrogate at 16.00.

R.W. Beaton

Plate 191 Below The "Silver Jubilee" was the first British streamlined train, entering service on 30th September, 1935 between Kings Cross and Newcastle Central. It ran Mondays-Fridays only, leaving Newcastle at 10.00 and arriving at Kings Cross at 14.00. In the down direction it left Kings Cross at 17.30 on the same 4 hour timing averaging 67.08 mph. Initially four Gresley A4 Pacifics were specially built for the service, Nos. 2509 *Silver Link*, 2510 *Quicksilver*, 2511 *Silver King* and 2512 *Silver Fox*, all finished in silver-grey to match the train. What a fine sight No. 2510 *Quicksilver* makes on the down train near Potters Bar in 1937. Sadly the train was withdrawn at the outbreak of war and never reinstated.

E.E. Smith

Plate 192 Right In July 1937 the LNER added another streamlined train to the highly successful "Silver Jubilee" and this was named the "Coronation" in honour of the Coronation of King George VI and Queen Elizabeth in that year. The nine coach set was very striking in appearance with light blue upper panels and dark blue, known as "garter blue", for the lower panels. A unique "beaver tail" observation car (see plate 226) was incorporated at the rear of the train in summer. The train left Kings Cross at 16.00 arriving Edinburgh Waverley at 22.00 and left Edinburgh Waverley at 16.30 reaching Kings Cross at 22.30. Five streamlined class A4 Pacifics were specially allocated to the "Coronation" service and one of them, No. 4488 *Union of South Africa*, is climbing to Potters Bar on the down train shortly after its introduction in Summer 1937.

E.E. Smith

Plate 193 Below The most famous of all, the "Flying Scotsman", which makes the 392.9 mile journey between Kings Cross and Edinburgh Waverley every week-day. From June 1862, almost without interruption there has been a 10.00 departure from Kings Cross to Edinburgh Waverley which received the title "Flying Scotsman" shortly after the grouping. In May 1928 it was scheduled to make the longest non-stop run in the world made possible with corridor tenders allowing a crew change en route. In the early 1930s Gresley class A3 Pacific No. 2796 *Spearmint* is seen on the up train near Peascliffe Tunnel.

F. G. Carrier

Plate 194 Above In Spring 1936 the down "Flying Scotsman" is seen behind Gresley class A4 Pacific No. 2510 *Quicksilver* accelerating northwards from Doncaster near Arksey. This was one of four 'A4s' which ran for about 9 months without any numbers at the front end (see also plate 255).

A.G. Ellis Collection

Plate 195 Below An unusual sight on 19th September, 1955 with 'V2' 2-6-2 No. 60821 heading the up train. It is seen rushing down from Stoke Summit towards Peterborough running 40 minutes late and almost certainly deputising at short notice for a failed Pacific.

Peter Groom

Plate 196 Above Holden GER class D15/2 4-4-0 No. 8889 with extended smokebox is approaching Norwich Thorpe at Thorpe Junction on 29th May, 1939 with a train from Yarmouth.

J.P. Wilson

Plate 197 Right A scene at Spalding on 16th September, 1933 with former GCR and GNR motive power in the shape of Robinson class B5 4-6-0 No. 5187 and Ivatt large-boilered Atlantic No. 4407 respectively.

H.C. Casserley

Plate 198 Above Class B12/3 4-6-0 No. 61577 is leaving Kings Lynn in July 1959 heading a Hunstanton train.

N. Stead

Plate 199 Below Another class B12/3, No. 61570, is seen accelerating the Lowestoft portion of the 13.30 from Liverpool Street away from Ipswich at East Suffolk Jn on 10th October, 1951. The line to Bury St Edmunds and Cambridge can be seen on the right of the picture.

R.E. Vincent

Plate 200 Above Class D16/3 4-4-0 No. 62566 is leaving
Ipswich on 8th October, 1952 with a stopping train for
Cambridge.

A.G. Ellis Collection

Plate 201 Below Another 'D16/3', No. 62596 with original
footplating unlike No. 62566 above which was rebuilt with
modified footplating, is leaving South Lynn shortly after
nationalisation.

E.E. Smith

Plate 202 Above Stoke was on the cross-country Cambridge — Colchester line, and about 1956 Holden GER class E4 2-4-0 No. 62789 is seen simmering in the station. One hundred of these engines were built 1891-1902 (GER class T26) to satisfy the Great Eastern's need for some mixed traffic engines suitable for working cross country passenger trains such as seen here.

E.E. Smith

Plate 203 Below An unidentified class D16/3 4-4-0 is heading a Peterborough — March train at King's Dyke Crossing on 3rd October, 1959.

N. Stead

Plate 204 *Above* Class D16/3 4-4-0 No. 62567 is seen at Wisbech about 1958, thought to be heading a Kings Lynn — Peterborough train.

E.E. Smith

Plate 205 *Below* Class B1 4-6-0 No. 61050 is rounding the north side of Wensum triangle from Norwich Thorpe with a cross country train from Yarmouth and Lowestoft to the Midlands on 23rd July, 1955. The Thompson 'B1s' together with the Gresley 'B17s' supplemented existing motive power on the GE section after the war.

R.E. Vincent

Plate 206 Above Sunday morning at Hammerton Street, Bradford, shortly after nationalisation.

L. Overend

Plate 207 Below About 1960, four Worsdell class J71 0-6-0Ts are lined up at Darlington together with a Riddles class J94 0-6-0ST and a Thompson class B1 4-6-0.

E.E. Smith

Plate 208 Above Holmes NBR class J36 0-6-0 No. 65216 *Byng* inside Carlisle Canal.

E.E. Smith

Plate 209 Above Inside Wrexham shed about 1936. Parker MS&LR class N5 0-6-2T No. 5539 is standing in front of Robinson GCR class C13 4-4-2T No. 5050. Another N5 can be seen on the left.

E.E. Smith

Plate 210 Right Worsdell class J21 0-6-0 No. 65064 is standing under the coaling plant at Darlington on 19th May, 1952.

R.E. Vincent

Plate 211 *Left* Cromer on 25th August, 1955, with class J39/2 0-6-0 No. 64889 and class B1 4-6-0 No. 61048.

G.W. Morrison

Plate 212 *Above* From left to right at March on 4th May, 1958 are class K1 2-6-0 No. 62020, class B17/6 4-6-0 No. 61633 *Kimbolton Castle*, class B17/6 4-6-0 No. 61657 *Doncaster Rovers*, 'Austerity' 2-8-0 No. 90279 and the cab of class K3/2 2-6-0 No. 61860.

G.W. Morrison

Plate 213 *Left* Ivatt GNR class J52 0-6-0ST No. 4224 simmers at New England on 21st May, 1938.

J.G. Dewing

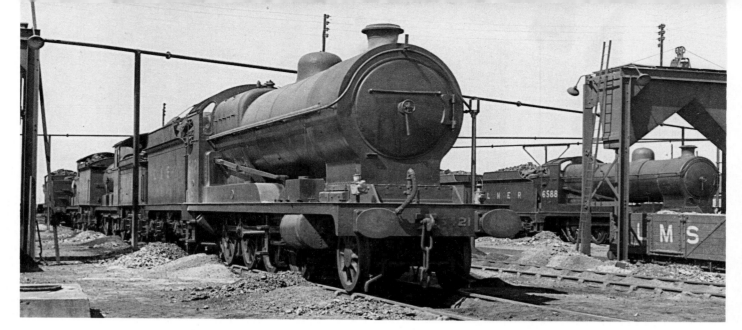

Plate 214 *Above* Robinson GCR class O5 2-8-0 No. 5421 dominates this picture taken at March in 1948.

E.E. Smith

Plate 215 *Left* A collection of 0-6-0Ts at Alexandra Dock, Hull in 1953.

E.E. Smith

Plate 216 *Below* Resplendent in green livery, Robinson class B4 4-6-0 No. 6097 *Immingham*, thought to be at Lincoln on 4th June, 1939.

S. Dewsbery

Plate 217 Above Large-boilered Ivatt class C1 4-4-2 No. 4445 resting between turns at Doncaster.

E.E. Smith

Plate 218 Below Kipps on 8th June, 1957 with Gresley non-condensing class N2/3 0-6-2T No. 69596 on the left and Holmes class J36 0-6-0 No. 65325 under the coaling plant.

G. W. Morrison

Plate 219 *Above* Inside the roundhouse at York on 11th April, 1964 are, from left to right, class V2 2-6-2 No. 60828, Peppercorn class A1 Pacifics Nos. 60150 *Willbrook* and 60155 *Borderer* and class B1 4-6-0 No. 61021 *Reitbok*.

G.W. Morrison

Plate 220 *Below* Two Gresley Pacifics, both as subsequently fitted with double chimneys, seen at Haymarket. On the left class A3 No. 60093 *Coronach* and on the right class A4 No. 60004 *William Whitelaw*.

N. Stead

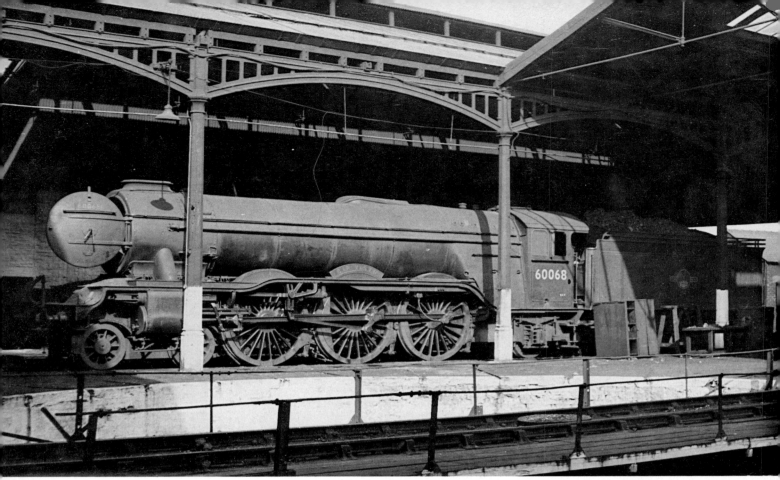

Plate 221 *Above* At rest inside Carlisle Canal is double-chimneyed Gresley class A3 4-6-2 No. 60068 *Sir Visto*.

P.J. Robinson

Plate 222 *Right* On its home shed of Blaydon on 18th September, 1955 is Raven class Q6 0-8-0 No. 63391.

G.W. Morrison

Plate 223 *Below* Thornton on 12th April, 1959. On view from left to right are "Shire" class D49/1 4-4-0 No. 62708 *Argyllshire*, Reid NBR class J88 0-6-0T No. 68334, class D30/2 4-4-0 No. 62418 *The Pirate*, class K3/2 2-6-0 No. 61955 and an unidentified "Shire" 4-4-0.

G.W. Morrison

Plate 224 Above Between duties at Mallaig on 22nd July, 1959 is class K2/2 2-6-0 No. 61764 *Loch Arkaig.*

G.W. Morrison

Plate 225 Below An all out effort is required to turn the 116 tons 11 cwt of class B17/1 4-6-0 No. 2829 *Naworth Castle* at Yarmouth on 26th June, 1938.

S. Dewsbery

Plate 226 Above Under the shadow of Ben Nevis at Fort William on 1st September, 1958. The observation coach is being turned to return on the 16.20 to Glasgow Queen Street and is attached to class J36 0-6-0 No. 65313.

G.W. Morrison

Plate 227 Below A bird's eye view of Grantham on 27th April, 1952 with the High Dyke freight locos on the left, the main line roads in the centre and the ashpits on the right.

P.H. Wells

Plate 228 Above Inside Darlington Works.

S.E. Teasdale

UNDER REPAIR

Plate 229 Below An A4 Pacific under repair at Doncaster Works.

S. Dewsbery

Plate 230 Left Grimsby and Immingham Tramcar No. 15 at Grimsby Corporation Bridge station on 19th May, 1954.

R.E. Vincent

Plate 231 Right What an ignominious end for five large-boilered C1 Atlantics at Doncaster.

N. Stead

Plate 232 Below Class Y3 Sentinel 0-4-0T, Departmental No. 38 (formerly BR No. 68168) shunting across the main street in Lowestoft on 20 April 1954. These two-speed geared engines were introduced in 1927 to a Sentinel Wagon Works design.

R.E. Vincent

KINGS CROSS

Plate 233 Below Gresley Pacific No. 60026 *Miles Beevor* makes an impressive departure from platform 3 of the terminus with an evening train to the north in the early 1960s.

M. Welch

Plate 234 *Above* On 5th July, 1952, Peppercorn class A1 Pacific No. 60122 *Curlew* is awaiting departure on the "Aberdonian" alongside the customary crowd of spotters.

B. Morrison

Plate 235 *Below* Royal class B2 4-6-0 No. 61671 *Royal Sovereign* returning to its base at Cambridge on an afternoon train from the Cross on 17th June, 1957.

R.E. Vincen

Plate 236 Above Whilst allocated to Hitchin, class L1 2-6-4T No. 67745 stands inside the terminus at the head of the 18.25 local to Baldock on 11th January, 1952.

B. Morrison

Plate 237 Right Another evening scene inside the station, this time an arrival at platform 5 in 1937 in the shape of "Klondyke" No. 3989.

E.E. Smith

Plate 238 Above From their delivery late in 1920, the Gresley class N2 0-6-2Ts were to be found on suburban workings from Kings Cross until early 1962, being the mainstay of the services for about 40 years and affectionately known as "Met Tanks". On 17th June, 1957 class N2/4 No. 69556 is carriage shunting and not setting off for Hertford as might first appear.

R.E. Vincent

Plate 239 Below On 18 April, 1952 Gresley A4 Pacific No. 60003 *Andrew K. McCosh* eases out of Gas Works Tunnel and into the terminus with the up "Tees-Tyne Pullman".

R.W. Beaton

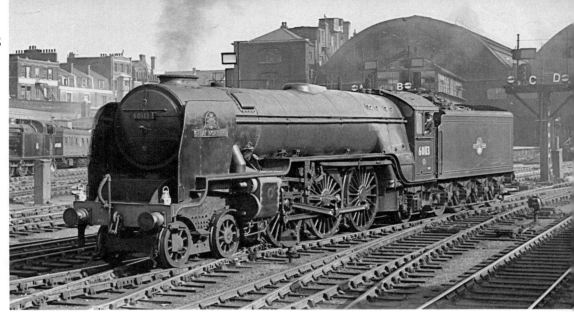

Plate 240 Above On purely personal grounds Edward Thompson selected Gresley's pioneer A1 Pacific *Great Northern* for rebuilding, and in September 1945 it appeared with a new 250 lb/sq.in. boiler, new valve gear and outside cylinders set well back behind the leading bogie. This rebuild was not reclassified but the remaining A1 Pacifics with 180 lb/sq.in. boilers became class A10 and it was not until January 1947 that *Great Northern* became class A1/1 to make way for the new Peppercorn Pacifics. It is seen at Kings Cross on 17th June, 1957 as BR No. 60113.

R.E. Vincent

Plate 241 Above In 1929 Raven class A2 Pacific No. 2404 *City of Ripon* was rebuilt with a modified 'A1' boiler, firebox and cab. In 1936, as reclassified A2/2, it is seen at Grantham shed with Gresley 8-wheeled tender.
T.G. Hepburn

Plate 242 Right Thompson class A2/3 Pacific No. 60512 *Steady Aim* at Grantham shortly after nationalisation, before the fitting of a smokebox number and with its original unlipped chimney.
M.F. Carrier

STREAMLINED SIX-COUPLED

Plate 243 Left Gresley class B17/5 4-6-0 No. 2870 *City of London* at Norwich on 26th June, 1938.

S. Dewsbery

Plate 244 Centre Gresley class A4 4-6-2 No. 4903 *Peregrine* at Doncaster on 2nd July, 1938. This was the last class A4 to be built and it is seen shortly after delivery when still brand new. It was renamed *Lord Faringdon* in March 1948.

S. Dewsbery

Plate 245 Bottom Gresley class W1 4-6-4 No. 10000 at Doncaster shed in 1938.

S. Dewsbery

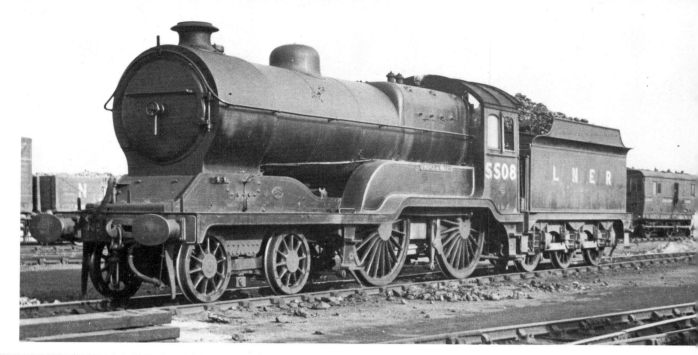

Plate 246 Top Robinson
"Director" class D11 4-4-0 No.
5508 *Prince of Wales* at
Doncaster on 18th September,
1937.

S. Dewsbery

Plate 247 Centre Robinson "Sir
Sam Fay" class B2 4-6-0 No.
5427 *City of London* at Gorton
in June 1937. Later in 1937 No.
5427 lost its name when it was
given to the streamlined class
B17 as seen in plate 243.

S. Dewsbery

Plate 248 Right Ivatt class D2
4-4-0 No. 4332, seen about 1936
at Boston.

E.E. Smith

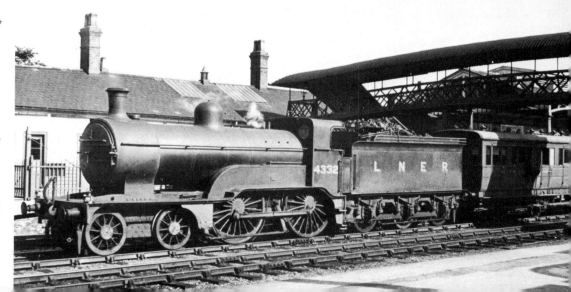

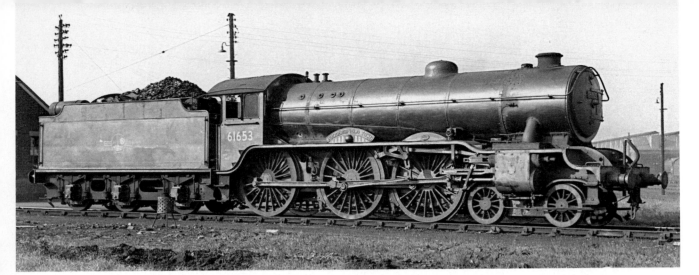

Plate 249 Top Gresley class B17/6 No. 61653 *Huddersfield Town*, as fitted with a 100A B1 type boiler, at March in October 1959.

N. Stead

Plate 250 Centre Class B12/3 4-6-0 No. 61570 at Stratford on 25th May, 1957.

R.E. Vincent

Plate 251 Left Vulcan Foundry built class B1 4-6-0 No. 1175, seen in pristine LNER green livery just before nationalisation.

M.F. Carrier

Plate 252 Left Class J3 0-6-0 No. 4154 at New England about 1936. This was one of the many Stirling/Ivatt GNR class J4 engines rebuilt by the LNER to class J3.

E.E. Smith

Plate 253 Below Holden class E4 2-4-0 No. 62789 at Beccles on 6th September, 1952. Only 18 of the class of 100 survived to carry BR numbers.

R.E. Vincent

Plate 254 Left M. Stirling H&BR class J28 0-6-0 No. 2418 believed to be at Doncaster in the mid 1930s. Only twenty of these domeless engines were built between 1911 and 1914 (H&BR class L) and the class became extinct in 1938.

F.G. Carrier

Plate 255 Above An interesting picture taken at Kings Cross on 14th September, 1935. No. 2509 *Silver Link* was the first of Gresley's A4 Pacifics completed at Doncaster in September 1935 and it had arrived at Kings Cross for the very first time the day before this picture was taken, having run light engine from Doncaster. It is thought that this picture was taken when it had returned after working its first train, the 07.10 Kings Cross — Cambridge slow.

F.G. Carrier

Plate 256 Below The late afternoon sun glints on Gresley class A3 Pacific No. 60106 *Flying Fox* in its final form with double chimney and smoke deflectors at Grantham on 21st July, 1962.

G.W. Morrison

Plate 257 Right Class D16/3 4-4-0 No. 8900 *Claud Hamilton* as rebuilt with boiler similar to the 'Super Clauds', but with round topped firebox in place of the Belpaire and modified footplating.

A.G. Ellis Collection

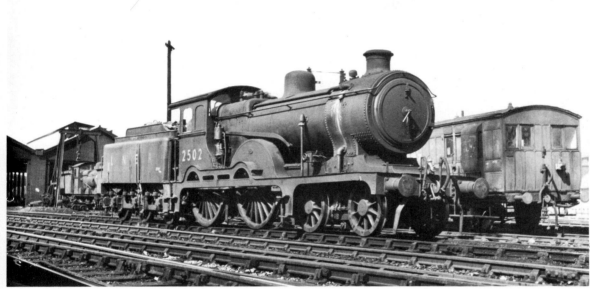

Plate 258 Left Class D15 4-4-0 No. 2502 (1946 number-formerly No. 8891) at Dereham just before nationalisation, seen as rebuilt superheated with extended smokebox but retaining the original footplating. It is attached to a former oil carrying tender.

E.E. Smith

Plate 259 Below Pollitt MS&LR class D6 4-4-0 No. 5880 at Immingham in May 1938 (GCR class 11A). Thirty-three of these 7'0" engines were built 1897-99 but none survived nationalisation, the last one being withdrawn immediately before, in December 1947.

J.G. Dewing

A TRIO OF ATLANTICS

Plate 260 Left Raven NER three-cylinder class C7 No. 2172. These engines were introduced in 1911 and were a slightly heavier version of the early class C6 of Worsdell, seen below. The fifty engines of this class were the prime express passenger motive power for the NER at the grouping.

F.G. Carrier

Plate 261 Centre Worsdell NER class C6 No. 702 at Gateshead in the early 1930s. These two-cylinder engines were introduced in 1903 but only twenty were built.

F.G. Carrier

Plate 262 Bottom Reid NBR class C11 4-4-2 No. 9906 *Teribus* seen in the mid 1920s. Twenty-two of these fine Atlantics were built between 1906 and 1921 and were NBR classes H and I. Sixteen class H were superheated and became LNER class C11, six were built to class 1 and these were initially LNER class C10, but by 1925 these six had all been rebuilt superheated to class C11. They were all withdrawn between 1933 and 1939.

A.G. Ellis Collection

Plate 263 Right Gresley class N2/2 0-6-2T No. 69549 at Doncaster on 17th August, 1958 after a visit to the Works. This was one of the sixty pre-grouping engines built 1920-21 (GNR class N2) with right hand drive, short chimney and condensing apparatus, although fifteen of these engines subsequently had the condensing apparatus removed. A further forty-seven engines were built after the grouping, all with left hand drive but not all fitted with condensing apparatus.

G.W. Morrison

Plate 264 Left Gresley class J50/3 0-6-0T No. 68977 at Doncaster in ex-works condition on 11th May, 1958. In 1922 ten J50s were built (GNR class J23), a further sixty-two were built from 1924-39 during which time thirty J51s which were built from 1913-19 (also GNR class J23) were rebuilt to class J50. All one hundred and two survived nationalisation and the last one was withdrawn in 1965 from Departmental stock.

G.W. Morrison

Plate 265 Right The last of the ninety-nine Reid NBR class N15 0-6-2Ts which was built at Cowlairs in April 1924 seen at Thornton on 8th June, 1957 as BR class N15/1 No. 69224.

G.W. Morrison

Plate 266 Above Gresley class V2 2-6-2 No. 60800 *Green Arrow* standing in the shed yard at Grantham on 27th August, 1958 waiting to take an afternoon train from the north on to Kings Cross. This engine was the first class V2 to appear from Doncaster in June 1936, as No. 4771, and fortunately it has been officially preserved in working order by BR after being withdrawn from service in August 1962.

Peter Groom

Plate 267 Below One of the most famous steam locomotives of all time, No. 4472 *Flying Scotsman*. It was the first of Gresley's class A1 Pacifics to be completed at Doncaster after the grouping and entered traffic on 24th February, 1923 as No. 1472, preceded only by Nos. 1470 and 1471 which both entered traffic during the last year of the GNR. *Flying Scotsman* was so named in February 1924 in connection with its appearance at the 1924 Empire Exhibition and renumbered 4472. After being withdrawn from service in January 1963 as reboilered class A3 No. 60103, it was purchased privately and restored to LNER livery. It is seen here before being reboilered and as fitted with a streamlined non-corridor tender in July 1938.

F.G. Carrier

Plate 1 Maunsell 'Lord Nelson' Class 4-6-0 No 30853
Sir Richard Grenville with Bulleid modifications including
larger tender, improved cylinders and multiple jet blastpipe
with large diameter chimney. It is seen on shed at Eastleigh
on 29th September, 1961.

G. W. Morrison

Plate 2 The up 'Golden Arrow' is approaching Folkestone
Junction on 18th April, 1952 behind Bulleid 'West Country'
4-6-2 No 34104 *Bere Alston*. This was one of nineteen
'West Country' Pacifics which were built after nationalisation with large 5,500 gallon capacity tender. It is seen in
standard dark BR Brunswick green livery with orange and
black lining and lion and wheel emblem on the tender.

A. Cawston, D. Cobbe collection

by

J.S. WHITELEY and G.W. MORRISON

Oxford Publishing Co.

Plate 3 On 14th August, 1937, Maunsell 'King Arthur'
Class 4-6-0 No 769 *Sir Balan* is leaving Dover Marine at the
head of an up boat train. It is seen with a Urie eight-wheeled
tender, Ashford-style cab built to comply with the composite SR loading gauge and standard design of Maunsell smoke
deflectors.

A. Cawston, D. Cobbe collection

ACKNOWLEDGEMENT

The authors have derived great pleasure from compiling this album, and in so doing are much indebted to the many
photographers who have made their collections freely available and who have offered such valuable assistance during its
preparation. We should also like to offer our thanks once again to Margaret Morley for typing the manuscript.

Contents

Introduction

The Southern Remembered is the third volume in this series, and has been prepared with a similar theme to *The LMS Remembered* and *The LNER Remembered*, already published. It includes pictures showing steam locomotive designs which were inherited by the Southern Railway on its formation in 1923, and also designs which were conceived during its twenty-five years' existence until nationalisation on 1st January, 1948.

The Southern Railway came into being on 1st January, 1923, and numerically was the smallest of the 'Big Four' companies, inheriting approximately 2,300 locomotives at the grouping, compared with approximately 10,500 locomotives by the LMS, 7,700 by the LNER and 4,050 by the GWR. On formation of the Southern Railway, locomotives of three major companies were brought into one ownership, those of the London and South Western Railway, the South Eastern and Chatham Railway and the London, Brighton and South Coast Railway, together with some small companies in the Isle of Wight and the West of England. The Southern Railway also differed fundamentally from the LMS, LNER and GWR in having taken over some electrified lines, and then subsequently embarking upon a programme of further main line electrification which was undertaken at the expense of steam locomotive construction and development.

Contributions from the three major Southern constituent companies were roughly as follows: The London and South Western Railway operated approximately 1,020 route miles, had about 930 locomotives and was the only one to employ six-coupled tender locomotives on express passenger services. The London, Brighton and South Coast Railway operated approximately 450 route miles and preferred the use of tank locomotives on its relatively short main lines, having some 435 tank locomotives and only about 180 tender locomotives. The South Eastern and Chatham Railway had approximately 640 route miles and owned some 725 locomotives, having developed the four-coupled wheel arrangement on tender locomotives for express passenger use.

R. E. L. Maunsell had been Chief Mechanical Engineer of the South Eastern and Chatham Railway from 1913, and was appointed to the post of Chief Mechanical Engineer of the Southern Railway on its formation in 1923. The locomotives he took over were a very mixed bag of about 125 different classes, several of which had already outlived their usefulness, and he was intent upon a scheme of standardisation. He was largely unable to complete this, however, mainly because of the serious economic depression in the post-First World War years, and also the Southern Railway's continued programme of electrification. He did, however, manage to produce some extremely good designs during his 15 years in office, and will no doubt be remembered by many people for his magnificent 'Schools' 4-4-0s, possibly the finest 4-4-0s ever to run in this country.

When Maunsell retired in 1937 he was succeeded by O. V. S. Bulleid who had previously been acting as assistant to Nigel Gresley, the CME of the LNER. Bulleid's task was no easier than Maunsell's, as he arrived on the scene when the prospects of a Second World War were soon to become an ominous reality, and the Southern Railway was still continuing with its programme of main line electrification. Although Bulleid did not produce very many designs during his ten years or so in office before nationalisation on 1st January, 1948, he was responsible for improving several existing designs and will certainly be remembered for his magnificent, if slightly unconventional, Pacifics. It was because of his determined efforts that the SR eventually possessed more Pacifics than the LMS, and almost as many as the LNER, and his 'Merchant Navys' and Light Pacifics succeeded in transforming the express passenger services of the Southern Railway.

J. S. Whiteley
February 1980

Plate 4 Above Between 1887 and 1895 William Adams built 90 inside cylinder 0-4-2 engines of Class 'A12' and 'O4' for the LSWR. They were general purpose engines and were used on a variety of duties from secondary expresses to freight work. No E602 is passing Clapham Junction on 25th May, 1931 during the removal of the overhead electrification.

H. C. Casserley

Plate 5 Below Often referred to as 'Jubilees', Adams Class 'A12' 0-4-2 No 555 is seen near Botley on 15th October, 1938 heading a local train from Eastleigh to Portsmouth. The first of this class of 6 ft 0 in engines was withdrawn in 1928, only four survived nationalisation and were withdrawn later in 1948.

H. C. Casserley

Plate 6 *Above* Class 'A12' 0-4-2 No 598 is leaving Andover Junction in 1938 on an up stopping train to Basingstoke. The original stovepipe chimneys were replaced by Drummond chimneys during the early 1900s.

C. R. L. Coles

Plate 7 *Left* On 2nd May, 1931, Adams 0-4-2 No E599 awaits the 'right away' from Guildford. These 'A12s' were the last 0-4-2 tender engines in service in this country.

H. C. Casserley

Plate 8 *Right* One of the famous Brighton 'Gladstones', No B172 *Littlehampton* at Brighton on 14th March, 1933. These Class 'B1' 0-4-2 engines were the last of William Stroudley's express passenger designs for the LBSCR. A total of 36 were built between 1882 and 1891 with 26 being taken into Southern Railway stock at the grouping. The last six engines of the class, Nos 172-177, were completed at Brighton Works after Stroudley's death, between November 1890 and April 1891. Nos 172 and 173 were the last two to be built and incorporated some of Robert Billinton's modifications. No 172 was the last of the 'Gladstones' to be withdrawn from service, in September 1933, and it is seen here with Marsh boiler and chimney.

A. G. Ellis collection

Plate 9 Left Between 1900 and 1908 one hundred and nine of Wainwright's very successful Class 'C' 0-6-0s were built for the SECR. They had 5 ft 2 in coupled driving wheels, inside cylinders, and were designed for mixed traffic duties. One of these engines was rebuilt by Maunsell in 1917 as a Class 'S' 0-6-0ST, and of the remainder all but two survived nationalisation, the last one being withdrawn from the Southern Region of BR in 1963. The example seen here has been re-numbered 1713 by the addition of 1000 to all SECR locomotives from 1931.

E. E. Smith

Plate 10 Below Wainwright Class 'C' 0-6-0 seen as BR No 31719 on 7th May, 1949, but still lettered 'Southern' on the tender, is heading an up freight at Wandsworth Common.

R. W. Beaton

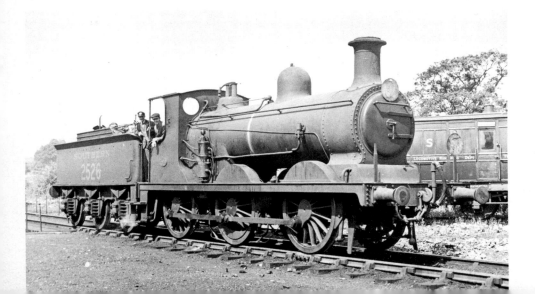

Plate 11 Left Numerically the largest class of 0-6-0 built for the LBSCR were R. J. Billinton's Class 'C2', 55 of which were built between 1893 and 1902. They were all built by the Vulcan Foundry at Newton-le-Willows and as a result were always known as 'Vulcans'. No 2526, seen here in the early 1930s, was one of the 45 'C2s' which were eventually rebuilt with larger boilers over a period of 32 years, from 1908 until 1940 (see Plate 12). Only three of the unrebuilt engines were in service at nationalisation, and the last one was withdrawn in 1950.

E. E. Smith

Plate 12 Right Billinton's 'C2s' had 160 lb/sq in boilers, but increased loadings, and accelerated timings prompted Marsh to rebuild them to Class 'C2X', using a 'C3' 170 lb/sq in boiler. Forty-one of the conversions were done at Brighton Works, but the last four were carried out at Ashford. Class 'C2X' No 2445 is seen in the early 1930s, and the last of these 'Large Vulcans' was withdrawn in 1962.
E. E. Smith

Plate 13 Left No 2448 was one of the 'Large Vulcans' to be fitted with one of the fifteen 'C2X' boilers which had L. B. Billinton's top feed apparatus, housed in an additional dome. Only six of these boilers were originally fitted to Class 'C2Xs', the remainder being fitted to five Class 'C3s' and four Class 'B2X'. These boilers were interchangeable and the second dome was retained after the top feed was discarded. No 2448 is seen at New Cross on 30th April, 1937 with side feed, dual braking and cut down boiler mountings.
A. G. Ellis collection

Plate 14 Below The Class 'C2X' 0-6-0s with larger boilers and extended smokebox were far stronger engines than the original 'C2s' and capable of handling the heaviest goods trains. BR No 32446 is heading a down freight at Wandsworth Common on 8th August, 1949.
R. W. Beaton

Plate 20 Left The 'K' Class Moguls were mainly confined to the Brighton line and throughout their working life no major modifications were made, although the boiler pressure was raised to 180 lb/sq in. BR No 32340 is seen shunting in Lewes sidings near Southerham Junction on 12th June, 1962 in its last year of service. All seventeen engines were withdrawn *en bloc* late in 1962 as part of the Southern Region's dieselisation programme.

D. Cobbe

Plate 21 Right In 1917 the first of Maunsell's two cylinder Class 'N' 2-6-0s appeared for the SECR. They were designed as mixed traffic engines with a superheated taper boiler of 200 lb/sq in. Twelve were in service at the grouping with three more entering service in 1923, all fifteen being built at Ashford, Nos 810–821 and A823–A825. In 1919 the Government decided on construction of the class for national use and employment was found for the staff of Woolwich Arsenal Ordnance Factory following the end of the First World War. An order was placed for 100 complete sets of parts for the Maunsell Class 'N' 2-6-0s but in the event only 50 sets of parts were purchased by the SR and assembled at Ashford 1924/5, Nos A826–A875, with boilers built by the North British Locomotive Company. A further 15 engines were built at Ashford 1932/3 and numbered 1400–1414 and these all had larger 4,000 gallon tenders. No 839 seen here was one of the Woolwich engines.

A. G. Ellis collection

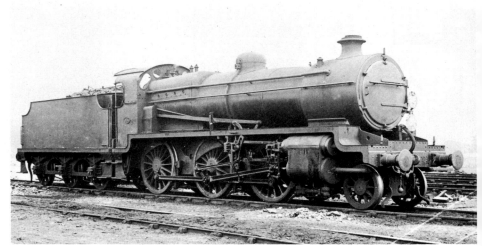

Plate 22 Below From 1933 the 'N' Class were fitted with smoke deflectors. No 1823 was one of the 1923 Ashford engines and is seen at St. Leonards West Marina shed on 10th July, 1939.

J. P. Wilson

Plate 23 *Above* The Woolwich engines were sent to the West of England when new and one of them, No 31835, is leaving Padstow on 17th May, 1962 with a local train for Wadebridge.

D. Cobbe

Plate 24 *Left* Another one of the Woolwich engines, No 31860 is heading the 09.50 Wadebridge—Bodmin North in May 1962. No 31408 was the last engine of the class to be withdrawn in 1966.

D. Cobbe

Plate 25 *Right* In 1897 Class 'T7' 4-2-2-0 No 720 was built at Nine Elms Works for the LSWR to a design of Dugald Drummond. This was his first express locomotive for the LSWR and incorporated two inside cylinders which drove the leading driving wheels and two outside cylinders the trailing drivers, a 'double-single' design. The design was not a success and in an attempt to improve matters the four cylinders were reduced to 14 in and a larger boiler fitted. At the same time five similar 'double-singles' were introduced in 1910, and these became Class 'E10'. The performance of all six engines however rarely compared with those of 4-4-0s of similar dimensions and as a result they suffered early withdrawal in 1926/7. Class 'T7' No E720 is seen in this photograph.

A. G. Ellis collection

Plate 26 Left Stirling/Wainwright Class 'B1' 4-4-0 No 1444 leaving Bromley on 29th August, 1931. The twenty-nine Class 'B' 4-4-0s were James Stirling's final design for the SER before he retired in 1898 and they were all built in 1898/9, nine at Ashford and the remainder by Neilson, Reid & Co. To improve their performance Wainwright decided to reboiler them with boilers of 170 lb/sq in working pressure. Between 1910 and 1927 all but two were reboilered, becoming Class 'B1', and all the 'B1s' were subsequently fitted with extended smokeboxes. As such they were capable of handling all but the hardest of main line duties. Withdrawal commenced in 1933 but was interrupted during the war years and the last one was withdrawn in 1951.

H. C. Casserley

Plate 27 Right LBSCR Class 'B4' 4-4-0 No 2068 in Southern green livery at Brighton in October 1937 Thirty-three of these engines were built by Robert J. Billinton between 1889 and 1902, and twelve were subsequently rebuilt to Class 'B4X' from 1922 (see *Plate 29*). The 'B4s' had 6 ft 9 in coupled drivers, two inside cylinders and all but two members of the class (Nos 2044 and 2046) had 180 lb/sq in saturated boilers. The first 'B4' was withdrawn in 1934 and at the outbreak of the Second World War two of the eight surviving 'B4s' (Nos 2051 and 2068) were loaned to the LNER. These two engines were returned to the Southern in 1944 and were withdrawn shortly afterwards. Twelve engines survived nationalisation and the last one was withdrawn in 1951.

A. G. Ellis collection

Plate 28 Below R. J. Billinton Class 'B4' No 2047 at Polegate on 20th October, 1934. It is seen after being renumbered by the Southern. To avoid duplication of numbers, the SR decided upon a renumbering scheme in 1931 whereby 1000 was added to the number of SECR engines, 2000 added to LBSCR engines, with LSWR engines being left with their original numbers. After the grouping and prior to this renumbering scheme the SR had adopted prefixes to the numbers with 'E' signifying LSWR engines (Eastleigh), 'B' LBSCR engines (Brighton) and 'A' SECR engines (Ashford). Isle of Wight engines bore the prefix 'W'.

H. C. Casserley

Plate 29 Right One of the twelve 'B4s' which were rebuilt by L. B. Billinton to Class 'B4X' between 1922 and 1924. These rebuilds had a K-type superheated Belpaire boiler, the same diameter driving wheels but slightly enlarged 20 in cylinders. No 2073 is at Eastleigh in May 1936 with vacuum brake, Maunsell superheater, cut-down dome and Southern green livery.

A. G. Ellis collection

Plate 30 Below On 12th July, 1939 Class 'B4X' No 2067 is entering St. Leonards Warrior Square on a Tonbridge–Hastings train. No 2067 also has a cut-down dome but has Westinghouse air brake. All twelve engines were withdrawn in 1951, although several members of the class had spent lengthy periods in store after nationalisation.

J. P. Wilson

Plate 31 Right Considered by many to be the most handsome of H.S. Wainwright's designs for the SECR were his Class 'D' 4-4-0s, and a total of fifty-one were built between 1901 and 1907. Twenty-two were built at Ashford and the remaining twenty-nine were built by outside contractors. From 1921 several were rebuilt by Maunsell (see *Plate 181*). The last Class 'D' was withdrawn in 1957 but fortunately one is preserved and can be seen at the National Railway Museum at York.

E. E. Smith

Plate 32 *Above* For many years the Wainwright Class 'D' 4-4-0s handled top main line duties, and in BR days in 1953 No 31591 is leaving the now demolished Reading South station with a three coach 'bird-cage' set for Paddock Wood. The GWR station can be seen in the background to the right of the engine.

M. W. Earley

Plate 33 *Left* BR Class 'D' No 31734 is emerging from Bletchingley Tunnel near Godstone with another 'bird-cage' set forming a Redhill—Tonbridge train on 27th April, 1952. After nationalisation on 1st January, 1948, 30000 was added to the numbers of SR engines, a few LSWR engines on the duplicate list being the exception.

J. G. Dewing

Plate 34 Right The Class 'D15' 4-4-0 was the largest and last of Drummond's designs for the LSWR and ten were built at Eastleigh between February and December 1912. His successor on the LSWR was Robert Urie and he superheated them all between 1915 and 1917. These ten 4-4-0s were the principal motive power on the Bournemouth line until they were displaced by the new 'N15' 4-6-0s in 1925/6. They were then transferred to the Portsmouth line and performed extremely well until they were replaced by the 'Schools' in the late 1930s. During this period three were shedded at Fratton and the remainder at Nine Elms. Their original eight-wheeled tenders were exchanged for six-wheeled tenders from Class '700' 0-6-0s due to the restricted dimensions of Fratton roundhouse and turntable. BR No 30464 is seen with Urie chimney as latterly fitted to most of the class, and the last one was withdrawn in 1956.

E. E. Smith

Plate 35 Left Wainwright's Class 'E' 4-4-0s for the SECR were slightly larger than his 'Ds' and twenty-six were built at Ashford 1905—9. Some of these were also the subject of rebuilding by Maunsell, from 1919 (see *Plate 183*). The last Class 'E' was withdrawn in 1955 and No 31516 is seen at Brighton on 10th June, 1950.

J. G. Dewing

Plate 36 Below The Class 'E' 4-4-0s were built with Belpaire fireboxes and No 1176 is leaving Charing Cross with an Ashford train on 14th July, 1937.

J. P. Wilson

Plate 37 Left Between 1903 and 1920 Stirling built eighty-eight Class 'F' 4-4-0s for the SER. They were all built at Ashford and had inside cylinders and 7 ft 0 in coupled driving wheels. From 1903 Wainwright started rebuilding them with an improved domed boiler and new 18 in x 26 in cylinders in an attempt to improve the secondary services of the South Eastern and Chatham sections. They quickly became successful and a total of seventy-six were rebuilt to Class 'F1' by 1920, one of which was scrapped after a collision in 1919. By 1925 all the seventy-five 'F1s' had been fitted with extended smokeboxes and No 1043 is heading a train to Reading at Waterloo on 18th July, 1937.

J. P. Wilson

Plate 38 Below Class 'F1' No 1062 is leaving St. Leonards West Marina on 10th July, 1939 on a 'Sunny South Express'. Only eight 'F1s' survived nationalisation and the last one was withdrawn in 1949.

J. P. Wilson

Plate 39 Right Class 'G' 4-4-0 No A680 waiting to leave Maidstone West on 23rd April, 1927 with a train for Charing Cross via Strood and Gravesend. This engine was one of five 4-4-0s bought by the SECR in 1900 from the Great North of Scotland Railway. Ten were built by Neilson, Reid & Co for the GN of SR in 1899 to a design of Pickersgill, but in the event five were not required and as a result were purchased by the SECR becoming Class 'G'. They were all withdrawn between 1925 and 1927.

H. C. Casserley

Plate 40 *Left* Drummond LSWR 'K10' 4-4-0 No 385 with the characteristic Drummond wingplates at the front. Forty of these inside-cylinder 4-4-0s were built 1901–2 for mixed traffic duties, thirty-one survived nationalisation, and the last one was withdrawn in 1951.

E. E. Smith

Plate 41 *Below* Class 'K10' No 389 is near Fareham in 1938 heading a Southampton–Portsmouth train.

C. R. L. Coles

Plate 42 *Below* Wainwright's last design to appear on the SECR was the Class 'L' 4-4-0. The design had been prepared just before his retirement, but when R. E. L. Maunsell became CME of the SECR on 12th November, 1913, he modified it slightly. Twelve were built by Beyer Peacock & Co. (Nos 760–771) in 1914, and the remaining ten by Borsig of Berlin (Nos 772–781), also in 1914, with these engines being finally assembled at Ashford by Borsig fitters. No 1768 is approaching Hastings with a down Ashford train on 9th July, 1939.

J. P. Wilson

Plate 43 Above All twenty-two Class 'L' 4-4-0s were taken into BR ownership in 1948 and the last one was withdrawn in 1961. No 31767 is working hard on a Hastings—Tonbridge semi-fast shortly after leaving West St. Leonards in the late 1950s.

J. Stredwick

Plate 44 Below Drummond LSWR Class 'L11' 4-4-0 No 441 approaching Havant with a Brighton—Bournemouth express in 1938.

C. R. L. Coles

Plate 45 Right Forty Class 'L11' 4-4-0s were built by Drummond for the LSWR between 1903 and 1907. They were similar to his earlier Class 'K10', with 5 ft 7 in coupled driving wheels and 18½ in x 26 in inside cylinders. They all survived nationalisation and the last one was withdrawn in 1952.

E. E. Smith

Plate 46 Below A combination of two Drummond LSWR 4-4-0s at Bedhampton in 1938. Class 'L11' No 169 is piloting a Class 'S11' on an excursion from Bournemouth to Brighton.

C. R. L. Coles

Plate 47 Below Drummond LSWR Class 'L12' 4-4-0 No 421 approaching Havant in 1938 heading a Brighton–Bournemouth express. Twenty 'L12s' were built 1904–5 and were rebuilt with superheater by Urie from 1915, similar to the later 'D15s' as seen in *Plate 34*. No 421 has the rather ugly Urie chimney and extended smokebox.

C. R. L. Coles

Plate 48 Left In 1946 a Brighton–Bournemouth express is nearing Barnham Junction behind Class 'L12' 4-4-0 No 428. All twenty 'L12s' were in service at nationalisation and the last one was withdrawn in 1955.

C. R. L. Coles

Plate 49 Below Another class of Drummond LSWR 4-4-0 which was rebuilt by Urie with superheaters was the 'S11'. Ten of these 6 ft 0 in engines were built in 1903 primarily for use in the West of England and the last one survived until 1955. No 395 is leaving Havant in 1935 on a Portsmouth–London Bridge train.

C. R. L. Coles

Plate 50 Left William Adams built several classes of 6 ft 7 in outside-cylinder 4-4-0s for the LSWR and the Class 'T3' seen here in 1936 was one of his later ones. Twenty were built 1892–3 and although they were all in service at the grouping none survived nationalisation. No 563 was the last to be withdrawn in 1945, and happily has been preserved.

A. G. Ellis collection

Plate 51 Right Adams LSWR Class 'T6' was the last of several of his classes of 7 ft 1 in 4-4-0s. Ten were built 1895–6 and the last one was withdrawn in 1943.
A. G. Ellis collection

Plate 52 Above Drummond LSWR Class 'T9' 4-4-0 No 314 passes beneath the overhead electrification at Clapham Junction on 9th April, 1928. The 'T9' was Drummond's first coupled express passenger locomotive for the LSWR. It was a 6 ft 7 in development of his earlier Class 'C8' ordinary passenger locomotive and a total of sixty-six were built between 1899 and 1901 at Nine Elms and by Dübs & Co. of Glasgow. Between 1922 and 1929 the entire class had been rebuilt with superheaters and extended smokeboxes. The excellent free running characteristics of these engines soon gained them the nickname of 'Greyhounds'.

H. C. Casserley

Plate 53 Right Drummond 'Greyhound' No 119 at Eastleigh on 28th June, 1935. This engine had gained an excellent reputation over the years and was often rostered for special duties. Earlier in 1935 it had been selected for special treatment and was completely repainted in green livery with beautifully lined out wheels, highly burnished metalwork and plaques with the royal coat of arms for the leading splasher, as seen here. On 17th July, 1935 it hauled the King's Royal Train to Portsmouth for the Silver Jubilee Naval Review and subsequently was always kept as the 'royal' engine.

A. G. Ellis collection

Plate 54 Above In 1900 and 1901 the last batch of fifteen 'T9s' were built at Nine Elms with slight variations from the earlier examples including wider cabs and wider driving wheel splashers. No 312 was one of this batch and is entering Victoria on 8th July, 1939 on a relief train from the Kent coast.
J. P. Wilson

Plate 55 Left BR No 30705 is heading a Reading–Reigate local train between Betchworth and Reigate on 30th March, 1957. This was one of the earlier 'T9s' with separate coupling rod splashers and narrower cab. All sixty-six engines were in service at nationalisation and the last one was withdrawn in 1961. One, however, has been preserved and can be seen at the National Railway Museum.
R. E. Vincent

Plate 56 Right Adams LSWR Class 'X2' 4-4-0 No 590 at Eastleigh on 15 December, 1936. This was one of his earlier 7 ft 1 in 4-4-0s. Twenty were built 1890–2 and the last one was withdrawn from service in 1942.
A. G. Ellis collection

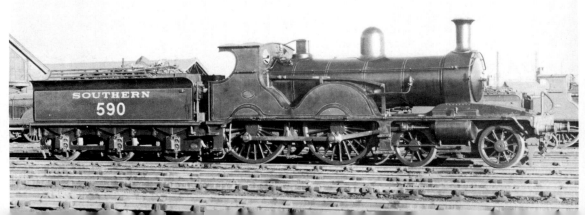

Plate 57 Right Douglas Earle Marsh took up office as the Locomotive, Carriage and Wagon Superintendent of the LBSCR on 1st January, 1905, having previously been Chief Assistant Mechanical Engineer and Manager of the Great Northern Railway Doncaster Works under H. A. Ivatt. It was, therefore, no surprise that his Class 'H1' Atlantics, the first one of which appeared in December 1905, were more than a little similar to Ivatt's large-boilered Atlantics of the GNR. In fact, no secret was made of the fact that a set of Doncaster drawings were used during construction, with appropriate modifications marked in red ink. The main differences were a longer piston stroke and the working pressure raised from 175 to 200 lb/sq in. No 2041 *Peveril Point* is seen at Brighton in the late 1930s with boiler mountings cut down to the composite gauge, and Maunsell chimney.

E. E. Smith

Plate 58 Above In 1938 Class 'H1' 4-4-2 No 2037 *Selsey Bill* is passing St. Quintin Park on the West London Extension line with a Birmingham—Eastbourne Summer Saturday 'Sunny South Express'. Five of these excellent two-cylinder Atlantics were built in 1905 and 1906 and were superheated between 1925 and 1927. With electrification of the Brighton line in 1933 their future was in doubt, but fortunately they were found work on the remainder of the Central Section and thereafter gave extremely good performances. The last one was withdrawn from service in 1951 having done more than 1 million miles.

C. R. L. Coles

Plate 59 Right Late in 1947 Class 'H1' No 2039 *Hartland Point* emerged from Brighton works experimentally modified by Bulleid prior to the construction of his 'Leader' class. It was fitted with sleeve valve gear, new cylinders, outside steampipes and a multiple-jet blastpipe and large diameter chimney. It is seen in this state at Brighton on 4th June. 1948 with Westinghouse air pump on the side of the smokebox. Only for a very short period early in 1949 did it ever appear on a public passenger train and it was eventually scrapped at Eastleigh in 1951.

A. G. Ellis collection

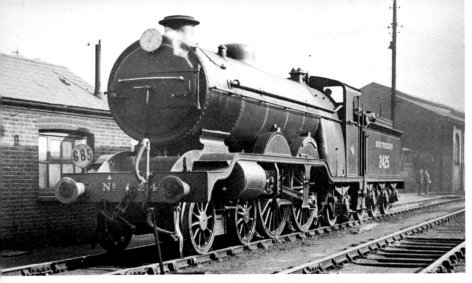

Plate 60 Left In June 1911 shortly before Marsh's resignation due to ill health, the first of his six Class 'H2' superheated Atlantics appeared from Brighton works. Apart from incorporating the Schmidt superheaters, the other main differences were larger cylinders, working pressure reduced to 170 lb/sq in (although this was subsequently increased to 200 lb/sq in) and straight running plate between the cylinders and coupled wheels. No 2425 *Trevose Head* is at Brighton about 1939 with Maunsell superheater, apparent by the snifting valve on the smokebox top.

E. E. Smith

Plate 61 Below Class 'H2' 4-4-2 No 2421 *South Foreland* is running into Victoria on 15th May, 1938 with a Newhaven boat train.

J. P. Wilson

Plate 62 Right After nationalisation the remaining Brighton Atlantics were living on borrowed time and spent periods in store. Stays of execution were however granted, and the last one, 'H2' No 32424 *Beachy Head* survived until April 1958. BR No 32425 *Trevose Head* is seen heading the 17.40 London Bridge—East Grinstead near Upper Warlingham on 23rd May, 1952.

C. R. L. Coles

Plate 63 Above On 5th October, 1952 Class 'H2' No 32424 *Beachy Head* awaits departure from Brighton with the return RCTS all-Pullman Brighton Works Centenary Special.

E. E. Smith

Plate 64 Below The last of the 'H2' Atlantics were very much in demand in their latter days for use on specials. On 3rd May, 1953 No 32425 *Trevose Head* is passing Norwood Junction on an SLS special from Victoria to Portsmouth, via Sutton.

B. C. Bending

Plate 65 Left Class 'H15' 4-6-0 No E331. This was one of five engines which Urie rebuilt from Drummond's LSWR Class 'F13' 4-6-0s, Nos E330—E334, although in the event they did not emerge from Eastleigh until 1924—5. The 'F13' 4-6-0s were four-cylinder engines and rather poor performers, the rebuilt engines had two outside cylinders and retained very little of the original Drummond design, having basically the same appearance as his earlier 'H15' which was rebuilt in 1914 from Drummond's LSWR Class 'E14'.

A. G. Ellis collection

Plate 66 Right No E522 was one of ten 'H15' 4-6-0s which were built in 1924, Nos E473—E478 and E521—E524. They were ordered by Urie just before the grouping as improved versions of his 'H15s', but Maunsell subsequently approved the order and they appeared with 'N15'-type taper boiler (see *Plate 72*), high running plate and stovepipe chimney.

A. G. Ellis collection

Plate 67 Left Class 'H15' 4-6-0 No E476 in full cry on a West of England train. These ten 'H15s' all had Urie 5,000 gallon tenders unlike the rebuilt engines as seen in *Plate 65* which retained the Drummond eight-wheeled tenders.

A. G. Ellis collection

Plate 68 Right No 30489 is seen at Nine Elms on 13th September, 1958. This was one of a batch of ten Class 'H15' 4-6-0s built 1913—14 by Urie for the LSWR at Eastleigh. It was his first 4-6-0 to appear on the LSWR and they were designed as mixed traffic engines with 6 ft 0 in driving wheels, two outside cylinders and Walschaerts valve gear. They were extremely useful engines and were hardly modified during their entire existence apart from the addition of smoke deflectors by Maunsell.

G. W. Morrison

Plate 69 Above Urie Class 'H15' 4-6-0 No 30483 is passing Clapham Junction on 14th March, 1952 heading the 12.54 Waterloo–Basingstoke.

R. E. Vincent

Plate 70 Left Sister engine No 30482 is passing Vauxhall on a Southampton train.
A. G. Ellis collection

Plate 71 Below No 30488 is drifting downhill to Weymouth, passing Bincombe Tunnels near Upwey Wishing Well Halt, heading a Bournemouth–Weymouth train on 16th August, 1952. All ten of these 'H15s' were withdrawn between 1955 and 1961.

R. W. Beaton

Plate 72 Right Between 1918 and 1923 twenty of Robert Urie's 'N15' 4-6-0s were built at Eastleigh for express passenger use on the Waterloo–Bournemouth and Salisbury lines. No E736 seen here as named *Excalibur* was the first to be delivered in August 1918. This design was chosen for further construction by Maunsell after the formation of the Southern, and a further fifty-four were built 1925–7 with modifications including a redesigned front end which improved their performance considerably. Maunsell's 'N15s' were named after Arthurian legends and soon became known as the 'King Arthur' class. The original Urie LSWR engines were included in the class when they themselves were given names of persons and places associated with the Knights of the Round Table.

Lens of Sutton

Plate 73 Above Urie 'Arthur' No 737 *King Uther* is waiting to leave Waterloo in 1935 on a Bournemouth train. By this time the engine has been fitted with standard SR smoke deflectors, a Maunsell smokebox and modified chimney. The Urie engines could always be distinguished from the rest of the 'Arthurs' by the high-arched South Western cab, and the last one was withdrawn in 1958.

C. R. L. Coles

Plate 74 Right In 1920 and 1921 Urie built twenty Class 'S15' 4-6-0s for the LSWR, Nos 496–515, for use on heavy goods traffic. The 'S15' was his third outside-cylinder 4-6-0 design for the LSWR and was similar in appearance to his earlier 'N15s' although it had 5 ft 7 in coupled wheels compared with 6 ft 7 in coupled wheels of the 'N15'. No E500 is standing at Eastleigh on 7th June, 1932 after being fitted with superheater, smoke deflectors and ugly stovepipe chimney.

A. G. Ellis collection

Plate 75 Above In August 1961 Class 'S15' 4-6-0 No 30508 is hauling a heavy down freight near Winchfield. It is fitted with Maunsell chimney but still has its Urie bogie tender.

W. P. Conolly

Plate 76 Below The Urie 'S15' was chosen by Maunsell for further construction and another twenty-five were built from 1927 (see *Plate 140*). The Urie engines could be distinguished by the slightly raised running plate over the cylinders, as seen on No 30506 near Pirbright Junction in 1960 on a down West of England train.

D. Cross

Plate 77 Left James Stirling designed this four-coupled crane tank for service at Folkestone Harbour. It was built in 1881 by Neilson, Reid & Co. and it remained at Folkestone until 1905 when it was transferred to Ashford. In 1929 after overhaul and fitting of a Westinghouse brake it was transferred to the Lancing Carriage Works and renumbered 234S. It was numbered 1302 in 1938 after an enclosed cab was fitted, and was finally withdrawn in 1949 having done a total mileage of only 118,163.

A. G. Ellis collection

Plate 78 Below In 1890 this 0-4-0ST was built by Hawthorn, Leslie & Co. for the Southampton Dock Co. It had 3 ft 2 in coupled wheels and was absorbed into LSWR stock late in 1891 after purchase of the Dock Company's holdings, remaining in the Docks until 1901. In March 1901 it was taken into General Stock as No 458 being transferred to the Southampton Town Quay and also used for light shunting at Winchester. *Ironside* was renumbered 3458 in November 1931 and thereafter spent much of its time at Guildford, and is seen there on 1st September, 1951. It was the last survivor of the Southampton Dock locomotives and was finally withdrawn in June 1954.

B. Morrison

Plate 79 Left Adams/Drummond LSWR Class 'K14' 0-4-0T No 147 *Dinard* at Southampton in September 1934. Twenty Class 'B4' 0-4-0Ts were built by Adams 1891–3 for dock shunting, and a further five similar 'K14s' were built by Drummond in 1908. All twenty-five were in service at nationalisation.

A. G. Ellis collection

Plate 80 Below Class 'B4' 0-4-0T No 30096 is shunting in Winchester goods yard on 25th February, 1963. The last engine of this class of 3 ft 9¾ in 0-4-0Ts was withdrawn in 1963.

P. Harrod

Plate 81 Left Drummond LSWR Class 'C14' 0-4-0T No 3741 at Eastleigh on 7th June, 1932. Ten of these engines were built in 1906 as 2-2-0T Rail Motor engines and were rebuilt by Urie as 0-4-0Ts between 1913 and 1923. Only three survived until the grouping in 1923 and the last of these 3 ft 0 in engines was withdrawn in 1959.

A. G. Ellis collection

Plate 82 *Above* On 10th June, 1950 Stroudley LBSCR Class 'D1' 0-4-2T No 2252 is leaving Brighton on a Horsham train. This famous class of 'D-Tanks' eventually comprised 125 engines, numerically the largest class the LBSCR ever possessed. They were built between 1873 and 1887 as a standard passenger tank engine for heavy suburban and secondary main line use.

J. G. Dewing

Plate 83 *Left* Stroudley Class 'D1' 0-4-2T No B612 is at New Cross in 1926. Of the 125 'D1s', 35 were built by Neilson & Co. late in 1881 and early in 1882 due to the pressure of work at Brighton at that time. Only twenty were still in service at nationalisation and the last one was withdrawn in 1950.

A. G. Ellis collection

Plate 84 *Left* The only class of 0-4-4T designed by Robert Billinton for the LBSCR was the 'D3', and thirty-six were built at Brighton 1892–6 to replace Stroudley's 'D-Tanks' on outer suburban and secondary passenger services. They were initially known as 'D Bogies' and No 2367 is standing at Tunbridge Wells on 17th October, 1935.

A. G. Ellis collection

Plate 85 Above In 1946 Class 'D3' 0-4-4T No 2393 is approaching Hurst Green Halt, near Oxted, on an auto-train from Tunbridge Wells. The last 'D3' was withdrawn in 1955 after a somewhat undistinguished career.

C. R. L. Coles

Plate 86 Right In 1909 when further reboilering of the 'D3s' was necessary, Marsh fitted the large 'I2' pattern to two engines, Nos 396 and 397, these two engines being reclassified 'D3X'. They were not particularly successful and no further engines were rebuilt as Class 'D3X'. No 2396 as rebuilt 'D3X' is at Tunbridge Wells on 23rd October, 1935 and suffered early withdrawal in May 1937. The other 'D3X' survived until July 1948

A. G. Ellis collection

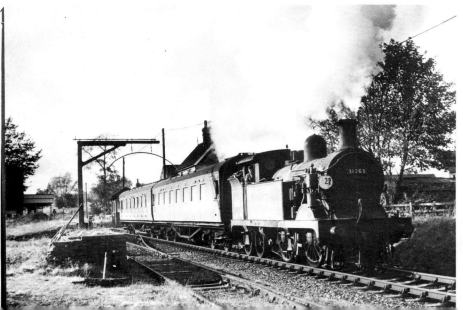

Plate 87 Top Between 1904 and 1915 sixty-six of Wainwright's Class 'H' 0-4-4Ts were built for the SECR. These excellent 5 ft 6 in tank locomotives were built to cope with the ever increasing amount of suburban passenger traffic and all but two survived nationalisation.

E. E. Smith

Plate 88 Centre On 3rd August, 1951, Class 'H' 0-4-4T No 31239 still lettered 'Southern' is shunting at Tonbridge.

R. E. Vincent

Plate 89 Left Push-and-pull fitted Class 'H' 0-4-4T No 31263 is leaving Grange Road on 4th November, 1962 with a Three Bridges—East Grinstead train. The last of these very useful engines was withdrawn in 1964.

P. Harrod

Plate 90 Above Drummond's only 0-4-4Ts for the LSWR were the Class 'M7' and 'X14', a total of one hundred and five being built between 1897 and 1911. They had 5 ft 7 in driving wheels and were designed for light passenger suburban duties. Class 'M7' No 36 is inside Eastleigh shed in the 1930s.

E. E. Smith

Plate 91 Below The Class 'X14s' were introduced in 1903 with detail alterations from the 'M7s', all subsequently being classified 'M7'. No 30057 is fitted for push-and-pull working and is leaving Swanage for Wareham on 27th October, 1962. The last 'M7' was withdrawn in 1964.

G. W. Morrison

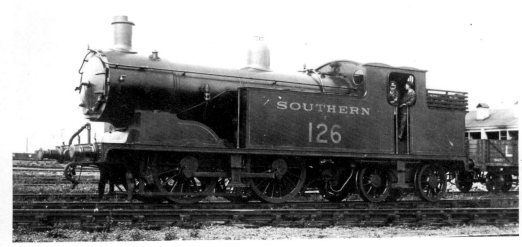

Plate 92 Left One of the Class 'X14' 0-4-4Ts, No E126, seen here, was rebuilt in 1921 by Urie with a superheater and extended smokebox but no further engines were selected for rebuilding.

A. G. Ellis collection

Plate 93 Right Adams LSWR Class 'O2' 0-4-4T No 30177 at Feltham on 14th September, 1958. Sixty of these engines were built 1889—95 at Nine Elms to replace the older Beattie well-tanks on branch line work. Between 1923 and 1949 twenty-three of these engines were transferred to the Isle of Wight (see *Plate 201*) and were given larger coal bunkers.

G. W. Morrison

Plate 94 Below Between 1876 and 1882 twenty Beattie LSWR Class '0330' 0-6-0STs were built by Beyer, Peacock & Co. for shunting duties. No 0328 is seen with original boiler and Salter safety valves on the dome. At the end of 1894 it was placed on the duplicate list as No 228 to make way for the Adams 'O2' Class 0-4-4Ts, was subsequently renumbered 328, being withdrawn as No 0328 in June 1929. The last of the class was withdrawn in 1933.

A. G. Ellis collection

Plate 95 Right In 1874 the first of Stroudley's Class 'E1' 0-6-0Ts was introduced on the LBSCR for goods services. They were similar in certain aspects of design to his 'D-Tanks' and a total of seventy-two were built at Brighton until 1883. After Stroudley's death, Robert Billinton built six modified 'E1s' at Brighton in 1891, and after the grouping several were rebuilt as 0-6-2Ts and classified 'E1R' (see *Plate 178*). The last of these 4 ft 6 in engines was withdrawn in 1961.

E. E. Smith

Plate 96 Below The only Adams 0-6-0T design for the LSWR was his Class 'G6', and a total of thirty-four were built from 1894 until 1900, when Drummond had succeeded him. As can be seen from *Plate 95*, they were very similar in appearance to Stroudley's Class 'E1' 0-6-0Ts. They were built for freight and shunting duties and were the 0-6-0T version of his Class 'O2' passenger tank locomotive. No 268 is at Eastleigh on 7th June, 1932.

A. G. Ellis collection

Plate 97 Below L. B. Billinton designed his Class 'E2' 0-6-0T to replace some of Stroudley's earlier 'E1s', and ten of these 4 ft 6 in engines were built at Brighton 1913—16. No 32107 is at Stewarts Lane shed on 6th June, 1950, and was one of the last five which were built with extended side tanks. All ten engines were withdrawn between 1961 and 1963.

R. E. Vincent

Plate 98 Left In 1888 James Stirling introduced his Class 'R' 0-6-0T for shunting work, and also for working the Folkestone Harbour and Canterbury and Whitstable branches. A total of twenty-five were built at Ashford for the SER until 1898. Between 1910 and 1922 Wainwright rebuilt thirteen of these 5 ft 2 in engines to Class 'R1' using domed 'H' class boilers. No 1335 was one of the 'R1s' which were fitted with Wainwright's 'pagoda' style of cab.

E. E. Smith

Plate 99 Right Class 'R1' 0-6-0T No 31069 banking a boat train away from Folkestone Harbour on 25th May, 1953. All thirteen 'R1s' entered British Railways stock, and the final survivors of the class were collected at Folkestone for use on the gruelling climb to Folkestone Junction from the Harbour. The last engine of the class was withdrawn in 1960.

B. C. Bending

Plate 100 Left R. J. Billinton's first 0-6-2T for the LBSCR was his Class 'E3', 'small radials' as they were often known. Sixteen of these 4 ft 6 in engines were built at Brighton 1894—5 based on Stroudley's solitary radial tank which was built in 1891. Although designed for light goods services, Westinghouse air brakes were fitted to enable them to work secondary passenger services in place of the 'D-Tanks'. The last 'E3' was withdrawn in 1959.

E. E. Smith

Plate 101 *Above* When R. J. Billinton ordered more 0-6-2Ts the wheel diameter was increased by 6 in to 5 ft 0 in for use as mixed traffic engines. These 'E4s' were so successful on both goods and passenger services that a total of seventy-five were built at Brighton between 1897 and 1903. These 'large radials' had a slightly higher pitched boiler than the 'E3s', and No 32507 is seen leaving Tonbridge on 19th July, 1951.

A. G. Ellis collection

Plate 102 *Left* Class 'E4' 0-6-2T No 32487 is at Nine Elms on 14th October, 1962 showing the extended smokebox. The last of these engines was withdrawn in 1963 but No 473 can be seen preserved on the Bluebell Railway in LBSCR colours with the name *Birch Grove*.

G. W. Morrison

Plate 103 *Right* Between 1909 and 1911 Marsh reboilered four Class 'E4s' using the larger 'I2' pattern boiler, and these engines became Class 'E4X'. They were expensive to reboiler, were never particularly outstanding and as a result no more were done. All four 'E4Xs' survived nationalisation but were mainly confined to shunting duties. The last one was withdrawn in 1959.

E. E. Smith

Plate 104 Above R. J. Billinton's next radial tank for the LBSCR was his Class 'E5', and thirty of these 5 ft 6 in 0-6-2Ts were built 1902–4. He incorporated the 'C2' boiler, increased the fuel and water capacity, and fitted a tapered chimney. No 2588 is shunting empty stock at Victoria in 1936. They were all built at Brighton and the last one was withdrawn in 1956.

C. R. L. Coles

Plate 105 Below Following the rebuilding of four Class 'E4s', Marsh reboilered four 'E5s' in 1911 using larger 'C3' boilers, and these four rebuilds were classified 'E5X', the last of which was withdrawn in January 1956. No 32401 is shunting at Brighton on 19th July, 1952 carrying a 'C3' boiler with a second dome which formerly housed top-feed apparatus.

R. W. Beaton

Plate 106 Right The last of R. J. Billinton's 0-6-2Ts for the LBSCR was his Class 'E6'. These were 4 ft 6 in goods engines and were based on the design of his passenger 'E5'. Twelve were built at Brighton and had tapered chimneys similar to the 'E5s'. Unfortunately, Robert Billinton was never to see one in service as he died on 7th November, 1904 just before the first engine left Brighton Works. No 32418 is at Newhaven on 7th October, 1962, shortly before being withdrawn from service.

G. W. Morrison

Plate 107 Below The only class of 0-6-4 tank locomotive to run on the SR was the Class 'J', five of which were built in 1913 at Ashford with 5 ft 6 in coupled wheels. It was Wainwright's last design of tank engine, and although they all survived nationalisation, the last one was withdrawn by 1951. No 1596 is at Ashford on a down train on 12th July, 1939.

J. P. Wilson

Plate 108 Right These 2-4-0 well tanks were one of Joseph Beattie's most successful designs for the LSWR. Originally eighty-five were built between 1863 and 1875 and were subsequently rebuilt by Adams, Urie and Maunsell. Only three saw the 20th century and were retained for use on the Wenford Bridge line (see *Plate 208*), finally being withdrawn in 1962 as BR Nos 30585–7.

A. G. Ellis collection

Plate 109 Left In June 1917 Maunsell's Class 'K' 2-6-4T No 790 emerged from Ashford, and was the only example of the class to run in SECR days. The design was basically a tank engine version of his 'N' Class 2-6-0, and after the formation of the SR a further nineteen were built in 1925 and 1926, all being named after rivers. No A792 *River Arun* is seen at Brighton. When the class had been in traffic for some time reports of bad riding became commonplace, and after several derailments it was decided to convert the entire class to 2-6-0 tender engines of Class 'U'. They were all rebuilt in 1928 (see *Plate 180*).

A. G. Ellis collection

Plate 110 Left The first of a class of seventy-one 4-4-2Ts designed by William Adams for the LSWR appeared in 1882. They were transferred to the LSWR duplicate list in 1904, with the prefix 'O' added to the number, and became Class O415. During the 1920s they were all withdrawn with the exception of two, Nos 3125 and 3520, and these were retained for use on the Axminster–Lyme Regis branch. In 1946 they were joined by No 3488 which was repurchased by the SR from the East Kent Railway. After nationalisation they were renumbered 30582–4. No 30583 posing here can still be seen preserved on the Bluebell Railway in LSWR colours.

N. Stead

Plate 111 Below BR No 30582 is leaving Axminster for Lyme Regis on 27th June, 1958.
J. P. Wilson

Plate 112 *Above* Twenty-seven Marsh Class 'I3' 4-4-2Ts were
built for the LBSCR 1907–13, and BR No 32030 is leaving
Tonbridge on 19th July, 1951. These Atlantic tanks gave
excellent performances, twenty-one being built with 6 ft 9 in
coupled wheels and the remainder with 6 ft 7½ in coupled
wheels. All but one survived nationalisation and the last one
was withdrawn in 1952.

A. G. Ellis collection

Plate 113 *Below* Marsh Class 'I3' 4-4-2T No 2025 leaving
Havant in 1935 with a Portsmouth—Brighton train. This
engine was superheated when built, although several were
originally saturated, being superheated between 1919 and
1927.

C. R. L. Coles

Plate 114 Above The Class 'H16' 4-6-2T was designed by Urie for heavy freight work on the LSWR, and five were built just before the grouping, in 1921–2. They were 5 ft 7 in outside cylinder engines and BR No 30520 is seen at Surbiton on 16th October, 1955.

A. G. Ellis collection

Plate 115 Below No 30518 is shunting at Clapham Junction on 6th June, 1951. All five 'H16s' were withdrawn in 1961–2.

R. E. Vincent

Plate 116 Left The only other Pacific tanks on the SR were Classes 'J1' and 'J2' designed by Marsh for the LBSCR. Class 'J1' 4-6-2T No 2325 is arriving at Eastbourne on a 'Sunny South Express' on 11th July, 1939. Only one Class 'J1' was built, in 1910, named *Abergavenny* until 1924, and it survived until 1951.

J. P. Wilson

Plate 117 Right A second 'J-Tank' was completed at Brighton in 1912, No 326 which was named *Bessborough* until 1925. These two 4-6-2Ts were developments of Marsh's Class 'I3' 4-4-2Ts, and Class 'J2' No 326 incorporated some of Billinton's modifications, including Walschaerts valve gear in place of Stephenson's which was used on the 'J1'. No 2326 is seen at Eastleigh on 15th March, 1937, and was also withdrawn in 1951.

A. G. Ellis collection

Plate 118 Above In 1913 L. B. Billinton decided to enlarge the design of the 'J-Tanks' replacing the trailing truck by a bogie, and seven of these Class 'L' 4-6-4Ts were built at Brighton for the LBSCR, two in 1914, three in 1921 and two in 1922. They were the only tank locomotives of Baltic wheel arrangement to run on the SR, and were extremely impressive looking engines. They did excellent work on the Central Section until electrification prompted Maunsell to take the decision to rebuild them as 4-6-0 tender engines of Class 'N15X', for service on the Western Section (see *Plate 172*). No B329 *Stephenson* was one of three to be named and is superbly turned out in Southern green livery.

A. G. Ellis collection

Plate 119 Right Urie LSWR Class 'G16' 4-8-0T No 30495 at Feltham on 2nd December, 1962. Four of these massive looking engines were built in 1921 for dealing with transfer freight at Feltham hump marshalling yards, and they were withdrawn between 1959 and 1962.

G. W. Morrison

SOUTHERN DESIGNS

Plate 120 Above The Southern Railway came into being on 1st January, 1923 and R. E. L. Maunsell was appointed Chief Mechanical Engineer. His main objective was to reduce the vast number of classes which he inherited at the grouping by a programme of standardisation. In 1923 more big engines were needed, and Maunsell decided to improve Urie's 'N15s' for further construction. No E765 *Sir Gareth* seen here was one of twenty engines (Nos E763–E782) which were built in 1925 by the North British Locomotive Company, with Ashford-style cab for the composite loading gauge. It is seen at Dover Marine about 1927 on a train for Victoria.

Lens of Sutton

Plate 121 Left Before the grouping, Eastleigh Works had an order for rebuilding ten four-cylinder Drummond 4-6-0s. Nothing had been done at the grouping and Maunsell was able to alter the order and have ten new Class 'N15s' built utilising the Drummond tenders. These ten engines (Nos E448–E457) appeared in 1925, and No E450 *Sir Kay* is seen as built to the former LSWR loading gauge with high arched cab.

Lens of Sutton

Plate 122 Left Various smoke deflection experiments were made by Maunsell, and in 1926 No E772 *Sir Percivale* is at Dover Marine fitted with German-type smoke deflectors and sloping front to the running plate. Maunsell finally decided on a medium-sized design of smoke deflector which was then fitted to the majority of large SR tender engines, as seen on the following pages.

Lens of Sutton

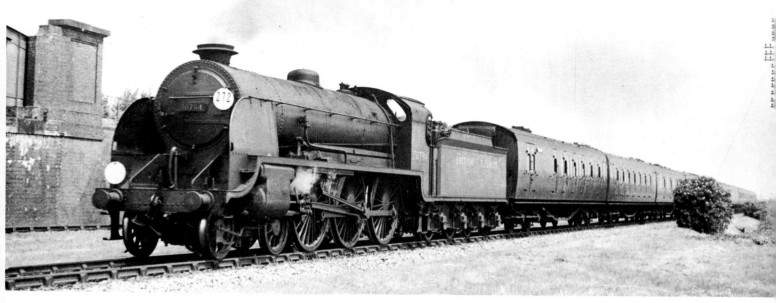

Plate 123 Above Class 'N15' 4-6-0 No 30784 *Sir Nerovens* was one of two 'King Arthurs' fitted with spark-arresting chimneys, and it is passing Battledown Flyover on 25th June, 1949 on a down Bournemouth express. Whilst these engines were fitted with these chimneys they gained the nickname 'Beefeaters'.

R. E. Vincent

Plate 124 Right Further orders were placed for 'N15s' during 1925–6. Ten more were built by North British in 1925 (Nos E783–E792) and fourteen at Eastleigh in 1926–7 (Nos E793–E806) making a total of fifty-four new 'N15s', plus twenty Urie 'N15s' which were modified by Maunsell (Nos E736–E755). No 30804 *Sir Cador of Cornwall* seen at Eastleigh on 15th August, 1961, was one of the 1926–7 batch built at Eastleigh with smaller six-wheeled tenders for use on the Central Section.

G. W. Morrison

Plate 125 Right No 30791 *Sir Uwaine* was built by the North British Locomotive Co. with Maunsell cab and large Urie double-bogie tender. It is approaching Basingstoke on 2nd June, 1951 with a relief from Waterloo to Bournemouth and Weymouth.

R. E. Vincent

Plate 126 *Above* These North British built 'N15s' were often referred to as 'Scotch Arthurs', and one of them, No 767 *Sir Valence*, is leaving Dover Marine with a boat train on 14th July, 1939.

J. P. Wilson

Plate 127 *Below* No 30763 *Sir Bors de Ganis* passes a busy scene at Bournemouth Central with an express from Weymouth to Waterloo.

E. E. Smith

Plate 128 *Top right* The Class 'L1' 4-4-0 was introduced in 1926 as a development of the SECR Class 'L'. Fifteen were built by the North British Locomotive Co. in 1926, (Nos A753–A759 and A782–A789), primarily for use on Folkestone expresses. They differed from the 1914 Class 'Ls' by having smaller cylinders, higher boiler pressure of 180 lb/sq in, Maunsell superheaters and improved cabs. They were the last new design of inside-cylinder 4-4-0 express engines in this country and proved very successful. No 31782 is at Ashford on 21st April, 1951 after removal of the smoke-box top snifting valves which was almost the only alteration to their appearance throughout their entire existence. The last one was withdrawn in 1962.

J. G. Dewing

Plate 129 *Below* After the success of the 'King Arthurs', Maunsell was confronted with the need for a more powerful locomotive capable of handling 500 ton Continental expresses on the Eastern Section. He eventually settled on a four-cylinder
4-6-0 with only a slight increase in weight on the 'King Arthurs'. The 33 sq ft grate of the 'Lord Nelsons' was the largest of
any British 4-6-0 when the class was first introduced, with the Belpaire firebox 18 in longer than the 'King Arthurs'. No E850
Lord Nelson appeared from Eastleigh in 1926 and ran for about two years whilst Maunsell studied the design very carefully.
No 853 *Sir Richard Grenville* is leaving Dover with an up boat train on 14th August, 1937 after being fitted with smoke
deflectors and flat-sided 5,000 gallon tender.

A. Cawston, D. Cobbe collection

Plate 130 Above After the prototype 'Lord Nelson' had been studied in service and proved satisfactory to Maunsell, more of the class were ordered in March 1927. This order comprised ten locomotives for the Eastern Section, and they were delivered between June 1928 and April 1929 (Nos E851–E860). Five further 'Lord Nelsons' were built at Eastleigh Works (Nos E861–E865) and they entered traffic between September and November 1929. No 850 *Lord Nelson* is approaching Petts Wood in 1938 on an up Continental express.

C. R. L. Coles

Plate 131 Below The 'Lord Nelsons' were soon working on the Western Section and the 'Bournemouth Belle' was a regular 'Lord Nelson' duty. No 861 *Lord Anson* makes a fine sight on the down train in the mid 1930s.

E. E. Smith

Plate 132 Above No 863 *Lord Rodney* is passing Bromley on 26th February, 1939 on the down 'Golden Arrow' which at this period consisted of four Pullman coaches, six corridor coaches and two six-wheeled brakes. The engine has just been fitted by Bulleid with Lemaître multiple-jet blastpipe and early type of large diameter stovepipe chimney in an attempt to improve draughting.

H. C. Casserley

Plate 133 Right Earlier, in August 1934, Maunsell fitted No 862 *Lord Collingwood* with twin Kylchap blastpipes in an attempt to improve draughting, and it is seen approaching Shorncliffe on an up boat train with the distinctive type of double chimney which was also fitted to No 865.

A. Cawston, D. Cobbe collection

Plate 134 Below In January 1937 No 857 *Lord Howe* was fitted with a very different boiler, a round-topped firebox with nickel-steel plates, and a combustion chamber in connection with Maunsell's thoughts of a Pacific design. This boiler was built at Eastleigh and had a strange hump-back appearance with a very small dome. It had a single snifting valve behind the chimney and the engine was fitted with special curved smoke deflectors.

A. G. Ellis collection

Plate 135 Left After the draughting arrangements for the 'Lord Nelsons' were improved by Bulleid, he fitted wide diameter chimneys which were more pleasing than the stovepipe seen in *Plate 132*. No 30864 *Sir Martin Frobisher* is at Nine Elms in the mid 1950s. The larger, high-sided, self-trimming tenders were fitted to the 'Lord Nelsons' in the late 1930s, and after Bulleid's cylinders were fitted, the outside steampipes no longer protruded through the lower part of the smoke deflectors.

E. E. Smith

Plate 136 Right No 30858 *Lord Duncan* is heading a Sunday Waterloo—Bournemouth West train, diverted via Alton due to engineering work on the main line. It is on the single track section from Alton to Winchester Junction alongside the single track Meon Valley line.

N. W. Sprinks

Plate 137 Below No 30857 *Lord Howe* is on an up van train from Eastleigh to Nine Elms, between Farnborough and Brookwood, on 5th February, 1962. By this date, this was one of the last regular 'Lord Nelson' turns. A standard boiler replaced the large round-top combustion chamber boiler, seen in *Plate 134*, in 1945, together with straight deflector plates.

P. Harrod

Plate 138 Above In July 1939 No 853 *Sir Richard Grenville* is passing Ashford on an up boat train, not long after being fitted with large diameter chimney, but still with low-sided tender and Maunsell cylinders.

S. Dewsbery

Plate 139 Below No 30864 *Sir Martin Frobisher* is reduced to a four-coach local on the Western Section in the mid 1950s. All the 'Lord Nelsons' were withdrawn 1961–2, but fortunately the prototype, *Lord Nelson*, has been saved from the scrapyard and at the time of writing is being restored at Steamtown, Carnforth.

E. E. Smith

Plate 140 Left Together with the 'N15s', the other class of Urie 4-6-0 which Maunsell selected for further construction was his 'S15' goods engine. They were improved in much the same way as the 'N15s' and externally were very similar to the later 'King Arthurs'. Twenty-five Maunsell 'S15s' were built, Nos 823–837 at Eastleigh 1927–8, and Nos 838–847 in 1936, also at Eastleigh. No 30830 is on Goring Troughs heading a Didcot–Southampton freight on 11th May, 1964 fitted with Urie 5,000 gallon bogie tender, and smoke deflectors which were added in the mid 1930s.

P. Harrod

Plate 141 Right No 30842 is ex-works at Eastleigh on 12th April, 1963. This was one of the 1936 batch which included engines for use on the Eastern and Central Sections which were fitted with 4,000 gallon six-wheeled tenders. No 30842, however, is fitted with the flat-sided version of the Urie 5,000 gallon tender.

G. W. Morrison

Plate 142 Below Class 'S15' 4-6-0 No 30834 is passing Woking in July 1961 heading an up freight for Nine Elms Goods.

W. P. Conolly

Plate 143 *Above* Class 'S15' No 30836 is heading a down freight between Reigate and Betchworth on 30th March, 1957. The class survived until 1966 and No 30841 (now named *Greene King*) has been preserved.

R. E. Vincent

Plate 144 *Below* The Class 'U' two-cylinder 2-6-0s were designed by Maunsell for use on secondary passenger services. They were 6 ft 0 in engines and twenty were built at Brighton in 1928 (Nos A610–A619), ten at Ashford in 1929 (Nos A620–A629) and a further ten at Ashford in 1931 (Nos A630–A639). The class was multipled in 1928 by the re-building of twenty Class 'K' 'River' tanks (see *Plates 109* and *180*), Nos A790–A809. Although work on the Class 'U' Mogul was under way when the decision to convert the 'River' tanks was taken, it was one of the rebuilds which appeared first, in March 1928.

G. W. Morrison

Plate 145 Above In 1928 the solitary three-cylinder 2-6-4T No A890 *River Frome* was converted to a 2-6-0 tender engine along with the two-cylinder 'River' tanks. No A890 emerged from Ashford in 1928 and was reclassified 'U1'. It proved very successful, and as a result Maunsell ordered a further twenty of these three-cylinder Moguls, Nos A891—A900 and 1901—1910 being built at Eastleigh in 1931. No 1902 is seen at Eastbourne in September 1931 when only a few weeks old.

A. G. Ellis collection

Plate 146 Left Class 'U1' 2-6-0 No 1906 is at Dover shed on 14th July, 1939, after the fitting of short smoke deflectors.

J. P. Wilson

Plate 147 Below The sole re-built Class 'U1' could be distinguished from the other 'U1s' by the slightly raised running plate over the outside cylinders, and it is seen as BR No 31890 leaving Hurst Green Halt on 5th May, 1951 on the 16.18 from London Bridge.

L. N. Owen

Plate 148 Right Maunsell then turned his attention to heavy shunting engines, and in 1929 eight of his three-cylinder Class 'Z' 0-8-0T engines were built at Brighton (Nos 950-957). They were very efficient engines and were to be found at various places on the SR, ending up at Exeter on banking duties between St. David's and Central stations. They were all withdrawn in 1962 and during their 33-year existence their external appearance hardly changed. No 30953 is at Ashford on 26th September, 1953.

R. E. Vincent

Plate 149 Left The Class 'V' 'Schools' 4-4-0s were designed by Maunsell with the severe restrictions of the Hastings line in mind, and the first batch of ten were built at Eastleigh in 1930 (Nos E900—E909). These three-cylinder 4-4-0s had 6 ft 7 in coupled wheels and a round-topped boiler of 220 lb/sq in. They were an immediate success and probably rank as the finest 4-4-0s ever to run in Britain. They were all named after public schools and No E907 *Dulwich* is seen on 24th October, 1930 when still only a few weeks old.

A. G. Ellis collection

Plate 150 Below 'Schools' Class 4-4-0 No 918 *Hurstpierpoint* is passing Ashford on an up train in July 1939. The 'Schools' were ordered in two batches, of ten, and twenty, although the second batch was increased to thirty during construction. This second batch comprised Nos E910—E929 (built 1932—4), and Nos E930—E939 (1934—5), all constructed at Eastleigh. Only the first batch of engines ran without smoke deflectors and they were added to these ten engines 1932—3.

S. Dewsbery

Plate 151 Above In 1937 ten 'Schools' were transferred from Fratton to Bournemouth, and No 928 *Stowe* makes a superb spectacle passing West Weybridge in 1939 on a Bournemouth express.

C. R. L. Coles

Plate 152 Below BR No 30923 *Bradfield* (named *Uppingham* until August 1934) leaves Ash with the 14.50 Reading–Redhill local on 31st October, 1962 after displacement from main line services.

P. Harrod

Plate 153 Right After O. V. S. Bulleid had succeeded Maunsell as CME of the SR, he modified three 'Schools' (Nos 914, 931 and 937) with Lemaître multiple-jet blastpipes. In 1939 he experimented further with No 937 *Epsom* and fitted an extended smokebox as seen here on 14th July, 1939 at Dover shed. It is in Malachite green livery, including the smoke deflectors, and has a particularly large stovepipe chimney which was fitted at this time.

J. P. Wilson

Plate 154 Above The decision was taken by Bulleid to equip several of the 'Schools' with Lemaître multiple-jet blastpipes and large diameter chimneys, and eventually twenty-one were dealt with, the remainder retaining Maunsell's original single blast-pipe and chimney. No 30939 *Leatherhead* fitted with improved lipped large diameter chimney is approaching Hildenborough on 3rd August, 1951 with a down Hastings train.

R. E. Vincent

Plate 155 Right No 30909 *St. Paul's* is approaching Tonbridge on 19th July, 1951 with an up Hastings express.

A. G. Ellis collection

Plate 156 Above Whilst allocated to Bricklayers Arms, 'Schools' 4-4-0 No 30939 *Leatherhead* is heading the 09.15 Charing Cross—Dover express between Hither Green and Grove Park on 22nd May, 1952.

C. R. L. Coles

Plate 157 Below Probably the least flattering angle for a 'Schools' fitted with a large diameter chimney shows No 30937 *Epsom* approaching Hildenborough on the 16.10 Ashford—Charing Cross on 3rd August, 1951. All the 'Schools' were withdrawn in 1961—2 but fortunately three have been preserved.

R. E. Vincent

Plate 158 Above Following on from his Class 'Z' tank engine of 1929, Maunsell's next tank locomotive design was for heavy transfer freight workings and for this he designed his Class 'W' 2-6-4T. Twenty-five of these were built, five at Eastleigh in 1932 (Nos 1911–1915), and the remaining twenty at Ashford 1935–6 (Nos 1916–1925). They were very powerful three-cylinder engines and Maunsell was able to make use of certain parts of the 'River' tanks after they had been converted to tender engines. To increase the brake power the bogie was fitted with brakes as can be seen in this picture of No 31911 at Eastleigh on 15th August, 1961. This was one of the Eastleigh engines which was fitted with right-hand drive, all the Ashford engines having left-hand drive. They were all withdrawn 1963–4.

G. W. Morrison

Plate 159 Right The Class 'Q' 0-6-0 goods engines were the last of Maunsell's designs for the SR and did not appear until his successor, O. V. S. Bulleid, had taken over as CME on Maunsell's retirement. They were designed as an inexpensive modern replacement for the variety of ageing 0-6-0s which the SR inherited, and a total of twenty were built at Eastleigh in 1938–9, Nos 530-549. They had 5 ft 1 in coupled wheels and were often called upon to perform passenger duties. Bulleid later fitted some of the 'Qs' with the multiple-jet blast-pipe and large diameter chimney, as seen here, in order to improve their performance. No 30542 is heading the thrice weekly goods from Bentley to Bordon on 31st August, 1964. They were withdrawn between 1962 and 1965 and one example has been preserved.

P. Harrod

Plate 160 Above O.V.S. Bulleid took up office as CME of the SR on 1st October, 1937, having been Gresley's assistant on the LNER. In March 1938 authority was given for the construction of ten express passenger locomotives and Bulleid produced a totally new design of unorthodox air-smoothed appearance. The first of these three-cylinder 'Merchant Navy' Pacifics appeared early in 1941. These first ten engines were numbered 21C1–21C10 and were all built at Eastleigh 1941–2. They were followed by a further ten from Eastleigh in 1944–5, Nos 21C11–21C20. The final batch of ten 'Merchant Navy' Pacifics were built at Eastleigh after nationalisation, in 1948–9, and these never carried the Bulleid numbering system, instead they became BR Nos 35021–30. The first twenty Pacifics were renumbered 35001–35020 by British Railways in 1948. No 35005 *Canadian Pacific* is seen in full cry on the down 'Atlantic Coast Express' passing Brookwood on 26th March, 1949, whilst experimentally fitted with a Berkley American mechanical stoker, hence the prolific smoke effect!

R. W. Beaton

Plate 161 Below No 35019 *French Line C.G.T.* is at Nine Elms on 13th September, 1958. This was one of the second batch of engines which had several detail changes compared to the first ten engines, including a modified cab front. By 1958 the casing ahead of the outside cylinders had been removed.

G. W. Morrison

Plate 162 *Above* 'Merchant Navy' Pacific No 35011 *General Steam Navigation* is heading the down 'Bournemouth Belle' near Earlsfield on 10th April, 1949, still in SR malachite green livery. These 6 ft 2 in Pacifics with a working pressure of 280 lb/sq in gained an excellent reputation as fast, free-steaming engines, but in the end their unorthodox features and unconventional design led to BR taking the decision to rebuild them more in line with Riddles BR standard designs, and the first BR rebuild appeared early in 1956 (see *Plate 185*).

R. W. Beaton

Plate 163 *Below* Bulleid's second design for the SR was his Class 'Q1' 0-6-0, the first of which appeared in March 1942. A total of forty were all delivered in 1942; Nos C1—C16 and C37—C40 were built at Brighton and Nos C17—C36 were built at Ashford. They were renumbered by BR in 1948 becoming 33001—40. They were designed during World War Two to meet the needs of heavier wartime loads over the same secondary routes as Maunsell's 'Qs'. The 'Q1s' were very functional, workmanlike engines, but hardly the most handsome ever to grace SR metals. No 33020 is at Chichester on 3rd October, 1965.

G. W. Morrison

Plate 164 *Right* The inside-cylinder 'Q1s' were fitted with a large 230 lb/sq in boiler, multiple-jet blastpipe and hideous stovepipe chimney. No 33031 is at the head of a Tonbridge—Redhill freight on 4th April, 1953, between Edenbridge and Godstone.

R. E. Vincent

Plate 165 Left In 1945 the first of Bulleid's Light Pacifics appeared which were similar in appearance to his earlier 'Merchant Navys'. They were required for use on restricted secondary routes over which the heavier 'Merchant Navys' were prohibited, particularly in the West of England, which prompted the SR to call them the 'West Country' class. Sixty-six 'West Country' Pacifics were built, Nos 21C101–21C148 (renumbered 34001–48 by BR in 1948) and Nos 34091–109. They were built at Brighton and Eastleigh between 1945 and 1950 and No 34051 *Winston Churchill* is on shed at Bournemouth on 28th October, 1962.

G. W. Morrison

Plate 166 Below Bulleid's 'Battle of Britain' Light Pacific was essentially the same class as the 'West Country', but the SR decided to split the class for publicity purposes. Forty-four 'Battle of Britain' class 4-6-2s were built between 1946 and 1951 making a total of one hundred and ten Bulleid Light Pacifics, and here No 34075 *264 Squadron* is heading a Victoria—Dover express past St. Mary Cray on 23rd April, 1949. It is in Bulleid livery but has BR numbering and lettering painted in SR style.

R. W. Beaton

Plate 167 Right 'West Country'
Class 4-6-2 No 34019 *Bideford*
is passing Pokesdown on
21st August, 1965 heading a
Weymouth–Waterloo train.
J. S. Whiteley

Plate 168 Above In 1962 'Battle of Britain' No 34064
Fighter Command was fitted with a Giesl Oblong Ejector
and characteristic narrow chimney, as seen here at Eastleigh
on 12th September, 1964. It improved the draughting
considerably but no more engines were so fitted.
G. W. Morrison

Plate 169 Below On 18th May, 1964 'West Country'
No 34015 *Exmouth* speeds through Basingstoke with
an up express.
J. S. Whiteley

Plate 170 Left 'Battle of Britain' 4-6-2 No 34066 *Spitfire* is climbing Parkstone Bank with rear end assistance on 29th July, 1966 with a Poole—Newcastle train.

G. W. Morrison

Plate 171 Below Between 1957 and 1961 seventeen of the forty-four 'Battle of Britains' and forty-three of the sixty-six 'West Countrys' were rebuilt, all at Eastleigh (see *Plate 186*). No 34068 *Kenley* was one of the 'Battle of Britains' which was not rebuilt, and it is seen in Folkestone Warren on 29th May, 1961 on a relief Dover express. The last of Bulleid's Light Pacifics was withdrawn in 1967, but several have been preserved.

D. Cobbe

Plate 172 Above Between 1934 and 1936 Maunsell rebuilt all seven of L. B. Billinton's Class 'L' 4-6-4Ts as 4-6-0 tender engines when they were displaced from the Central Section because of electrification. They were classified 'N15X', and Maunsell attached them to 5,000 gallon Urie bogie tenders for use on the Western Section. One of the Baltic tanks was named *Remembrance* in memory of the men of the LBSCR who gave their lives in the First World War, and it is seen as rebuilt 'N15X' No 2333 heading an up Bournemouth express in 1939.

C. R. L. Coles

Plate 173 Left Only two of the Baltic tanks were named at the time they were converted to tender engines. These engines retained their names and the other five were named when they were rebuilt. No 2328 *Hackworth* was one of the five engines named on rebuilding and it is pictured at Eastleigh on 21st January, 1936 shortly after emerging as a 4-6-0 tender engine.

A. G. Ellis collection

Plate 174 Below Class 'N15X' 4-6-0 as BR renumbered 32332 *Stroudley* is at Raynes Park in May 1950 heading a Waterloo-Salisbury train. Although very nicely proportioned engines, the 'N15Xs' rarely performed as well as the 'King Arthurs', and the last one was withdrawn in 1957.

W. P. Conolly

Plate 175 Left In 1910 Drummond ordered five 4-6-0s with 6 ft 7 in coupled wheels for Bournemouth services of the LSWR. They were built at Eastleigh in 1911, numbered 443–447 and classified 'T14'. Five further engines, Nos 458–462, were built between December 1911 and April 1912, also at Eastleigh. They worked the Bournemouth services until after the First World War, and were superheated between 1915 and 1918. Because of their front end appearance they gained the nickname 'double-breasters' and were also often nicknamed 'paddleboxes' because of their enormous splashers, having more than a passing resemblance to paddle-steamers. No E446 is seen in the mid 1920s with extended smokebox which was fitted by Urie.

A. G. Ellis collection

Plate 176 Right Between 1930 and 1931 these four-cylinder engines were further rebuilt by Maunsell. In an attempt to cure persistent hot boxes he removed the large splashers, lifted the running plate over the coupled wheels and fitted mechanical lubricators. All ten were dealt with between 1930–1 and No 446 is seen as modified, at Waterloo in 1937.

C. R. L. Coles

Plate 177 Below No 458 was the first 'T14' to be withdrawn in 1940 after suffering air raid damage during the war. The remaining nine survived nationalisation but the last one was withdrawn in 1951. Even after rebuilding their problems were not entirely solved, particularly their unreliable steaming, and as a result they were rarely used on front line express passenger work. No 459 is passing Byfleet in summer 1938 heading a relief down Bournemouth train.

C. R. L. Coles

Plate 178 *Above* Class 'E1R' 0-6-2T No 32608 running into the platform at Torrington with one coach forming the 08.52 to Halwill. The class of ten 'E1Rs' were designed for use on local passenger services in the West Country and were tested over several SR West Country branches, including very briefly the ex PDSWJR Callington branch. They had been rebuilt by Maunsell 1927–8 from Stroudley LBSCR 'E1' 0-6-0Ts (see *Plate 95*) by adding a pony truck at the rear and extending the coal bunker. The last one survived until 1959.

R. E. Vincent

Plate 179 *Left* Twenty Class 'I1' 4-4-2Ts were built by Marsh for the LBSCR 1906–7 at Brighton Works for secondary passenger and suburban services. They were not successful engines and as they were of little use on the Central Section the decision was taken to re-boiler them using the spare boilers of the 'B4' 4-4-0s which had been rebuilt as Class 'B4X'. Maunsell carried out this rebuilding between 1925 and 1932 and succeeded in improving these Atlantic tanks quite considerably. 'I1X' 4-4-2T No 2600 is at Horsham in October 1934 and was the first of the class to be withdrawn in 1944 with badly fractured frames. The last one was withdrawn in July 1951.

A. G. Ellis collection

Plate 180 *Right* In 1928 Maunsell rebuilt twenty of his Class 'K' 2-6-4 'River' tanks which he originally built for the SECR in 1917. These rebuilds became part of the Class of 'U' 2-6-0 tender engines and one of them, No 31800, is shunting in Farnham yard on 28th June, 1965.

P. Harrod

Plate 181 Above Class 'D1' 4-4-0 No 31739 is restarting from Warren Halt on 30th May, 1961 on a Dover train. Twenty-one of these engines were rebuilt between 1921 and 1927 for accelerated services on the Chatham and Kent Coast lines. They followed the successful rebuilding of the Wainwright 'E' Class (see opposite page) and were very similar in appearance.

D. Cobbe

Plate 182 Below On 7th August, 1949 Class 'D1' 4-4-0 No 31736 is near Balham heading a Victoria—Tunbridge Wells train. These 'D1s' gave excellent service and the last one was on duty until 1961.

R. W. Beaton

Plate 183 Above In 1919 and 1920 Maunsell rebuilt eleven of Wainwright's SECR Class 'E' 4-4-0s for use on Continental expresses via the Chatham Section from Victoria. It was important to keep the weight down, and he succeeded in producing a more powerful engine than the 'E' which was only slightly heavier. These rebuilt 'E1s' were outstanding 4-4-0s and No A179, which was the prototype rebuilt at Ashford in 1919, is seen shortly after the grouping on a down Continental express.

A. G. Ellis collection

Plate 184 Below Class 'E1' 4-4-0 No 31067 is emerging from Chislehurst Tunnel in September 1960 on a Hop Pickers' Special, and by this time the top feed apparatus and the smokebox snifting valves have been removed. This engine was the last of the Class to survive and was withdrawn in 1961.

D. Cross

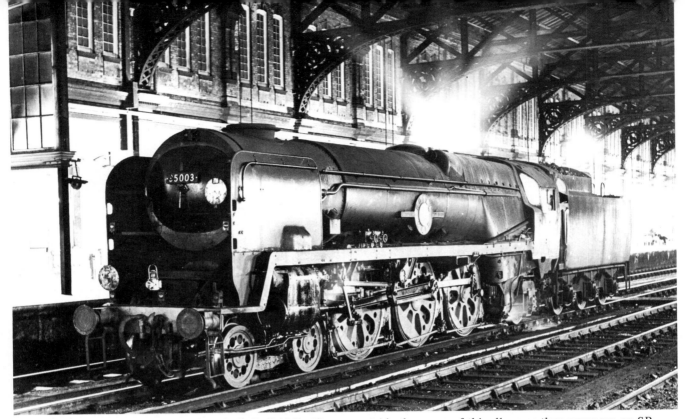

Plate 185 Above Strictly speaking the rebuilt Bulleid Pacifics are outside the scope of this album as they never ran on SR metals. All thirty 'Merchant Navy' Pacifics were rebuilt by BR 1956–9 in an attempt to improve their oil and coal consumption. Their air-smoothed casing was removed and with their high running plate and large smoke deflectors externally they resembled the Riddles BR Standard Pacifics. In this evening picture of No 35003 *Royal Mail* at Bournemouth Central on 20th August, 1965, the distinctive Bulleid wheels which were retained can be seen, together with the large diameter multiple-jet chimney. These rebuilt 'Merchant Navys' had a tragically short life, the last one being withdrawn in 1967, but fortunately several have been preserved.

J. S. Whiteley

Plate 186 Below The most obvious difference between the rebuilt 'Merchant Navys' and the rebuilt Light Pacifics was in the positioning of the nameplates. The 'Merchant Navys' had them attached to the boiler sides whereas the Light Pacifics had them attached to a backplate which was fixed to the running plate. Rebuilt 'West Country' No 34096 *Trevone* is restarting from Seaton Junction on 22nd July, 1962 heading the 16.00 Waterloo–West of England.

J. S. Whiteley

Plate 187 Above 'Schools' Class 4-4-0 No 30920 *Rugby* accelerates away from the former SECR terminus at Cannon Street on 5th June, 1958 heading the 17.05 to Hastings. Rebuilt 'West Country' Pacific No 34021 *Dartmoor* stands on the left-hand side on the 17.14 to Ramsgate. Diesel-electric multiple units were just about to take over these services at this date.

R. C. Riley

Plate 188 Below Spotlessly clean 'King Arthur' 4-6-0 No 30796 *Sir Dodinas le Savage* is leaving Cannon Street on 30th May, 1958 with the 17.47 to Dover, shortly before being transferred to the Western Section.

R. C. Riley

Plate 189 Left An evening scene inside Waterloo with one of Wainwright's handsome Class 'D' 4-4-0s, No 31746, standing on the 20.13 parcels to Reading.

B. Morrison

Plate 190 Below Waterloo was the LSWR terminus in London before the grouping, and one of Drummond's fine looking LSWR engines completes the picture. Class 'K10' 4-4-0 No 385 is leaving with a Reading train on 25th September, 1938.

J. P. Wilson

Plate 191 Above A comparison of SR and LSWR 'N15' 4-6-0s at Waterloo on 4th July, 1952. On the left Maunsell No 30783 *Sir Gillemere* prepares to depart on the 17.30 to Bournemouth, whilst on the right Urie LSWR No 30755 *The Red Knight* with large diameter chimney and vertical smoke deflectors stands on a West of England train.

J. P. Wilson

Plate 192 Below Shafts of morning sunlight illuminate 'Schools' 4-4-0 No 30929 *Malvern* standing inside Victoria on a Newhaven boat train in 1954.

W. P. Conolly

Plate 193 Above 'Lord Nelson' Class 4-6-0 No 855 *Robert Blake* leaves the 'Chatham side' of Victoria heading the 14.00 boat train on 10th July, 1937. The train is just starting its 1 in 62 climb to the Grosvenor Bridge.

J. P. Wilson

Plate 194 Right Victoria was a joint SECR and LBSCR terminus and in 1946 Marsh Class 'H2' 4-4-2 No 2422 *North Foreland* prepares to leave with a Newhaven boat train.

C. R. L. Coles

Plate 195 Below On 19th July, 1937 Marsh Class 'I3' 4-4-2T No 2030 leaves the 'Brighton side' of Victoria with a Brighton via Uckfield train.

J. P. Wilson

Plate 196 Above Charing Cross was the terminus for the SECR at the grouping and 'Schools' 4-4-0 No 915 *Brighton* is leaving on 14th July, 1939 heading the 11.15 to Dover and Deal. The SECR coat of arms can be seen on the roof.

J. P. Wilson

Plate 197 Below On 30th September, 1938 Maunsell Class 'D1' 4-4-0 No 1502 is entering Charing Cross.

H. C. Casserley

Plate 198 Above The Hayling Island branch from Havant on the mainland was the province of the Stroudley LBSCR 'Terriers' as rebuilt to Class 'A1X'. No 2635 is seen near Langstone in 1939. This engine had an interesting history; it was built in June 1878 as LBSCR No 35 *Morden*, placed on the duplicate list in November 1908 as No 635, and rebuilt to Class 'A1X' in April 1922. In 1946 it was withdrawn for use at Brighton Works as No 377S, and following the closure of Brighton Works it was returned to BR general stock in January 1959 as No 32635 in Stroudley yellow livery, being finally withdrawn in March 1963.

C.R.L. Coles

Plate 199 Above No 2644 was rebuilt to Class 'A1X' in 1912 and it is seen in 1938 shortly after leaving Havant on a Hayling Island train.

C. R. L. Coles

Plate 200 Left One of the features of the Hayling Island branch was the Langstone bridge. On 23rd August, 1952 Class 'A1X' No 32661 is crossing with the 16.26 Hayling Island–Havant formed of three ex-LSWR coaches.

N. W. Sprinks

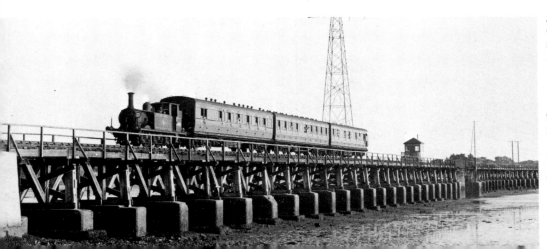

Plate 201 Above An aerial view of Ventnor on the Isle of Wight gives it almost a model-like appearance. Adams Class 'O2' 0-4-4T No W21 *Sandown* is leaving on a train for Ryde on 28th August, 1965. Prior to the grouping, there were three separate systems each with its own locomotives, the Isle of Wight Railway, the Isle of Wight Central Railway, and the Freshwater, Yarmouth and Newport Railway. Ventnor, seen here, was on the Isle of Wight Railway.

G. W. Morrison

Plate 202 Right Another of the Adams LSWR Class 'O2' 0-4-4Ts which was drafted to the Isle of Wight after the grouping, No W35 *Freshwater* is standing at Ryde (St. John's Road) in September 1961 on a Ventnor train.
W. P. Conolly

Plate 203 *Above* Inside St. John's Road shed at Ryde on 3rd August, 1964 sees three Adams Class 'O2' 0-4-4Ts, No W35 *Freshwater*, No W16 *Ventnor*, and No W29 *Alverstone*.

P. Harrod

Plate 204 *Above* Some of Stroudley's LBSCR 'Terriers' found their way to the Isle of Wight, and on 17th March, 1936 No W13 *Carisbrooke* in immaculate green livery with copper-capped chimney is seen at Ryde.

A. G. Ellis collection

Plate 205 *Above* Another Stroudley LBSCR class to be drafted to the Isle of Wight was the 'E1' 0-6-0T. Four were transferred there in 1932 and No W2 *Yarmouth* is at Newport in 1932.

A. G. Ellis collection

Plate 206 *Above* Beyer Peacock built some 2-4-0Ts for the Isle of Wight Railway between 1864 and 1883. One of them, No W16 *Wroxall* is at Newport in March 1931.

A. G. Ellis collection

Plate 207 *Above* Another one of Stroudley's 'Terriers', No W2 *Freshwater*. This engine ran on the Freshwater, Yarmouth and Newport Railway and was returned to the mainland in 1949 assuming BR No 32646.

A. G. Ellis collection

Plate 208 Above A delightful picture of Class '0298' 2-4-0WT No 30586 near Dunmere on the Wenford Bridge mineral railway in Cornwall. Three of these engines which were originally built by Beattie for the LSWR in 1874–5 were retained for working this line by the SR and lasted well into BR days, the last one being withdrawn in 1962.

D. Cobbe

Plate 209 Above On 15th April, 1950 BR No 30757 *Earl of Mount Edgecumbe* is heading the midday down train which consists of LSWR push-and-pull gated stock, between Calstock and Gunnislake on the line of the ex Plymouth, Devonport and South Western Junction Railway. Two of these 0-6-2Ts were built by Hawthorn, Leslie & Co. in 1907 for the opening of the PDSWJR on 2nd March, 1908, and continued to work on this line until after nationalisation, being finally withdrawn in 1957.

R. E. Vincent

Plate 210 Below No E188 *Lew* which was built by Manning, Wardle in 1925, similar in design to three earlier 2-6-2Ts which were built for the Lynton and Barnstaple Railway in 1897. These 1897 engines were withdrawn in 1935 on closure of the line, and in that same year *Lew* was sent to Brazil for use on a coffee plantation.

A. G. Ellis collection

Plate 211 Above As well as the two 0-6-2Ts, the PDSWJR also purchased this 0-6-0T from Hawthorn, Leslie & Co. in 1907. It was originally PDSWJR No 3 but is seen after the grouping as No 756 *A. S. Harris* and was withdrawn in 1951.

A. G. Ellis collection

Plate 212 Above Bournemouth trains use the former LSWR terminus at Waterloo and 'Battle of Britain' 4-6-2 No 21C159, later named *Sir Archibald Sinclair*, prepares to leave on the down 'Bournemouth Belle'. The locomotive was only three months old when this photograph was taken on 16th July, 1947.

J. P. Wilson

Plate 213 Below 'Lord Nelson' 4-6-0 No 865 *Sir John Hawkins*, fitted with distinctive double chimney with raised lip containing the Kylchap blastpipe, is seen leaving Waterloo on the down 'Bournemouth Belle' in 1938.

C. R. L. Coles

Plate 214 Above On 12th May, 1953 all the 'Merchant Navy' Pacifics were withdrawn from service after a driving axle fracture on No 35020 *Bibby Line*. Six 'V2' 2-6-2s from the Eastern Region were loaned, along with other classes to act as temporary replacements. One of the 'V2s' No 60896 with Doncaster shed plate (36A) is seen passing Vauxhall on the up 'Bournemouth Belle' on 20th May, 1953.

N. W. Sprinks

Plate 215 Below A superb study of Maunsell 'King Arthur' No 451 *Sir Lamorak* getting into its stride at Vauxhall, soon after leaving Waterloo, with a down West of England express in 1939.

C. R. L. Coles

Plate 216 *Above* Drummond Class 'T14' 4-6-0 No 30446, as rebuilt 1930—1, working very hard past the maze of lines at Clapham Junction on a down Nine Elms—Southampton express freight on 22nd June, 1949.

R. W. Beaton

Plate 217 *Below* The 18.54 Waterloo—Basingstoke is seen behind one of Maunsell's handsome 'S15' 4-6-0s, No 30847. It is passing Earlsfield, between Clapham Junction and Wimbledon on 26th May, 1953.

R. E. Vincent

Plate 218 *Upper right* 'Lord Nelson' 4-6-0 No 864 *Sir Martin Frobisher* hurries through Raynes Park on the outskirts of London with a down West of England express. ▶

E. E. Smith

Plate 219 *Lower right* 'Remembrance' Class 4-6-0 No 32329 *Stephenson* pauses at Surbiton with an up stopping train. ▶

A. G. Ellis collection

Plate 220 Left 'Lord Nelson' No 861 *Lord Anson* at the head of the 'Bournemouth Belle Pullman' passing Walton-on-Thames in 1938.

C. R. L. Coles

Plate 221 Above 'Battle of Britain' Pacific No 34052 *Lord Dowding* climbing the 1 in 326 near Woking with a West of England express on 23rd July, 1949.

R. W. Beaton

Plate 222 Left Drummond Class 'T14' 4-6-0 No 444, as rebuilt, working hard on a Waterloo–Salisbury train near Woking on 23rd July, 1949. The two down lines are on the near side and the up lines are on the far side of the picture.

R. W. Beaton

Plate 223 Above In July 1960 one of the Urie 'S15s' No 30512 hurries up the main line at Brookwood with a summer relief. The signal gantry suggests a lot of activity on the line at this peak summer period.

D. Cross

Plate 224 Below A humble duty for Drummond Class 'T9' 4-4-0 No 30729 near the end of its life, heading a permanent way train at Brookwood in September 1960. The 'birdcage' coach is of interest, and the whole ensemble is near Pirbright Junction.

D. Cross

Plate 225 *Upper left* Urie Class 'H15' 4-6-0 No 30485 leaves Winchfield on a hot summer's day with a down train. The signalman has been quick to drop signals.

N. Stead

Plate 226 *Lower left* A semi-fast from Basingstoke to Yeovil nears Worting Junction, about three miles west of Basingstoke behind Urie 'S15' No 30508 in August 1960.

D. Cross

Plate 227 *Above* Under clear signals 'Merchant Navy' Pacific No 35015 *Rotterdam Lloyd* speeds the down 'Bournemouth Belle' on the approach to Basingstoke, 48 miles from Waterloo in June 1951.

R. E. Vincent

Plate 228 *Below* 'Lord Nelson' No 30864 *Sir Martin Frobisher* appears to be in a hurry as it passes Battledown flyover at Worting Junction with the 13.30 Waterloo—Weymouth on 7th September, 1948. The West of England main line leaves the Bournemouth line at Worting Junction and can be seen on the left hand side passing underneath the bridge carrying the up line from Southampton and Bournemouth.

A. Cawston, D. Cobbe collection

Plate 229 Upper left 'Schools' 4-4-0 No 931 *King's-Wimbledon* pulls away from Winchester with a down Waterloo—Bournemouth express on 20th July, 1939. This locomotive was one of the nineteen 'Schools' fitted with a multiple blastpipe and large-diameter chimney.

J. P. Wilson

Plate 230 Lower left The handsome lines of a Maunsell 'King Arthur' are clearly seen in this picture of No 30773 *Sir Lavaine* waiting to leave Eastleigh with the 17.15 to Portsmouth on 15th August, 1961. Eastleigh, of course, was famous for the Works of the LSWR situated between the lines to Portsmouth and Southampton, just south of the station.

G. W. Morrison

Plate 231 Above The station clock towers above this study of 'West Country' Pacific No 34105 *Swanage* as it prepares to leave Southampton Central with an express for the Midlands on 12th September, 1964.

G. W. Morrison

Plate 232 Right An Eastleigh to Bournemouth all-stations train drifts into Southampton Central headed by 'T9' 4-4-0 No 30117 in July 1959.

D. Cross

Plate 233 *Above* No 30850 *Lord Nelson* leaves Southampton Central under the impressive gantry at the west end, with the 13.28 Fareham—Bournemouth West consisting of vintage stock, on 26th July, 1949.

A. Cawston, D. Cobbe collection

Plate 234 *Below* Deep in the heart of the New Forest 'Lord Nelson' No 30856 *Lord St Vincent* hurries a Birkenhead—Bournemouth express down the bank, towards Hinton Admiral on 19th August, 1961.

G. W. Morrison

Plate 235 Above One of the 'U' Class 2-6-0s No 31793 which was rebuilt from a 'River' tank, pulls away from Hinton Admiral with an all stations Bournemouth West—Southampton train on 18th August, 1961.

G. W. Morrison

Plate 236 Below A scene at Bournemouth Central on 20th August, 1965 with 'Battle of Britain' Pacific No 34086 *219 Squadron* leaving with the northbound 'Pines Express' after the train had been routed away from the Somerset and Dorset line.

J. S. Whiteley

Plate 239 *Above* Drummond Class 'T9' 4-4-0 No 30715 crosses the River Camel between Wadebridge and Padstow with a local train in September 1959.

D. Cross

IN THE SOUTH WEST

Plate 240 *Below* Another 'Greyhound', No 30709, on Great Western metals as it pulls out of Exeter St. David's and starts the steep climb up to Exeter Central with a train for Templecombe on 24th June, 1958.

J. P. Wilson

Plate 241 Upper left Woolwich Arsenal 'N' Class 2-6-0 No 31832 makes a pleasing picture as it heads a local goods away from Exeter, just to the east of St. James's Halt in the early 1960s.

J. Stredwick

Plate 242 Lower left Another Woolwich Arsenal 'N' 2-6-0 No 31846 rounds the curve into Barnstaple Junction with a local freight from Ilfracombe on 13th August, 1955.

R. E. Vincent

Plate 243 Above The 17.15 to Ilfracombe pulls away from Barnstaple Junction on 8th July, 1964 headed by 'N' Class 2-6-0 No 31853.

D. Cobbe

Plate 244 Right The passengers wait patiently at Bere Alston for Class 'O2' 0-4-4T No 30236 to finish shunting the stock for the 10.50 departure to Callington on 7th April, 1953.

R. E. Vincent

Plate 245 Above The Callington to Bere Alston line crossed the River Tamar at Calstock on a magnificent viaduct on which Class 'O2' 0-4-4T No 30192 is crossing with the 16.23 from Callington on 25th September, 1954.

R. E. Vincent

Plate 246 Below On 7th April, 1953 Class 'O2' 0-4-4T No 30236 is at rest between duties at Callington Locomotive Shed.

R. E. Vincent

Plate 247 Right The pioneer 'West Country' Pacific No 34001 *Exeter* emerges from Mutley Tunnel at Plymouth at the head of the 11.35 Exeter St. David's–Plymouth North Road. The impressive tunnel mouth shows up well in this picture taken on 27th June, 1955.

R. E. Vincent

Plate 248 Above 'West Country' No 34024 *Tamar Valley* simmers gently at Wadebridge on 24th June, 1955 awaiting the green flag whilst heading an Okehampton—Padstow train.

R. E. Vincent

Plate 249 Below Class 'H' freight train approaching Mutley Tunnel, Plymouth, *en route* to Friary Station behind Class 'N' 2-6-0 No 31847 on 27th June, 1955.

R. E. Vincent

Plate 250 Above 'Battle of Britain' No 34061 *73 Squadron* passes along the sea-wall between Dawlish and Teignmouth on the former Great Western main line, with a train from Exeter on 13th August, 1952.

R. W. Beaton

Plate 251 Below On 2nd July, 1964 'Battle of Britain' No 34078 *222 Squadron* makes a vigorous departure from Padstow at 09.33 with a portion of the up 'Atlantic Coast Express'.

D. Cobbe

Plate 252 Left 'Battle of Britain' Class 4-6-2 No 34090
Sir Eustace Missenden, Southern Railway, with its
distinctive nameplate, is leaving the boat train sidings at
Folkestone Junction on 29th August, 1952 for Victoria,
its train having been brought up from the harbour by tank
engines.

A. Cawston, D. Cobbe collection

Plate 253 Above The most famous boat train of all, the
'Golden Arrow', seen awaiting departure from Victoria in
1947 behind 'West Country' Pacific No 21C119, later
named *Bideford*. In this post-war period the train left
Victoria at 10.00 and was allowed one hundred minutes
to Dover with a formation of ten Pullmans and two vans.
The channel was crossed to Calais and Paris was reached at
approximately 17.30.

C. R. L. Coles

Plate 254 Below A fine sight at Bickley on 8th August, 1949
with 'Battle of Britain' Class 4-6-2 No 34074, later named
46 Squadron, in full cry on the down train.

R. W. Beaton

Plate 255 Above On 9th August, 1937 'Lord Nelson' Class 4-6-0 No 858 *Lord Duncan* is working hard whilst approaching Shorncliffe on an afternoon boat train to Victoria.

A. Cawston, D. Cobbe collection

Plate 256 Below The up 'Night Ferry' is passing Bromley South on 3rd April, 1955 behind Class 'L1' 4-4-0 No 31754 and 'Battle of Britain' 4-6-2 No 34074 *46 Squadron*. This overnight service operated between Paris and London Victoria via Dunkerque and Dover, arriving at Victoria at 09.10. The train often comprised as many as two French vans and ten blue Wagons Lits of the International Sleeping Car Company, and regularly had an 'L1' piloting a Pacific.

B. C. Bending

Plate 257 *Above* 'West Country' Pacific No 34101 *Hartland* has steam shut off whilst passing Tonbridge on 11th October, 1953 heading the 13.20 Folkestone Harbour—Victoria boat train.

N. W. Sprinks

Plate 258 *Right* Beautifully turned out 'West Country' Pacific No 34092 *City of Wells* is approaching the summit at Knockholt on the down 'Golden Arrow' in September 1959.

D. Cross

Plate 259 *Below* On 14th July, 1939 No 850 *Lord Nelson*, soon after being fitted with large tender and large diameter chimney, is leaving Dover Marine with an up boat train.

J. P. Wilson

Plate 260 Above A line-up at Nine Elms in 1950 comprises 'West Country' Pacific No 34023 *Blackmore Vale* and rebuilt 'paddleboxes' Nos 444 and 447.

C. R. L. Coles

ON SHED

Plate 261 Below Another scene at Nine Elms sees 'Lord Nelson' 4-6-0 No 30861 *Lord Anson* outnumbered by Bulleid Pacifics in both rebuilt and unrebuilt form.

G. W. Morrison

Plate 262 Above Bognor shed on 5th May, 1934 sees Stroudley LBSCR Class 'D1' 0-4-2Ts Nos 2605, B615, 2299, and 2616.

A. G. Ellis collection

Plate 263 Left A footplate view of Eastleigh on 15th August, 1961.

G. W. Morrison

Plate 264 Below An impressive angle to view a 'Schools' with a multiple-jet blastpipe and large diameter chimney. No 30929 *Malvern* is on shed at Bournemouth in the mid-1950s whilst allocated to Bricklayers Arms.

E. E. Smith

Plate 265 *Above* A busy scene at Templecombe with a stranger on shed in the shape of Class 'Z' 0-8-0T No 30953. Somerset and Dorset Class '7F' 2-8-0 No 53807 has just passed underneath the West of England main line with a northbound local working.

E. E. Smith

Plate 266 *Below* Glorious Devon. On 10th October, 1953 Okehampton sees 'West Country' Pacifics No 34025 *Whimple* and No 34017 *Ilfracombe* on shed.

R. E. Vincent

Plate 267 Above A fine trio of LBSCR engines on shed at St. Leonards West Marina on 15th July, 1939. From left to right, Marsh Class 'H2' 4-4-2 No 2424 *Beachy Head*, L. B. Billinton Class 'B4X' 4-4-0 No 2060 and R. J. Billinton Class 'E4' 0-6-2T No 2561.

A. G. Ellis collection

Plate 268 Below A trio of Urie LSWR 'H16' 4-6-2Ts at Feltham on 2nd December, 1962.

G. W. Morrison

Plate 269 Above 'West Country' Pacific No 34102 *Lapford* is nearing the end of its days on 27th March, 1967. The nameplates have been removed for safe keeping and it is seen at Bournemouth shed.

G. W. Morrison

Plate 270 Below Hither Green on 13th September, 1958. From left to right, Class 'N' 2-6-0s Nos 31858, 31405 and 31859, and Class 'W' 2-6-4Ts Nos 31912 and 31913.

G. W. Morrison

Plate 1: A delightful picture, taken on 19th July 1938, near Welshpool, of 'Dukedog' No. 3202 (later No. 9002) heading a local train for Shrewsbury, along the Cambrian line, for which C. B. Collett built thirty of these locomotives as late as 1936. They were not entirely new, having been constructed from the frames of withdrawn 'Bulldog' class locomotives, with 'Duke' class boilers. They were extremely successful and lasted for more than twenty years.

J. G. Dewing

Plate 2: The 9.10 Paddington to Birkenhead express is pictured near Loudwater, on 18th March 1957, headed by 'King' class locomotive No. 6016 *King John* of Old Oak Common Depot.

J. D. Edwards

THE GREAT WESTERN REMEMBERED

J. S. Whiteley and G. W. Morrison

Oxford Publishing Co.

Plate 3: A Great Western classic photograph taken at Flax Bourton, which is between Bristol and Bridgwater, of 'Star' class 4-6-0 No. 4014 *Knight of the Bath*, at the head of a Wolverhampton (Low Level) to Paignton express in 1939.

C. R. L. Coles

ISBN 0 86093 204 4

Contents

Introduction

The Great Western Remembered is the fourth volume in a series, and is a companion volume to *The LMS Remembered, The LNER Remembered,* and *The Southern Remembered,* published in 1979 and 1980. It has been compiled on the same basis as the others by giving a photographic record of the company from the Grouping on 1st January 1923.

The Great Western Railway, of course, differed from the other companies as it was 1833 when it was planned in Bristol, and of the Big Four at the time of the Grouping, the Great Western took over eighteen comparatively small railway companies, the handing over taking a two year period. This resulted in the GWR inheriting a wide variety of small motive power. A large proportion of the locomotives which were inherited were already quite old, and the GWR was quick to sort out the motley collection of the older classes, by scrapping many, but also rebuilding others with standard Great Western features.

The Great Western always had an air of superiority, which tended to divide enthusiasts into those who worshipped it, and those who hated it, but if one looks at it dispassionately, it had good reasons for its attitude. Churchward had built what must be some of the finest express passenger locomotives ever to run in this country in the 'Saints' and the 'Stars', many of which put in fifty years service without any major modifications, and were still to be seen on express passenger work right up to their withdrawal. The same can also be said for the 2800 class 2-8-0s. The Collett era was really an extension of the firm basis set by Churchward, and so the outward appearance of GWR locomotives changed little over fifty years.

The GWR was always very publicity conscious, making much of the first-claimed 100m.p.h., with *City of Truro's* epic descent of Wellington Bank and the introduction of the first Pacific locomotive in this country in the shape of *The Great Bear*, which, as a locomotive, could hardly be considered a success, but certainly could as far as a publicity exercise was concerned. The various locomotive exchanges in the mid-1920s, when the 'Castles' demonstrated their superiority over LMS and LNER express locomotives, was also exploited to the full by the GWR Publicity Department.

From 1930 onwards, there were no major changes on the motive power side, the designs then in existence being basically sound enough to last until the end of steam, and the limelight then tended to be on the LMS and LNER who were both running their streamlined trains just prior to World War II. In spite of its deep-rooted steam traditions, the Western Region of British Rail was the first to eliminate steam from its main line operations, and indeed continued their forward-looking approach with the introduction of Inter-City 125 units.

The photographs selected for this book have been chosen to try and portray a balanced picture of the Great Western from 1923 onwards, and whilst most have not been published before, we felt that no Great Western album would be complete without a few of the late Maurice Earley classics. To all the other photographers who have put their collections at our disposal, we extend our thanks, and hope that Great Western enthusiasts will obtain as much pleasure from the book, as we have had in its compilation.

G. W. Morrison
October 1984

The Churchward Era

George Jackson Churchward was appointed Locomotive, Carriage and Wagon Superintendent of the Great Western Railway in 1902, succeeding William Dean, and so began the most significant period of locomotive design for the Great Western Railway, until his retirement in 1921.

His achievements in standardisation of design were never matched until the latter 1930s, when Sir William Stanier standardised designs for the LMS, followed by H. G. Ivatt and ultimately R. A. Riddles for British Railways.

Such was the excellence of his basic and rugged locomotives, that many lasted almost to the end of steam on British Railways, in some cases putting in over fifty years of service, and most without any major modifications.

The 2900 class 4-6-0 'Saints'

The prototype No. 100, later named *William Dean*, emerged from Swindon Works in 1902. The appearance of the locomotive caused quite a stir at the time, as it had none of the traditional lines of the period.

There were 77 of these magnificent locomotives constructed between 1902 and 1913, thirteen of them being built as 4-4-2s. These were all converted to 4-6-0s between April 1912 and January 1913. Few major alterations occurred throughout their working lives except for No. 2935 *Caynham Court*, which was fitted with rotary cam poppet valve gear and new cylinders in May 1931. No. 2925 *Saint Martin* was reconstructed with 6ft. driving wheels and larger cab in 1924, and became the prototype for the famous 'Hall' class, being renumbered 4900 and lasting in service until 1959. The first 'Saint' was withdrawn in 1931 and the last, No. 2920 *Saint David*, in 1953. Forty seven survived to enter service with British Railways in January 1948.

Plate 4 (left): Top link work for 'Saint' No. 2953 *Titley Court*, as it passes Chipping Sodbury on 30th June 1925, with an 'up' Bristol to Paddington express. When this photograph was taken, outside steam pipes had not been fitted, neither had whistle shields, which were added to the class from 1925. Comparison with *Plate 5* shows the extended safety-valve bonnet which was shortened after 1927.

H. G. W. Household

Plate 5 (below): After 39 years of service, 'Saint' No. 2951 *Tawstock Court* is seen at Gloucester Shed on 22nd June 1952, the month in which it was withdrawn from service. It was the first locomotive in the last batch of five to be constructed in 1913, and was one of the 33 members of the class to be fitted with a speedometer after 1937. Interchange of boilers with the 'Granges' took place after 1939, resulting in locomotives running with the smaller type of chimney, as is seen in this photograph.

L. Elsey

Plate 6 (right): A portrait of 'Saint' No. 2905 *Lady Macbeth* taken at Bristol (Bath Road) Shed 5th June 1938. This was one of the nineteen members of the class which had the older platforms with square 'drop ends'. After November 1930, the majority of the class was fitted with new front ends, which were given an estimated life of 25 years. No. 2905 was one of the class so fitted, which is indicated by the outside steam pipes. The locomotive is running in the 1934 livery with the circular totem of the letters GWR.

J. P. Wilson

Plate 7 (left): A 'down' Paddington to Swansea express is pictured near Burnham Beaches, on 25th April 1925, headed by 'Saint' No. 2907 *Lady Disdain*. Most of the early withdrawals from 1931 onwards tended, with a few exceptions, to be the locomotives which were not fitted with the new front ends. No. 2907 *Lady Disdain* was one of them, being withdrawn as early as 1933 after 27 years service.

H. G. W. Household

Plate 8 (below): On 10th July 1925, 'Saint' No. 2950 *Taplow Court* makes a splendid sight as it heads a 'down' Paddington to Swansea express on to the water troughs between Sodbury Tunnel and Chipping Sodbury Station.

H. G. W. Household

The 2800 class 2-8-0s

The prototype of this famous class, No. 97, appeared as early as June 1903. It was designed with many of the improvements incorporated in the second 'Saint', No. 98, and had the same type of boiler.

These locomotives have the distinction of being the first 2-8-0s in this country, and must surely rank as one of the most successful heavy freight locomotives ever to be built in the British Isles. The class ultimately consisted of 167 locomotives, 84 being built between 1903 and 1919, followed by a gap of 20 years before C. B. Collett constructed the remainder between 1938 and 1942. There were very few alterations to the original design except for side window cabs, outside steam pipes, and modified framing. Twenty members of the class were converted to oil burning between October 1945 and September 1947, but by January 1950 all had been reconverted to coal.

One member of the class, No. 2804, visited Scotland for trials on the Glenfarg Incline in January 1921, and No. 3803 took part in the 'Locomotive Exchange' trials of 1948. The prototype, which became No. 2800, is recorded as having covered 1,319,831 miles during its 55 years of service, and was in fact the first to be withdrawn in 1958. The last to be withdrawn was No. 3836, which was taken out of traffic in 1965.

Plate 9 (above): Having probably just received its last major overhaul, 2-8-0 No. 2861, built in June 1918, stands outside Swindon Works on 2nd September 1956, ready to resume duties from its home depot of Newport.

Gavin Morrison

Plate 10 (above): The class was not often used on passenger duties, but occasionally they appeared during busy summer Saturdays in Devon and Cornwall. In this photograph, No. 2836 is seen in August 1959 heading an 'up' empty stock train, south of Oxford.

J. D. Edwards

Plate 11 (left): No. 2830, which was the last of lot number 160 to be built in 1907, is seen after 45 years service working very hard through Leamington Spa on 25th September 1952, with a heavy 'up' freight.

B. Morrison

Plate 12 (right): No. 3805 has just received a major overhaul at Swindon and is seen at Westbury Shed on 1st October 1961, looking very smart in its unlined black livery. The side window cab can be clearly seen in this picture compared with *Plate 9*. The Collett-built locomotives were known as the 2884 class.

Gavin Morrison

Plate 13 (below): The gentleman taking the sea air along the wall at Teignmouth seems unimpressed by this fine sight of No. 3838 heading a 'down' freight towards Newton Abbot on 2nd October 1959.

L. Elsey

The Prairie Tanks
The 3100, 3150, 5100, 5101, 6100 and 8100 class 2-6-2Ts

Three hundred and six of these fine 2-6-2Ts were constructed over the lengthy period from 1903 to 1949.

The prototype, No. 99, had an interesting career. It appeared in 1903, and was thoroughly tested for over a year by Churchward before any further locomotives were constructed. No. 99 later became No. 3100, in December 1912. It ran as such until April 1929 when it became No. 5100. The side tanks were altered at this time from straight-topped to the sloping pattern, and it also received a long-cone boiler in 1910.

A start on rebuilding the first forty locomotives (Nos. 3100, 3111-3149), built between 1903 and 1906, was made in 1938, but the war interrupted the programme after only ten had been altered. The prototype, No. 99, finally became the first of the 8100 class in September 1938 when it was rebuilt using the original frames but having new front ends fitted, a boiler with high pressure, and 5ft. 6in. diameter coupled wheels.

The 1938 batch of rebuilds, Nos. 3100-3104 were also interrupted by the war, these being from the larger boilered 3150 series.

Some of the locomotives were constructed in 1949 so had as little as twelve years service. The vast majority of the class operated in the Wolverhampton/Birmingham areas, with the exception of the 6100s, which were almost exclusively used on the London suburban services.

Plate 14 (above): No. 3100, rebuilt from No. 3173 in December 1938, awaits scrapping on 8th September 1957, at Swindon Works. These five rebuilds were originally intended for banking duties, but by 1950 were regularly being used for suburban trains around Wolverhampton, Newport and Tondu.

Gavin Morrison

Plate 15 (below): No. 3102, with a newly-painted smokebox, is seen shunting in the yards of Wolverhampton, prior to leaving with a freight for Wrexham. The locomotive, which was a rebuild of No. 3181 in May 1939, was allocated to Wolverhampton (Stafford Road) Shed when this picture was taken on 20th July 1954. *B. Morrison*

Plate 16 (above): A 5101 class locomotive, No. 5152, prepares to leave Chipping Norton on 14th September 1963, as No. 6111 arrives with a Railway Enthusiasts' Club special.

J. R. P. Hunt

Plate 19 (below): A fine study of one of the original batch of Class 5100 locomotives built in 1906. No. 5132 is leaving Exeter St. David's on 5th June 1949, with a local train for Torquay. Note the absence of outside steam pipes; only six out of the batch of forty received them from 1943 onwards. This locomotive put in forty five years service, compared with twelve for some of the 5101 class.

J. P. Wilson

Plate 17 (above): Another 5101 class locomotive, built in November 1929, No. 5103, is ready to leave Ruabon on 9th August 1956 with the 17.04 local train to Llangollen.

B. Morrison

Plate 18 (left): A portrait of one of the post-war batch of Class 5101, No. 4144, is seen in the lined Brunswick green livery of British Railways at Cardiff (Canton) Depot on 3rd June 1962. This locomotive is one of several members of the class which have been preserved.

Gavin Morrison

Plate 21 (above): 6100 class No. 6132 looks very smart, on 14th October 1962, at Southall Shed in its unlined green livery with small emblem.

Gavin Morrison

Plate 20 (above): One of the seventy 6100 class loco-motives, No. 6103, built with 225lb. boiler pressure, is approaching High Wycombe on a local train from Banbury on 6th June 1953. The class was specifically-built for London suburban work, and all operated in the division until 1954. The introduction of diesel multiple units in 1960 saw their rapid demise.

B. Morrison

Plate 22 (below): No. 8100 was in fact the third 5100 class to be rebuilt, in September 1938. It went to Leamington after re-building, where it is seen on 17th June 1951, alongside railcar No. W22, built in 1940 with an AEC engine. For the history of No. 8100 (which contained the frames of the 1903 prototype 2-6-2T) reference should be made to the introductory notes on the Prairie tanks on *Page 10*.

B. Morrison

The 3800 class 4-4-0 'Counties'

Plate 23 (above): An official works photograph of No. 3821 *County of Bedford,* which was the first of the final batch of ten, and which varied from the original thirty in that they had curved drop-ends to the footplating *(compare Plates 24 & 25 below).* These locomotives were the only outside-cylindered 4-4-0s built by the Great Western. They were used initially on the Shrewsbury to Hereford route where the LNWR objected to the use of 4-6-0s. They were extremely rough-riding locomotives and probably the least successful of the Churchward engines. They were soon demoted to secondary work and withdrawn in the early 1930s.

OPC/British Rail Collection

Plate 24 (above): No. 3825 *County of Denbigh* is seen on express passenger duties on 18th July 1926, near Cheletenham (Racecourse) Station, with a Paignton to Wolverhampton train, which consists of quite a variety of coaching stock.

H. G. W. Household

Plate 25 (above): One of the members of the second batch of ten built in 1906, all of which were named after Irish counties, is seen on 9th July 1924, near Hatherley Junction, Cheltenham, hauling a Penzance to Wolverhampton express. The locomotive is No. 3804 *County Dublin,* and is paired to the tender off *The Great Bear* which it received in June 1924. Two other members of the class ran with this tender, possibly in an attempt to stabilise them.

H. G. W. Household

The 2221 class 4-4-2 'County' Tanks

Plate 26 (right): These locomotives were basically tank versions of the 'County' 3800 class, but had a smaller boiler. Thirty of the class were built between 1905 and 1912. They were primarily used on outer London suburban services, hence the large 6ft. 8½in. coupled wheels. They were rapidly withdrawn in the early 1930s, after the introduction of the 6100 class. No. 2235 is seen at Oxford on 1st July 1934.

R. C. Riley Collection

The 4000 class 4-6-0 'Stars'

Based upon the experience gained from the three 'De Glehn' Compound Atlantics and his two cylinder 4-6-0 'Saints', Churchward produced, in 1906, the first of what many have regarded as his finest class of locomotive, the 'Stars'. No. 40 (later numbered 4000) emerged as a 4-4-2 and ran in this condition, together with other differences from the rest of the class, until November 1909, when it became a 4-6-0. Seventy three of these locomotives, including No. 40, were built by 1923, thirty nine surviving to enter service with British Railways. They altered little in appearance during their existence, except for the addition of outside steam pipes. Right up to the end, they could be seen working heavy express trains, some members covering over two million miles during their life. Between 1925 and 1929, five were rebuilt as 'Castles', followed in 1940 by a further ten (Nos. 4063-72) which became 'Castles' Nos. 5083-92. After 1938, most of the class received 4,000 gallon high-sided tenders.

Plate 27 (above): On 25th April 1925, No. 4015 *Knight of St. John* is pictured near Burnham Beeches, Buckinghamshire, at the head of the 2.30p.m. Cheltenham to Paddington express, which was only allowed 75 minutes for the 77 miles from Swindon to Paddington.

H. G. W. Household

Plate 28 (right): No. 4034 *Queen Adelaide*, built in November 1910, passes along the sea wall near Teignmouth with the 'down' 'Cornish Riviera' express on 24th April 1924.

H. G. W. Household

Plate 29 (below): A 'Star', at the peak of its career, hauling the heavy 'up' 'Cornish Riviera' express. The locomotive is No. 4042 *Prince Albert*, built in May 1913, and lasting over 38 years. It is seen between Teignmouth and Dawlish, on 24th April 1924.

H. G. W. Household

Plate 30 (right): On 24th September 1955, the Talyllyn Railway Preservation Society's annual special makes a fine sight as it nears the top of Hatton Bank, headed by No. 4061 *Glastonbury Abbey* with its number specially painted on the buffer beam for the occasion by Tyseley Shed. The locomotive is fitted with the elbow steam pipes.

R. C. Riley

Plate 31 (below): The external condition of No. 4056 *Princess Margaret* is in sharp contrast to *Plate 32*. The locomotive is heading a 'down' express past Southall, on 10th August 1957, with the number painted on the buffer beam for working an enthusiasts' special.

R. C. Riley

Plate 32 (below): No. 4056 *Princess Margaret* was the last of the class to be withdrawn, in October 1957. Built in July 1914, it had the elbow-type outside steam pipes added in August 1949, and it also has the 4,000 gallon tender. Two members of the class, Nos. 4059 and 4062, ran with the Hawksworth flat-sided tenders, whilst in 1936, Nos. 4045 and 4022 had *The Great Bear* tender. No. 4056 spent its later days at Bristol (Bath Road) Shed where it is seen on 9th March 1952.

L. Elsey

The 4400, 4500 and 4575 class 2-6-2Ts

These fine little 2-6-2Ts were very similar. The 4400s had 4ft. 1½in. coupled wheels, but the 4500 and 4575 classes had the diameter of the coupled wheels increased to 4ft. 7½in., to give them a 60m.p.h. capability. Eleven of the 4400s were built in 1905, the first one, No. 4400, being built at Swindon and the rest at Wolverhampton. Fifty five of the Class 4500 were built between 1906 and 1915, and as was so often the case with Churchward's successful designs, a gap of nine years elapsed before a further 120 were constructed between 1924 and 1929. The last 100 engines had larger side tanks with 1,300 gallons capacity, compared to 1,000 gallons for the earlier locomotives. All entered service with British Rail. Nos. 4500-29 were originally built without outside steam pipes which were added from 1929 onwards. Auto-apparatus was fitted to fifteen members of the class between August and November 1953 for working in the South Wales valleys.

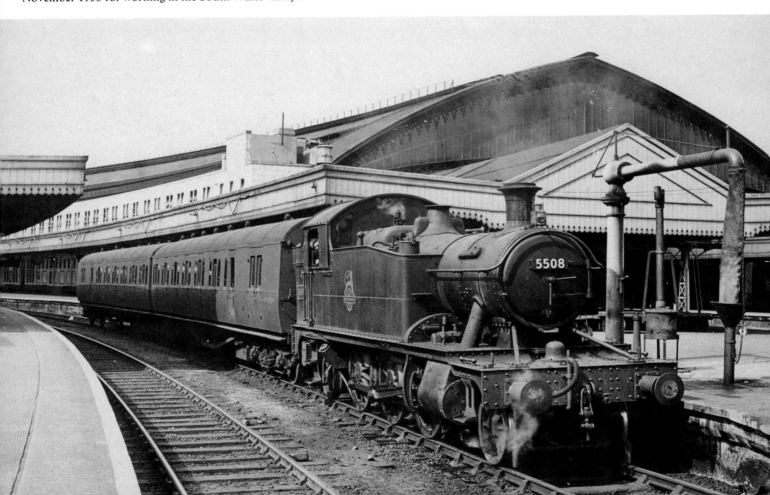

No. 111 4-6-2 *The Great Bear*.

Much has been written over the years about this locomotive. It appears that Churchward was instructed by the company's Directors, contrary to his own wishes, to build, as cheaply as possible, the largest locomotive in the country.

The locomotive was presented to the Directors at Paddington in January 1908, and immediately received considerable interest. As a publicity exercise, the locomotive was a huge success being the only British Pacific for fourteen years. Operationally, it was a different story; its size and weight restricted its use to the Paddington to Bristol line, with very few wanderings. It was restricted to 65m.p.h., and caused constant worry to the permament way engineering department. When costly repairs were due in January 1924, Collett grasped the opportunity to rebuild the locomotive as a 'Castle', which emerged as No. 111, but renamed *Viscount Churchill*. The eight-wheeled tender lasted a further twelve years in traffic and ran with many different classes.

Plate 35 (above):   An official photograph of the locomotive.
OPC/British Rail Collection

Plate 36 (right):   About one year after rebuilding from *The Great Bear*, it is seen as 'Castle' class locomotive No. 111, now *Viscount Churchill*, with a 3,500 gallon tender, at Slough on 25th April 1925.

H. G. W. Household

Plate 37 (below):   This is, no doubt, one of the publicity photographs taken of No. 111, showing its massive proportions. The total length of engine and tender over buffers was 71ft. 2¼in., almost 7ft. longer than a 'Star', and at 142 tons 15 cwt. in full working order, about 28 tons more than a 'Star'. Not only was the engine restricted to the Bristol line, but it was banned from using platform 1 at Paddington. It was always allocated to Old Oak Common.

OPC/British Rail Collection

The 4200 and 5205 class 2-8-0Ts

The increase in mineral traffic in South Wales in the early 1900s meant that there was a need for a tank version of the famous 2800 class. A 2-8-2T design was considered but rejected mainly on the length of the wheelbase, bearing in mind the environment in which the locomotives would work, so a 2-8-0T prototype appeared in 1910 as No. 4201. Fourteen months elapsed before any more were built, there being little variation between No. 4201 and the others, except for an increase of the coal bunker capacity and the fitting of top feed. The 5205 class, introduced in 1923, had outside steam pipes and an increased cylinder diameter to 19in., which increased the tractive effort. Fourteen of the 4201 series were rebuilt as 2-8-2Ts, to increase their operating capabilites, whilst Nos. 5255-5294 were also converted. Nos. 5275-5294 never entered traffic as 2-8-0Ts and were stored at Swindon prior to conversion. Due to wartime demands, a further batch of ten was built as late as 1940, being numbered 5255-5264.

Plate 38 (above): One of the last batch to be built in 1940, and in fact the second 2-8-0T to be numbered 5261, the original becoming 2-8-2T No. 7226, is seen in ex-works condition in the standard British Railways livery of unlined black on 3rd June 1962, at Cardiff (Canton) Shed. Note the raised running plate above the cylinders, compared with No. 4289 in *Plate 39*.

Gavin Morrison

Plate 39 (below): On 5th February 1953, No. 4289 is pictured near Ely, west of Cardiff on a 'down' freight. Two hundred and five of these locomotives were built, including the ones converted to 2-8-2T, all entering service with British Railways, the last one, No. 5235, being withdrawn in 1965.

S. Rickard

The 4300 class 2-6-0s

No prototype was considered necessary for these extremely successful Moguls, of which 324 were built between 1911 and 1932. They were, in fact, a tender version of the 3150 class 2-6-2Ts, and the first new GWR locomotives to be built with top feed. The second batch, built in 1913, Nos. 4321-40, had the frames lengthened by 9in., as did the remainder, but this batch also had enlarged cabs, similar to the 3800 'County' class.

Eighty eight of the 4300 series and twelve of the 8300 series were withdrawn between 1936 and 1939 and some parts, particularly the wheels and motion, were used on the 'Granges' and 'Manors'. From 1928, sixty five locomotives had their weight distribution altered and they became the 8300 class, but they reverted to their original condition in 1944 and to their original numbers. From No. 6362 onwards, outside steam pipes were fitted new, many of the earlier locomotives being modified from 1928 onwards. The first locomotive was withdrawn in 1936 and the last in 1965. One locomotive, No. 6320, was converted to oil burning in March 1947, reverting back to coal in August 1949.

Plate 40 (above): No. 6323 is seen on Bristol (Bath Road) Shed. This photograph was taken on 5th June 1938, before the outside steam pipes were added ten years later. Note the automatic tablet catcher on the tender. Seven locomotives ran with tablet catchers at various times and were used on the Minehead and Barnstaple branches.
J. P. Wilson

Plate 41 (below): A very dirty No. 5381, which became No. 8381 in 1928 and reverted back in 1944, is seen on a very lengthy freight passing Beaconsfield, en route to London, on 13th August 1956.
Gavin Morrison

Plate 42 (left): No. 6352 enters Lydney Junction on 19th May 1958, at the head of the 12.40p.m. slow passenger train from Carmarthen to Cheltenham.

J. D. Edwards

Plate 43 (below): The 1932 batch, numbered 9300-9319, was built with the same weight distribution as the modified 8300 locomotives. Between 1956 and 1959, they were altered back to the 5300 weight specification and became Nos. 7322-7341. No. 7324 is seen at Banbury Shed on 18th May 1958 (note the side window cab).

F. J. Bullock

Plate 44 (below): An unusual meeting at Oxford of the Midland Compound No. 1000 and Mogul No. 7317. This picture was taken during a locomotive change on a railtour from Nottingham to Eastleigh on 11th September 1960, returning via the Midland & South Western Joint Railway. The ex-works Mogul, in unlined green livery, gave a spirited performance, reaching the upper seventies down the bank through Winchester. Other locations where these two classes could have been regularly seen together would have been Chester, Birkenhead and, possibly, Crewe.

Gavin Morrison

The 4700 class 2-8-0s

The performance of *The Great Bear* on fitted freight work had been partly successful, and a request from the traffic department for a locomotive to work heavy fast vacuum-fitted freights led Churchward to produce the 4700 class. Only nine were built, No. 4700 appearing in 1919 with a standard No. 1 boiler. The remainder of the class were constructed with the new No. 7 boiler and with outside steam pipes, No. 4700 being altered accordingly. From 1932, the 3,500 gallon tenders were replaced with the 4,000 gallon type. Generally speaking, these very successful locomotives changed little in appearance. They spent most of their lives working at night on express freights between London, Wolverhampton and Plymouth. Their weight and size restricted their route availability, but in their latter years they were frequently seen, in the summer, working expresses between Paddington and Devon, and maintaining schedules on all but the fastest workings. They were the last of Churchward's famous designs, and it is a pity that one was not preserved.

Plate 46 (right): In 1953, the 5.14p.m. Paddington to Weston-super-Mare fast train is pictured crossing from the main to relief line at Twyford East box, and is headed by No. 4708.

M. W. Earley

Plate 47 (below): On express passenger duty, No. 4706 passes through the centre road at Newbury at the head of a Paddington to Paignton train on 29th August 1959.

L. Elsey

Plate 45 (above): No. 4705 is seen on Southall Shed on 28th April 1963, at the end of its working life of forty years. This locomotive achieved the highest mileage for a member of the class of 1,656,564 miles.

Gavin Morrison

The Collett Era

C. B. Collett was appointed Chief Mechanical Engineer of the Great Western Railway in 1922. During his twenty years in this capacity, he appreciated the excellence of G. J. Churchward's designs and concentrated much of his efforts in developing and expanding them. This policy resulted in the building of what are probably the most famous of Great Western Locomotives, namely the 'Castles' and 'Kings', which became the mainstay of Great Western express motive power through the glamorous pre-war years, and indeed virtually to the end of steam on the Western Region. His pannier tanks were equally famous if much less glamorous and his forward thinking attitude produced the streamlined diesel railcars, as early as 1934. He retired in 1941.

The 4073 class 4-6-0 'Castles'

One hundred & seventy one of these famous locomotives were built (including rebuilds) between 1923 and 1950. By the Grouping, the weight of trains dictated that something more powerful than a 'Star' was needed, but it had to be within the 20 ton axle load permitted by the Civil Engineer. Collett followed Churchward's cautious approach to the introduction of new locomotives, in that No. 4073 operated for six months on 'Star' diagrams before the second engine was completed. No. 4073 *Caerphilly Castle* was exhibited in 1924 close to the LNER *Flying Scotsman* at the British Empire Exhibition at Wembley, the GWR stating that it was the most powerful passenger locomotive in the country. This resulted in the comparative trials between the two types on each other's main lines, the 'Castle' substantiating the claims about it with ease. No. 5000 *Launceston Castle* also ran trials between Euston and Carlisle. Nos. 4000/09/16/32/37 and 5083-5092 were rebuilt from 'Stars', and there was little alteration to the appearance of the class until No. 7018 *Drysllwyn Castle* appeared with a double chimney in May 1956, and with three-row superheater. The next locomotive modified was No. 4090 having four-row superheater. Sixty five locomotives were so modified, and in this condition achieved some of their finest performances. The 3,500 gallon tenders were replaced by ones of 4,000 gallon capacity, Hawksworth flat-sided tenders being constructed for the final batch, from No. 7008 onwards, and these were freely interchanged. Five locomotives were converted to oil burning in 1946 and 1947 but were changed back by the end of 1948. The 'Castles' must be unique in British express locomotive design in that they were built over a period of 28 years with only minor alterations, and remained on top link work for 38 years.

Plate 48 (above): No. 5054 *Earl of Ducie* is seen on Carmarthen Shed on 9th September 1962, just after receiving what was probably its last major repair at Swindon.

Gavin Morrison

Plate 49 (below): No. 5017 *The Gloucestershire Regiment 28th, 61st* seen on 11th May 1956, at Gloucester Station. This locomotive was originally named *St. Donats Castle*, the alteration being made in April 1954. The locomotive covered 1,598,851 miles in its thirty years of service.

W. Potter, D. Cobbe Collection

Plate 50 (above): A pre-war picture, taken on 22nd July 1937, of No. 5042 *Winchester Castle* approaching Swindon on a 'down' Paddington to Bristol and Weston-super-Mare express. Built in July 1935, the locomotive saw thirty years of service covering 1,339,221 miles. *J. P. Wilson*

Plate 51 (below): The real No. 4082 *Windsor Castle* is seen on Royal Train duties from Weymouth to London as it passes Reading (West) Station in June 1938, fully decorated, and with the magnificent LNWR coaches. This locomotive took part in the Stockton & Darlington Centenary celebrations in 1925, and was unique in having the honour of being driven from Swindon Works to the station by His Majesty King George V with Queen Mary also on the footplate. It carried a plaque to commemorate the event. It was under repair in February 1952, and was therefore not available to haul the funeral train of King George VI, so the name, numbers and plaque were transferred to No. 7013 *Bristol Castle*. They were never replaced on the real No. 4082. *M. W. Earley*

Plate 52 (left): The down 'Torbay Express' leaves Exeter St. David's on 2nd June 1957, headed by an immaculate 'Castle', No. 5059 *Earl St. Aldwyn.*

F. J. Bullock

Plate 53 (below): One of the late M. W. Earley classic photographs of 'Castles' shows No. 5035 *Coity Castle* heading the 11.15a.m. ex-Paddington (Sunday) fast train for Weston-super-Mare and Taunton. It is seen in November 1951 passing Tilehurst. The River Thames can be seen in the background. The smart external condition was so typical of the way that Old Oak Common kept the express locomotives at this time.

M. W. Earley

Plate 54 (right): The 1.45p.m. Paddington to Hereford train passes the outskirts of Oxford at North Junction, headed by one of the immaculate Worcester 'Castles', No. 7005 *Sir Edward Elgar*, on 22nd October 1957. This locomotive was originally named *Lamphey Castle*. Only the leading four or five coaches would work forward to Hereford from Worcester.

J. D. Edwards

Plate 55 (left): On 4th March 1958, No. 5005 *Manorbier Castle* is seen at speed on the Swindon Test Plant rollers.

J. D. Edwards

Plate 56 (right): 'Castle' class locomotive No. 5056, *Earl of Powis*, of Old Oak Common Shed, hauls the 2.10p.m. express from Paddington to Birkenhead and is pictured near Seer Green. This locomotive was originally named *Ogmore Castle* but was renamed in September 1937.

J. D. Edwards

Plate 57 (above left): No. 5086 *Viscount Horne* enters Bristol (Temple Meads) on 4th June 1949, with a Penzance to Wolverhampton express. This was one of the ten 'Castles' which were rebuilt from 'Stars' between 1937 and 1940. The rolling stock looks to be nearly as dirty as the locomotive.

J. P. Wilson

Plate 58 (below left): Probably the most spectacular locations on the Great Western Railway for photography, are the tunnels between Dawlish and Teignmouth. Unfortunately the photographer was not blessed with a clean locomotive, but in spite of the external condition, No. 5058 *Earl of Clancarty* makes a fine sight, as it heads a 'down' express on 5th June 1949, at Horse Cove.

J. P. Wilson

Plate 59 (above): In March 1935, in keeping with the fashion of the late 1930s, No. 5005 *Manorbier Castle* was partially streamlined. These features were gradually removed from the end of 1935 onwards, until by 1946 the only evidence left was the snifting valve. It is seen at Westbourne Park on an 'up' express on 14th July 1937.

J. P. Wilson

Plate 60 (below): A Birkenhead to Bournemouth express, formed of Southern stock, leaves Leamington Spa headed by No. 5053 *Earl Cairns* on 19th February 1949.

J. P. Wilson

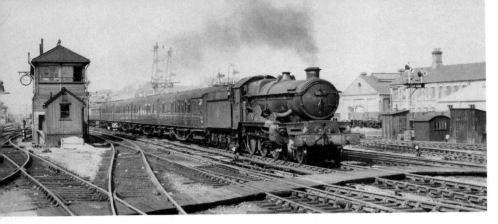

Plate 61 (left): The clock on the side of the signal box at the west end of Swindon Station indicated the time as 9.50a.m. as an unidentified 'up' express, headed by 'Castle' No. 5057 *Earl Waldergrave*, passes through on the fast line on 13th June 1959.

J. D. Edwards

Plate 62 (right): The 'down' 'Cambrian Coast Express' rushes through Beaconsfield on 20th September 1958, headed by No. 7013 *Bristol Castle*. This was, in fact, the original No. 4082 *Windsor Castle*, built in April 1924, but it changed identities in 1952 when it was not available to work the funeral train of King George VI *(See Plate 51)*. The locomotive is in its final condition with double blastpipe and chimney, and final pattern outside steam pipes with larger radius curves to allow clearance for the bulky four-row superheater header inside.

Gavin Morrison

Plate 63 (below): One of the well-kept Wolverhampton (Stafford Road) 'Castles', No. 5010 *Restormel Castle*, is seen approaching High Wycombe (Middle) signal box, with an 'up' morning express from Wolverhampton to Paddington on 11th April 1957.

J. D. Edwards

Plate 64 (right): On 29th April 1958, the 4.45p.m. Paddington to Hereford train is seen drifting into Oxford, past the cemetery, headed by a superbly-groomed Worcester 'Castle', No. 7005 *Sir Edward Elgar*. It is noticeable that even the buffer heads have been polished.

J. D. Edwards

Plate 65 (below): The last express passenger engine to be built by the Great Western at Swindon was 'Castle' class No. 7007, appropriately named *Great Western*, which was the same name as the first locomotive built in 1846. On 21st March 1960, No. 7007 is pictured leaving Oxford with a 'down' express from Paddington to Worcester, where the locomotive spent the majority of its working life.

J. D. Edwards

Plate 66 (above): On 14th July 1958, the 'down' 'Torbay Express' is seen passing through the cutting at Teignmouth Quay, headed by No. 5034 *Corfe Castle* which was built in 1935 and withdrawn in September 1962, having covered 1,250,714 miles.

R. C. Riley

Plate 67 (above right): An immaculate No. 5021, *Whittington Castle*, overshadowed by a large gasometer, arrives at Newquay with an excursion from Exeter on 21st July 1954.

L. Elsey

Plate 68 (above): Another view of No. 5034 *Corfe Castle* with the 'up' 'Torbay Express' passing along the sea wall at Teignmouth. The locomotive had received a good cleaning during the three days that separate this picture, taken on 17th July 1958, and that in *Plate 66*.

R. C. Riley

Plate 69 (left): Landore Depot at Swansea have certainly spent some time cleaning 'Castle' No. 4099 *Kilgerren Castle*. It was photographed at Swansea (High Street) from the window of the 5.25p.m. departure for Carmarthen, and was ready to leave on the 5.30p.m. for Paddington on 17th May 1958.

J. D. Edwards

Plate 70 (above): On 18th April 1964, only ten months before withdrawal and looking well cared for and complete with nameplate, No. 7011 *Banbury Castle* enters Evesham with a Worcester to Paddington express. It was built in 1949 by British Railways under the direction of Hawksworth, and is running with one of his flat-sided tenders.

J. R. P. Hunt

Plate 71 (above): One of the 65 'Castles' fitted with four-row superheaters and double chimney, No. 7023 *Penrice Castle*, makes a spirited departure, on 7th June 1964, from Bath (Green Park) on a railtour. This was one of the very few, if not the only occasion when a 'Castle' visited the old Somerset & Dorset terminus.

Gavin Morrison

Plate 72 (left): Another of the class with a double chimney and, since preservation, one of the best-known 'Castles'. No. 7029 *Clun Castle* is seen outside Swindon Shed on 26th April 1964. Withdrawn in December 1965, it only had a life of fifteen years in normal service, but happily it is now regularly used on steam specials.

Gavin Morrison

Plate 73 (below): On 3rd June 1962, only one month before withdrawal, No. 5053 *Earl Cairns* is seen at the back of Cardiff (Canton) Shed fitted with a Hawksworth tender. It was originally named *Bishop's Castle*, but altered to *Earl Cairns* in August 1937. It covered 1,293,786 miles in its 26 years of service.

Gavin Morrison

Plate 74 (below): No. 5062 *Earl of Shaftesbury* is stored, complete with nameplate, at Cardiff (Canton), on 3rd June 1962, the locomotive having run its last revenue-earning trip, as it was officially withdrawn two months after this photograph was taken. It was originally named *Tenby Castle* and was renamed in November 1937. *Tenby Castle* became No. 7026 in 1949.

Gavin Morrison

The 'Halls' became the 'maids of all work' on the Great Western from the latter 1920s until the end of steam.

The Churchward 4300 class Moguls had been giving excellent service, but the running department and the footplatemen tended to expect rather too much from them. Many years previous, Churchward had considered the 'Hall' design, but nothing happened until Collett put it into practice. The usual cautious approach, which had paid such handsome dividends so many times before, was again implemented. No. 2925 *Saint Martin* was selected in 1924 as the guinea pig, having the coupled wheels reduced in diameter from 6ft. 8½in. to 6ft., and also fitted with a side window cab. This locomotive, which was renumbered 4900, was tested with great success for nearly three years, when an initial order was then placed in 1928 for no less than eighty engines. There was little variance between No. 4900 and the production models, which had outside steam pipes and a raised boiler pitch. The first 42 locomotives were built with Churchward-type 3,500 gallon tenders, Nos. 4943-4957 then had the Collett type, and finally the remainder, with the odd exception, had the 4,000 gallon pattern. Two hundred and fifty nine of these locomotives were built up to 1943, when a further 71 modified locomotives were constructed by Hawksworth.

Eleven locomotives were converted to oil burning in 1946 and 1947, but all had been reconverted by March 1950.

All locomotives survived to enter service with British Railways, except No. 4911 *Bowden Hall*, which was destroyed by enemy action in April 1940. No. 4900 *Saint Martin* was the first to be withdrawn in 1959, with a total mileage for its career of 2,092,500 miles.

Plate 75 (above): On 25th July 1962, No. 6957 *Norcliffe Hall* pauses at Dainton Summit to pin down the brakes on this mixed freight, before descending the steep gradient to Totnes. This locomotive was one of the eleven 'Halls' converted to oil burning in April 1947, and carried the number 3952 after the conversion.
John Whiteley

Plate 76 (below): A superb night study of Cardiff Canton's No. 4956 *Plowden Hall*, as it waits for the road at Oxford on a fitted freight heading south, in the late evening of 8th August 1959.

J. D. Edwards

Plate 77 (above): Nottingham (Victoria) was the farthest north that Great Western locomotives ventured down the Great Central, except on very rare occasions, (see Plate 160). No. 5973 *Rolleston Hall*, built in May 1937, prepares to head south with a rake of southern stock on a return excursion to Poole, which it would probably work as far as Oxford.

J. P. Wilson

Plate 78 (below): A fine pre-war scene in 1938 at Reading (West) shows No. 5971 *Merevale Hall*, when only about a year old, heading an 'up' Weymouth express.

M. W. Earley

Plate 79 (left): No. 5967 *Bickmarsh Hall* is seen on Westbury Shed on 1st November 1961, fitted with a smaller diameter chimney, which some of the class carried after they had exchanged boilers from the later 'Modified Halls' during overhaul at Swindon. This locomotive was constructed in March 1937.

Gavin Morrison

Plate 80 (right): Another portrait taken at Westbury Shed, on 23rd April 1962, this time of No. 4920 *Dumbleton Hall*, obviously recently ex-works and, at this time, allocated to Plymouth (Laira). Happily this locomotive has been preserved and is currently being restored at the Dart Valley Railway.

Gavin Morrison

Plate 81 (left): 1st October 1961 sees a well-groomed Exeter-allocated 'Hall', No. 5976 *Ashwicke Hall* on Bristol (St. Philip's Marsh) Depot, attached to a Hawksworth 4,000 gallon tender. These tenders were constructed for the 'Modified Halls'.

Gavin Morrison

Plate 82 (above): The British Railways' lined black livery was extremely smart and No. 4908 *Broome Hall* shows it to advantage on 31st July 1956, as it leaves Par with an 'up' express on the stiff climb to Treverrin Tunnel.

L. Elsey

Plate 83 (below): A busy scene at Shrewsbury, as a commendably clean No. 4976 *Warfield Hall* leaves with a Hastings to Birkenhead express. An ex-LMS 8F, No. 48706, is seen alongside and No. 2933 *Bibury Court* awaits departure with the 16.50 train for Gobowen on 28th August 1952.

B. Morrison

Plate 84 (left): No. 6901 *Arley Hall* makes a smokey exit from Shrewsbury on 23rd June 1962, as it starts the long climb to Church Stretton with a freight, probably destined for South Wales.

John Whiteley

Plate 85 (right): A really dirty No. 6952 *Kimberley Hall,* built in 1943, makes a spectacular departure from Oxford on a Cowley to Birkenhead freight on 21st March 1960, and passes some new diesel multiple units.

J. D. Edwards

Plate 86 (left): On 27th August 1959, Llanelly-based 'Hall', No 5902 *Howick Hall* passes Oxford (North) Junction with an 'up' freight. The connection to the former LNWR line to Bletchley can be seen curving to the right, behind the leading wagons.

J. D. Edwards

Plate 87 (right): On 14th June 1958, the 4.18p.m. train from Swindon has just arrived at Didcot behind 'Hall' No. 4918 *Dartington Hall*, which appears to have recently visited the works. A 4300 class 2-6-0 No. 5397 is about to remove the empty carriage stock from the 2.42p.m. train from Paddington, in spite of the headlamp code indicating an express. The locomotive shed can be seen on the right, and this is now the headquarters of the Great Western Preservation Society.

J. D. Edwards

Plate 88 (above): On 30th September 1961, No. 5974 *Wallsworth Hall* of Westbury emerges from Bincombe Tunnel at Upwey Wishing Well Halt, as it descends rapidly down the line to Weymouth with a train from the Western Region.

Gavin Morrison

Plate 89 (right): On 23rd June 1962, a southbound parcels heads over the north/west joint route at Bayston Hill, just south of Shrewsbury, headed by No. 6934 *Beachamwell Hall*, fitted with a 'Modified Hall' boiler.

John Whiteley

The 6959 class 4-6-0 'Modified Halls'

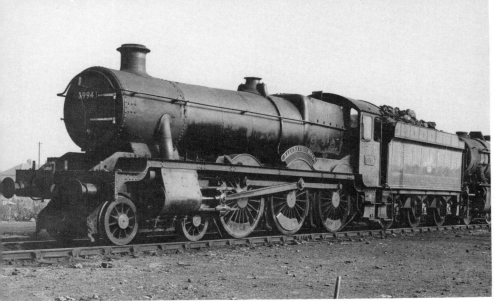

Hawksworth produced seventy-one of these 'Modified Halls' between March 1944 and November 1950. The main differences between these and 'Halls' were three-row superheaters fitted to the standard No. 1 boilers, main plate frames were used throughout with a simple plate frame bogie, and new pattern cylinders were fitted. Several different experiments were carried out on locomotives during construction, resulting in some small variances in the class. No. 6974 was the first to have the new pattern Hawksworth 4,000 gallon straight-sided tender. Nos. 6959-6970 were built during the war without cabside windows, which were subsequently fitted between 1945 and 1948, and they also ran without nameplates for two or three years. No. 6962 was the first to be withdrawn in 1963, some of the class only having fifteen years of service.

Plate 90 (above left): No. 6994 *Baggrave Hall* is pictured well coaled up on 14th October 1962, on Southall Shed, with a Collett-type tender.

Gavin Morrison

Plate 93 (above right): No. 7920 *Coney Hall* has just arrived at Birmingham (Snow Hill) with a morning commuter train from Leamington Spa on 10th March 1964.

J. R. P. Hunt

Plate 91 (centre left): Tyseley Junction is the setting for this picture of No. 7918 *Rhose Wood Hall*, taking the Stratford-upon-Avon line with an evening commuter train from Birmingham (Snow Hill) on 5th May 1964.

J. R. P. Hunt

Plate 94 (below right): The crew of 0-6-0 No. 3217 take a rest from duties on an engineer's train, and give a glance at No. 7919 *Runter Hall* heading for Birmingham, past Rowington, with an empty stock working during the summer of 1963.

J. R. P. Hunt

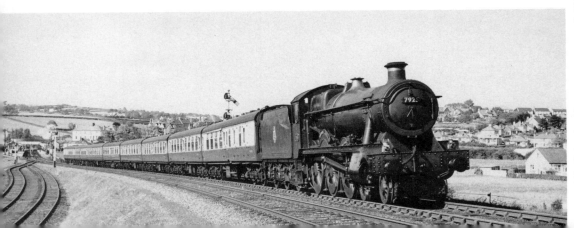

Plate 92 (below left): 8th August 1956 was a hot summer's day, and 'Modified Hall' No. 7925 *Westol Hall* is seen with no exhaust, hauling the 'down' 'Cornishman' out of Par, as it starts the steep 6½ mile climb to Burngullow.

L. Elsey

The 5600 class 0-6-2Ts

At the Grouping, the Great Western inherited many 0-6-2Ts from the railways of South Wales. Many of these were in poor condition, which resulted in a motive power shortage. Collett decided to scrap those in bad order, and rebuild the others with standard Churchward boilers and other standard parts. He also decided to continue the 0-6-2T wheel arrangement, which had not been used by the Great Western to any extent in the past.

No. 5600 appeared in November 1924, and two hundred had been built by 1928, the last fifty being built by Armstrong Whitworth. The majority of the class worked in South Wales, particularly in the Cardiff area, but these locomotives could also be found around Wolverhampton, Bristol, Swindon and Westbury.

They were extremely versatile locomotives, with impressive power and acceleration. The first withdrawals were in 1962, and all had gone by 1966. Several have been preserved.

Plate 95 (left): No. 5675, recently ex-works, pictured on 3rd June 1963 and in unlined green livery, is seen on Swansea East Dock Depot.

Gavin Morrison

Plate 96 (below): One of the preserved 5600 class locomotives, No. 6697, is seen on 19th April 1956, leaving Leamington Spa Yard with an 'up' freight. This was one of the Armstrong Whitworth locomotives built in 1928. It appears to have a tall safety-valve bonnet, although these were not originally fitted to the Armstrong Whitworth locomotives.

R. C. Riley

Plate 97 (right): No. 6628 enters Quakers Yard (High Level), on 10th August 1963, with a train from Aberdare to Pontypool Road. The locomotive was one of the Swindon-built batch of 1927.

J. R. P. Hunt

Plate 98 (below): No. 5667, built in June 1926 and in lined British Railways Brunswick green livery, is seen on 3rd June 1962 on Barry Shed, together with three pannier tanks.

Gavin Morrison

Plate 99 (right): A train of empty coal wagons is pictured on 12th May 1952, passing Penrhos Junction, just west of Caerphilly, headed by No. 5653 in the plain black livery.

R. C. Riley

The 6000 class 4-6-0 'Kings'

Volumes have been written in praise of these magnificent machines, which were really the ultimate development over twenty years of Churchward's 'Stars'. Much speculation surrounds the reasons for the building of the 'Kings', but the Publicity Department, no doubt, had much to do with it.

The 20 ton axle load restriction imposed by the Civil Engineer had stifled further development of the 'Castles', but with the limit being raised for the Plymouth and Wolverhampton routes to 22½ tons upon instruction from the General Manager, the way was clear for the 'Kings'.

Tests with No. 5001 *Llandovery Castle* resulted in a reduction in the coupled wheels diameter to 6ft. 6in. Another departure from the standard design was the leading bogie, with outside bearings for the leading axle, and inside for the trailing; this was necessary to give adequate clearance on curves.

No. 6000 *King George V* appeared in June 1927 in time to be shipped to America for the Baltimore & Ohio Railroad Centenary.

The Great Western had the most powerful express locomotive in the country, without it being a Pacific, with little variation within the class of thirty. After some small adjustments to improve the riding qualities, the 'Kings' settled down to give splendid service on the jobs for which they were designed.

It was in 1947 that Hawksworth fitted No. 6022 with a four-row superheated boiler and a mechanical lubricator, with some improvement in performance. After tests with No. 6001 in 1953, No. 6015 appeared in September 1955 with a double chimney and double blastpipe. The performance of this locomotive was superb, resulting in the whole class receiving the modifications, plus new cylinders, new half frames, valve gear and motion parts. It was in this condition that the 'Kings' gave their finest performances.

Plate 100 (above):   On 15th July 1937, a well-polished Wolverhampton (Stafford Road) 'King', No. 6006 *King George I*, prepares to leave Paddington at the head of the 7.10p.m. departure for Wolverhampton.

J. P. Wilson

Focus on No. 6000 *King George V*

Plate 101 (above): A close up of the bell, presented by the Baltimore & Ohio Railway to commemorate the visit of the locomotive to the centenary celebrations in 1927. Two cabside medallions were also presented. At this date, 23rd April 1962, the bell was mounted on a wooden plinth.

Gavin Morrison

Plate 102 (above): After working the 'down' 'Inter-City' from Paddington on 20th July 1954, No. 6000 *King George V* prepares to turn on the Wolverhampton (Stafford Road) turntable. The locomotive was ex-works in April 1954, and is seen with an inner sleeved chimney and modified outside steam pipes, and mechanical lubricator. During its 35 years of service, it covered 1,910,424 miles, being withdrawn in December 1962 for preservation at the Bulmer Railway Centre, Hereford.

B. Morrison

Plate 103 (below): The 'down' 'Cambrian Coast Express' pulls out of Paddington headed by No. 6000 *King George V* on 6th August 1960.

R. C. Riley

Plate 104 (above): In keeping with the trend of the mid-1930s, the Great Western decided to partially streamline No. 6014 *King Henry VII*, which totally ruined the classical looks of the locomotive. Fortunately, only 'Castle' class locomotive No. 5005 *Manorbier Castle* and *King Henry VII* received this treatment. No. 6014 emerged from Swindon Works in this condition in March 1935, but by January 1943 all signs of streamlining had gone, except the 'V' shaped cab. Of particular interest is the streamline fairing on the tender, which only lasted a matter of months.

British Rail/OPC Collection

Plate 105 (below): Restored to its former glory, but still with the 'V' shaped cab, and with its reporting number indicator fitted above the buffer beam, No. 6014 *King Henry VII* makes a splendid sight as it passes High Wycombe on 6th May 1957, heading the 2.10p.m. Paddington to Birkenhead express. The locomotive spent a great deal of its 34 years on this route. During its life, it covered 1,830,386 miles.

J. D. Edwards

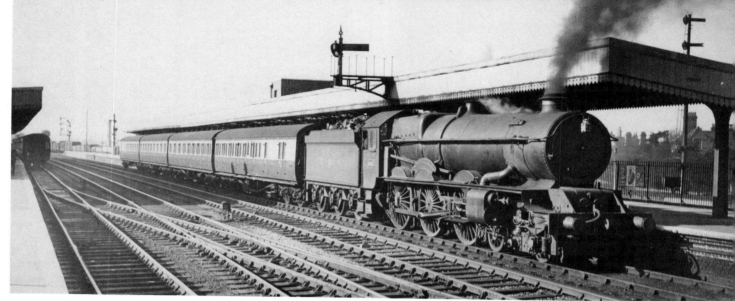

Plate 106 (above): Very light work for No. 6002 *King William IV* as it prepares to leave Leamington Spa with an 'up' local train on 19th February 1949. The unique front bogie design shows up well in this picture.

J. P. Wilson

Plate 107 (right): No. 6016 *King Edward V* receives attention at Old Oak Common before setting off for Paddington to work a 'down' express in 1953.

Gavin Morrison

Plate 108 (below): Journey's end for an express from Birkenhead to Paddington, on 15th July 1937, headed by No. 6006 *King George I*, which spent most of its working life at Wolverhampton (Stafford Road) Depot. It was in fact the first 'King' to be withdrawn, in February 1962.

J. P. Wilson

'Kings' on the 'Cornish Riviera Express'

Plate 109 (left): No. 6004 *King George III* glistens in the winter sunshine on 1st December 1957, as it passes under the bridge at Old Oak Common at the head of the 'down' train. This was the first 'King' to receive a cast-iron double chimney.
R. C. Riley

Plate 110 (below): No. 6000 *King George V* with its bell and plaques, beautifully turned out by Old Oak Common Shed, races out of Sonning Cutting with the regulator closed, giving a pleasing smoke effect, on the 'down' train in 1953.
M. W. Earley

Plate 111 (above): No. 6022 *King George III*, the first 'King' to be fitted with a four-row superheater, in February 1948, is seen in Sonning Cutting, at the location made famous by the late Maurice Earley.

M. W. Earley

Plate 112 (below): With a train of this size, plenty of assistance will be needed over the South Devon banks for No. 6017 *King Edward IV*, seen skirting the River Teign, just west of Teignmouth, with a 'down' express on 22nd June 1958.

L. Elsey

Plate 113 (above): On 5th June 1949, No. 6018 *King Henry VI* makes a magnificent sight as it leaves Exeter St. David's with a Bristol to Plymouth express. This locomotive took part in the 'Locomotive Exchanges' in 1948, and ran between King's Cross and Leeds.

J. P. Wilson

Plate 114 (below): A sad day for 'King' enthusiasts was 28th April 1963, when, No. 6018 *King Henry VI* was reinstated after withdrawal to work the last 'King' trip from Birmingham, via Southall, to Swindon. One of the authors was a passenger on the train, and still vividly remembers the fantastic climb of Hatton Bank. The locomotive is pictured on Swindon Shed, surrounded by Hymek diesels.

Gavin Morrison

Plate 115 (above): On 14th March 1957, the 'down' 'Inter-City' is seen departing High Wycombe, en route to Wolverhampton, headed by 'King' No. 6007 *King William III*. It was said to be virtually a new locomotive after rebuilding due to the Shrivenham collision of 15th January 1936.

J. D. Edwards

Plate 116 (below): 'King' No. 6001 *King Edward VII* approaches High Wycombe with the up 7.25 Wolverhampton to Paddington train on 21st March 1957. *J. D. Edwards*

Plate 117 (below): The 'down' 'Inter-City' express, without headboard, bursts out of White House Farm Tunnel headed by 'King' No. 6028 *King George VI* on 18th March 1957.

J. D. Edwards

Plate 118 (left): The final form for No. 6000 *King George V*, seen on Westbury Shed on 23rd April 1962.
Gavin Morrison

Plate 119 (above): On 5th June 1938, No. 6029 *King Edward VIII* is pictured on Bristol (Bath Road) Shed sporting the locomotive's pre-war livery. No. 6029 was named *King Stephen* until May 1936.
J. P. Wilson

Plate 120 (below): The end of the road for Nos. 6003 *King George IV* and 6024 *King Edward I*, seen stored at Cardiff (Canton) Depot on 3rd June 1962; both had done their last working and were withdrawn in that month. No. 6024 is preserved and is currently being restored.
Gavin Morrison

The 5700 class 0-6-0 Pannier Tanks

By 1929, there was a growing need to replace the hundreds of aged saddle and pannier tanks, which operated throughout the Great Western system.

No. 5700 appeared from the North British Locomotive Company works in 1929, and became the first of no fewer than 863 locomotives.

Seven different builders were used in the construction of these locomotives, spanning a period of 21 years. There were minor differences between certain batches but, externally, the most obvious was the improved cab and top feed to the boiler; these modifications commencing with locomotive No. 8750 in 1933. There were ten locomotives built with condensing apparatus for use on the Metropolitan line.

Thirteen of the locomotives were sold to the London Transport Executive; three remaining in service until 1971. The first withdrawals were in 1956, but some survived until 1966. Due to regional boundary alterations, a few were allocated to the London Midland Region, whilst some others finished on the Southern working empty carriage stock workings out of Waterloo, and on the Folkestone Harbour branch.

They were extremely successful machines, very powerful for their size, free running, and with excellent acceleration.

Plate 121 (right): This pleasing picture, taken in July 1959, is made interesting by the human element, and shows No. 8762, still with GWR lettering, carrying out shunting duties at Westbourne Park, London. *J. B. Snell*

Plate 122 (below): This excellent branch line scene shows No. 9647 at Chard (Central), on 27th June 1958, working a Taunton to Chard Junction train. This locomotive was built in 1946 at Swindon.

J. P. Wilson

Plate 123 (above): One of the 25 pannier tanks built by W. G. Bagnall in 1930 and 1931 was No. 8744, pictured at Westbury Shed on 1st October 1961.

Gavin Morrison

Plate 124 (above): Another W. G. Bagnall example is No. 6707, pictured at Swindon Works on 7th June 1959. The fifty locomotives in the 6700 series were only fitted with steam brakes and a simple three link coupling for shunting work. Many of the first batch of twenty five were stored, when new, for two years as there was no work for them. Most of this batch of locomotives spent their working life in South Wales.

Gavin Morrison

Plate 125 (right): No. 9707 was one of the eleven locomotives built with condensing apparatus for use on the Metropolitan line, which were always based at Old Oak Common Shed. They had a slightly increased water tank capacity, but a reduced coal capacity. The batch were fitted with ATC apparatus, which was raised when running on electrified track.

B. Morrison

Plate 126 (below): Spark arresting chimneys were fitted to thirteen of the pannier tanks. Nos. 5757 and 7713 had them fitted in 1937 and 1938, but the rest were altered during World War II. The locomotives used in military depots around Didcot were the ones to be modified. No. 5744 is pictured stored at Didcot with other pannier tanks in September 1959.

Gavin Morrison

Panniers at Work

Plate 127 (above): One of the locomotives built in 1930 by Armstrong Whitworth, No. 7788, is seen in 1945 in Sonning Cutting heading a pick-up freight to Reading (West) Junction Yard. The fireman looks anxiously to see if the injector is working.

M. W. Earley

Plate 128 (right): Someone appears to be about to leave the footplate on this picture of No. 4643, as it arrives at Park Junction with a train of pit props from Newport Docks on 11th March 1959.

S. Rickard

Plate 129 (below): On 16th May 1959, No. 7736, a North British-built pannier tank of 1929, pauses at Torpantau with a passenger train from Brecon to Newport, after completing the steep climb from Talyllyn Junction on the old Brecon & Merthyr line.

S. Rickard

The 2251 class 0-6-0s

The Churchward 2-6-0s and 2-8-0s had taken over main line freight duties, which left a shortage of small freight/mixed traffic locomotives for the lines on which the larger locomotives were prohibited. Collett produced 120 locomotives of the 2251 class. They replaced many of the famous 'Dean Goods' engines, and were well liked by the crews. No. 2251 appeared in 1930, whilst the last, No. 3219, emerged in 1948.

Plate 130 (above): No. 3212, with a Churchward 3,000 gallon tender, was built in 1947 and is seen at the back of Westbury Shed on 1st October 1961.

Gavin Morrison

Plate 131 (right): An 'up' pick-up freight from Banbury, on 4th March 1957, approaches the outskirts of High Wycombe, headed by No. 2297.

J. D. Edwards

Plate 132 (left): On 21st June 1959, No. 2247, built just at the end of World War II, is seen at Worcester Shed. Numbers 2281-2286 were built new with tenders from the 'Aberdares', which were of 4,000 gallon capacity, and originally came from the Robinson 2-8-0 RODs. Ten other members of the class were fitted with these tenders from time to time.

Gavin Morrison

Plate 133 (right): Collett 0-6-0 No. 2297 heads the 9.40a.m. Acton to Banbury pick-up away from High Wycombe on 15th April 1957.

J. D. Edwards

Plate 134 (below): On 10th September 1962, No. 3201 poses at Talyllyn Junction Station, in fully lined out passenger green livery. It is waiting for a connection off the Mid-Wales line, before heading up the valley to Torpantau, at the head of a Brecon to Newport local train.

Gavin Morrison

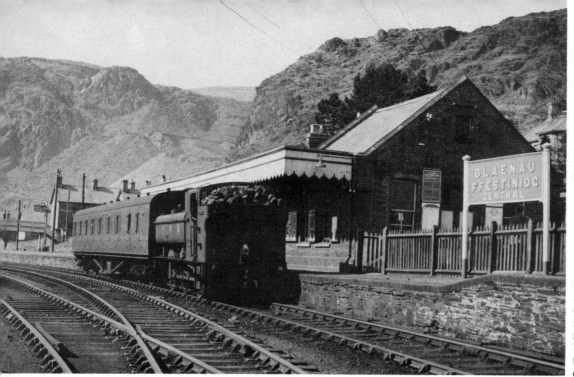

Plate 135 (left): On 30th March 1959, eleven years after nationalisation, No. 7428 still has GWR lettering on the tank sides. It is seen at Blaenau Ffestiniog (Central) ready to leave on a single coach train for Bala Junction. Fifty of the 7400 class locomotives were built between 1936 and 1950, and they had an increased boiler pressure of 180lb., compared to the 165lb. of the 6400 locomotives, which made them slightly more powerful.

Gavin Morrison

Plate 136 (below): In lined green BR livery, No 6416 prepares to leave Merthyr on 10th September 1962. All forty locomotives of the 6400 class were fitted for auto-train working, and were primarily used in the steeply-graded lines of the South Wales valleys. They were built between 1932 and 1937, and three examples have been preserved.

Gavin Morrison

Plate 137 (right): On 29th March 1959, No. 7428 comes off the train from Blaenau Ffestiniog (Central) at Bala, and heads for the shed. No. 8727 waits to take over for the short journey to Bala Junction, to connect with trains on the Ruabon to Barmouth line.

Gavin Morrison

Plate 138 (left): The 5400 class locomotives were designed for passenger work, particularly auto-train working. They had 5ft. 2in. coupled wheels, which were larger than the 5700 class (4ft. 7½in.) and were Collett's answer as a replacement for the aged 0-6-0 pannier tanks which had been auto-fitted late in life. They were fast with excellent acceleration, and could normally be seen sandwiched between four auto-trailers. No. 5410 is pictured on 25th February 1962, in fully lined out BR green livery, at Westbury, but out of use. Withdrawals started as early as 1956 with the demise of the branch lines, and the introduction of diesel multiple units.

Gavin Morrison

Plate 139 (right): No. 5418 operates push and pull duties in May 1952, on the West Ealing to Greenford line.

C. R. L. Coles

The 4800, 1400 and 5800 class 0-4-2Ts

These splendid little 0-4-2Ts were another of Collett's masterpieces. Ninety five were built during five years in the mid-1930s, and they could be seen at work over most of the Great Western system. There was some similarity with the Armstrong 517 class, but the locomotives were built with standard components used on the 5400 and 6400 classes. The 4800 locomotives, which later became the 1400s, were fitted for auto-working and with ATC, whilst the 5800 series had neither. Nos. 4800 to 4874 were renumbered due to the 481 numbers being required for oil burning 2800s. The final members of the class lasted until 1964, and four have been preserved.

Plate 140 (above left): On 16th June 1957, No. 1438 stands on Stourbridge Junction Shed during a visit by a group of enthusiasts from the north of England.

Gavin Morrison

Plate 141 (left): One of the non auto-fitted batch of twenty built in 1933 is seen at Bristol (Temple Meads) on 4th June 1949, with a High Siphon van, used for milk churn traffic.

J. P. Wilson

Plate 142 (below): Still sporting the Great Western livery, in August 1952, No. 1432 leaves Oswestry with the 11.20 train to Gobowen. This was an auto-train working for many years.

B. Morrison

Plate 143 (right): Fully lined out, in November 1953, No. 1411 prepares to leave Aylesbury Town with the 1.25p.m. train to Princes Risborough. Prior to 1953, these workings were shared with Eastern Region locomotives and stock. The locomotive has a top feed added to the boiler, and a large whistle shield to stop steam obscuring the cab windows.

N. W. Sprinks

Plate 144 (below): One of the Collett 0-4-2T locomotives fitted for auto-working is seen at Wallingford ready to leave for Cholsey & Moulsford on the main line. By 6th March 1959, the locomotive shed at Wallingford had closed. The capacity of the water tower should be more than adequate to fill the tanks of No. 1407.

J. D. Edwards

Plate 145 (left): A delightful setting for this photograph of No. 1437 and auto-car No. W1670W, recovering from a signal check at Princes Risborough, with the 2.42p.m. ex-Oxford on 1st April 1957. Both tracks are single lines, the one on the left being the Watlington branch.

J. D. Edwards

Plate 146 (below): The Hemyock branch was the home of a 1400 class engine for many years. It left the main line at Tiverton Junction with two delightful intermediate halts at Uffculme and Culmstock. On 8th October 1962, No. 1451 is pictured at Hemyock looking very smart in its fully lined out BR Brunswick green livery.

L. Elsey

Plate 147 (right): No. 7209 is pictured at Severn Tunnel Junction Shed on 26th April 1964. This locomotive was rebuilt from 2-8-0T No. 5284 in October 1934 and the first batch of twenty, Nos. 7200 to 7219, retained the curved platform above the cylinders.

Gavin Morrison

The 7200 class 2-8-2Ts

There were 54 of these fine machines rebuilt from the 4200 and 5205 class 2-8-0Ts, between August 1934 and December 1939. The frames on the first forty were increased in length by 4ft. 1in. at the rear to accommodate the trailing radial axle. Seven hundred additional gallons of water could be carried, with three tons more coal, which considerably extended the area of operation of the class. The first forty were rebuilt from the 5205 class, whilst the last fourteen were from the much older 4200 class. In fact, No. 4202, which became No. 7242, was 25 years old at rebuilding. They were extremely good machines, most being based in South Wales, and, in their early years, regularly worked trains to London and Exeter. No. 7235 was tried on the Lickey Incline, but had problems with platform clearance at Bromsgrove. The water capacity on the last fourteen members was 900 extra gallons, but only two tons extra coal.

Plate 148 (above right): Light work for Oxford-based 7200 class locomotive No. 7239, rebuilt from 5205 class No. 5274, heading for home at Kingham on 2nd March 1960.

J. D. Edwards

Plate 149 (right): No. 7230, ex-2-8-0T No. 5265, heads a westbound freight through Pengam Sidings, east of Cardiff.

S. Rickard

Plate 150 (above): No. 7216, which was originally 2-8-0T No. 5291, passes through Llantrisant with a heavy eastbound coal train on 14th August 1963.

J. R. P. Hunt

Plate 151 (below): The immaculate external condition of No. 7215, after a visit to the works, is unlikely to last long after a few weeks work around the South Wales coalfield. It is pictured at Swansea East Dock on 9th September 1962. *Gavin Morrison*

The 1366 class 0-6-0 Pannier Tanks

Only six of these delightful little tanks were built by Collett, in 1934, and were basically an improved version of the 1361 class, introduced by Churchward. They were used initially within Swindon Works, and later at Weymouth Docks as seen in these pictures. Finally they went to the Southern Region's Wenford Bridge mineral branch where they replaced the famous Beattie 2-4-0 well tanks. No. 1369 is preserved.

Plates 153 to 156: A series of pictures taken on 30th September 1961, at Weymouth Docks, of locomotives Nos. 1368 and 1369, handling two Channel Island boat trains. Clearance was extremely limited along the quayside, and railway staff had to frequently 'bounce' cars out of the way. They were fitted with bells to warn unwary pedestrians as, presumably, it was thought that a sharp blast on the whistle would frighten people too much.

Gavin Morrison

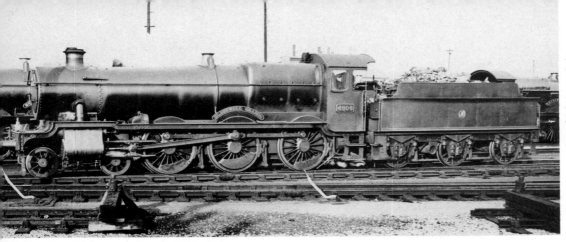

Plate 157 (left): No. 6806 *Blackwell Grange* stands on Bristol (Bath Road) Shed in its original livery, on 5th March 1938, with a 3,500 gallon Churchward tender, and with a short copper-capped chimney. Note the fire iron casing along the bottom of the firebox.

J. P. Wilson

The 6800 class 4-6-0 'Granges'

The 'Granges' were the result of the withdrawal of eighty 4300 class Moguls, although in fact only the wheels and motion were used. The locomotives had the same route availability as the 'Halls', and so were, in fact, more restricted than the Moguls. The coupled wheel diameter was 5ft. 8in., which was slightly smaller than the 'Halls'. The first four engines were initially fitted with a plain cast-iron chimney. The locomotives were used throughout the GWR system, on similar duties to the 'Halls'.

Plate 158 (below): Fresh from overhaul at Swindon Works in June 1959 is No. 6811 *Cranbourne Grange* in fully lined out Brunswick green livery, and still attached to one of the small 3,500 gallon tenders. The locomotive is fitted with a narrow chimney.

Gavin Morrison

Plate 159 (right): On 16th July 1964, No. 6871 *Bourton Grange* takes the centre road at Leamington Station at the head of a coke train. The locomotive is obviously recently ex-works and has the 4,000 gallon tender attached. It also carries a Midland Region shed-plate (2B).

J. R. P. Hunt

Plate 160 (below): A superb study of No. 6842 *Nunhold Grange* making a spirited ascent of Hatton Bank with a 'down' express on 27th September 1964.

J. R. P. Hunt

Plate 161 (left): Worcester-allocated No. 6851 *Hurst Grange* is seen re-starting a 'down' express for Chester at Shrewsbury on 9th August 1956.
B. Morrison

Plate 162 (below): An extremely dirty member of the class, No. 6868 *Penrhos Grange*, is seen at Eastleigh Station on 12th September 1964, as it pauses with a rake of Southern stock on a York to Bournemouth express. Great Western locomotives used to work through to Bournemouth, normally being attached to the trains at Banbury or Oxford.
Gavin Morrison

Plate 163 (right): An extraordinary working occurred on 15th August 1964, when No. 6858 *Woolston Grange*, working the Poole to Bradford /Leeds train, and which would normally have come off at Leicester or Nottingham, managed, due to an oversight by control, to reach Huddersfield. As can be seen from the cylinder casing, it hit the platform edge at Berry Brow, between Penistone and Huddersfield. The photographer was able to grab a quick picture of it on Hillhouse Shed, Huddersfield, before an astonished foreman ejected him from the premises and placed the locomotive well out of sight inside the shed, where it remained for two weeks before being towed to Crewe as an out of gauge load.

Gavin Morrison

Plate 164 (centre): No. 6831 *Bearley Grange* is pictured on 23rd July 1961, in Swindon Works yard with the preserved 'Dean Goods' and *Lode Star*, and fitted with a 4,000 gallon tender in fully lined out green livery.

W. Potter, D. Cobbe Collection

Plate 165 (bottom): No. 6831, as it ended its career, dumped without name and number plates, and with a 3,500 gallon tender at Oxley Depot some four years later, in October 1965.

Gavin Morrison

The 7800 class 4-6-0 'Manors'

The first of the class appeared in January 1938, twenty locomotives being built in the initial batch. Like the 'Granges', the first batch of 'Manors' utilised the wheels and motion from withdrawn 4300 class Moguls. It is ironic that these locomotives were the last built by Collett and, in their original form, were the least successful. A new standard boiler No. 24 was used and this proved to be a poor steam producer, and it was not until 1951 that tests with improved draughting were carried out with No. 7818 *Granville Manor* that the problems were solved. The locomotives were attached to 3,500 gallon Churchward tenders, although some acquired the 'intermediate' 3,500 gallon type. The 17 ton axle loading gave them an extensive route availability, which is no doubt why so many have been preserved. The class ultimately received fully lined Brunswick green livery from British Railways.

Plate 166 (left): No. 7814 *Fringford Manor*, built in January 1939, and recently ex-Swindon Works when this picture was taken on 8th September 1962, at Derry Ormond on the Carmarthen to Aberystwyth line.

Gavin Morrison

Plate 167 (below): No. 7802 *Bradley Manor* on 'special' duties for the Stephenson Locomotive Society at Oswestry Station, when it headed the last train over the Whitchurch to Oswestry section of the ex-Cambrian Railways, on 17th January 1965.

Gavin Morrison

Plate 168 (right): For many years, especially during the 1950s and early 1960s, Aberystwyth Depot always seemed to make a special effort to keep an immaculate 'Manor' available for working the 'Cambrian Coast Express' to Shrewsbury. No. 7803 *Barcote Manor* was frequently chosen for this special attention along with Nos. 7802 and 7819. It is seen on shed at Aberystwyth with a London Midland Region (6F) shed-plate, and fitted with an 'intermediate' 3,500 gallon tender.

J. Livesey

Plate 169 (left): The 'down' 'Cambrian Coast Express' split at Dovey Junction releasing carriages for Pwllheli. The Aberystwyth section went forward behind the locomotive which had brought the train from Shrewsbury. The three coach train was easy work for No. 7803 *Barcote Manor*, on 30th May 1964, as it drifts into Borth Station.

Gavin Morrison

Plate 170 (below): After working the 'down' 'Cambrian Coast Express' on 30th May 1964, No. 7803 *Barcote Manor* simmers gently on Aberystwyth Shed.

Gavin Morrison

Plate 173 (above): On a very warm day in May 1964, a very dirty No. 7800 *Torquay Manor* approaches Talerdigg Summit, on the Cambrian main line, with a Gainsborough Model Railway Society's special, en route to Aberystwyth to visit the Vale of Rheidol narrow gauge railway.

Gavin Morrison

Plate 174 (above): Another of the well-kept Aberystwyth 'Manors', No. 7819 *Hinton Manor*, prepares to leave Shrewsbury with the 'down' 'Cambrian Coast Express' on 31st March 1964.

J. Livesey

Plate 175 (below): A portrait of No. 7812 *Erlestoke Manor*, which is now preserved on the Severn Valley Railway. The photograph was taken on 8th September 1962, outside Aberystwyth Station.

Gavin Morrison

Plate 171 (above left): The 'Manors' were regular performers on the Midland South and West joint line from Cheltenham to Southampton. The locomotives were based at Gloucester and sub-shedded to Cheltenham. Nos. 7808 and 7818 were used in the later 1950s and early 1960s and, on 22nd April 1962, No. 7808 *Cookham Manor* was on Eastleigh Shed. The locomotive is now preserved at Didcot.

Gavin Morrison

Plate 176 (right): Waiting to depart from Aberystwyth with an express for Manchester on 8th September 1962, is No. 7822 *Foxcote Manor*, which was one of the batch of ten built as late as December 1950.

Gavin Morrison

Plate 172 (left): An unusual setting for this picture of No. 7809 *Childrey Manor* as it passes Wye Valley Junction on 18th October 1958, en route to South Wales with a 'down' vans train.

S. Rickard

The Hawksworth Era
The 1000 class 4-6-0 'Counties'

F. W. Hawksworth was Chief Mechanical Engineer from July 1941 to 1946, and he is probably best known for the 'County' class. The 'County' design, when it appeared in August 1945, was not so different from Great Western traditions as had been rumoured. The main new features were the double blast-pipe and chimney, a non standard coupled wheel diameter of 6ft. 3in., and a high boiler pressure of 280lb. The power from the two cylinders was roughly equivalent to the four cylinders of a 'Castle', this causing considerable increase in hammer blow, which together with the weight of the coupled wheels of 19 tons 14 cwt. per axle, resulted in the class having speed restrictions on all routes other than where the 'Kings' were permitted. In the early days, all tended to be allocated to sheds covering the Paddington to Penzance, and Paddington to Wolverhampon routes. These restrictions were lifted to some degree, resulting in the class having a wider sphere of operation. The reason for the construction of the class in the first place is not entirely clear, as the work they carried out was generally inferior to the 'Castles', and it is significant that only thirty were built. The first locomotive, No. 1000, was the first to emerge from Swindon in Great Western green livery after World War II.

Plate 177 (above): The distinctive nameplate attached to No. 1000, after running without one for approximately one year.
B. Morrison

Plate 178 (below): No. 1000 *County of Middlesex* is seen in British Railways lined black livery, ready to leave Paddington with a 'down' express on 8th July 1952. This locomotive was the only one to be constructed with a copper-capped double chimney and, in this state, was a poor performer. After tests and alteration to draughting in 1954, the rest of the class, which had single chimneys, were altered to squat copper-capped chimneys, which ruined the appearance but improved the performance.
J. P. Wilson

Plate 179 (above): On a lovely summer's evening in August 1958, No. 1025 *County of Radnor* drifts into Stratford-upon-Avon with empty stock, which was to form a returning excursion to Manchester (London Road).

B. Morrison

Plate 180 (below): A superb portrait of No. 1015 *County of Gloucester*, straight out of Swindon Works after overhaul, and painted in British Railways lined black livery. It is seen in Reading Shed yard in 1949 and it appears that the works have forgotten to fix the front numberplate, hence the chalked number on the buffer beam. This locomotive ran for thirteen months before being named.

M. W. Earley

The 9400 class 0-6-0 Pannier Tanks

Further to a request for more 5700 class pannier tanks in 1947, the General Manager, Sir James Milne, insisted that a more modern-looking locomotive should be produced, and so Hawksworth designed the 9400 class, with the No. 10 taper boiler. The locomotives were not so easy to operate whilst shunting, as the controls were not as accessible as in the 5700 panniers. They were also heavier than the 5700 class pannier tanks, and had to be restricted over some routes, but in spite of their disadvantages British Railways built a total of 210, the last ones appearing as late as 1956, which gave them very short lives indeed. Only the first ten were built at Swindon under the Great Western in 1947, the rest being constructed by R. Stephenson, Bagnall & Co., and the Yorkshire Engine Company. Many were withdrawn with less than ten years of service and some must have been in good mechanical order, so it is rather surprising that only two members of the class have been preserved.

Plate 189 (above): Swindon-built No. 9401 is seen leaving Stratford-upon-Avon with a stopping train to Worcester on 14th December 1957. This locomotive was loaned to the Eastern Region for trials in 1957, and was used at Temple Mills Yards, London.

R. C. Riley

Plate 190 (right): One of the Bagnall-built locomotives, No. 8422, is pictured on shunting duties at Swindon Junction Station on 15th October 1950. Fifty engines were constructed by this company between 1949 and 1954.

L. Elsey

The 1500 class 0-6-0 Pannier Tanks

Only ten of these heavy duty shunting pannier tanks were produced in 1949 at Swindon. Hawksworth departed from the normal Great Western tradition for panniers, in that the 1500 class was designed with outside cylinders and Walschaerts valve gear. The short wheelbase of 12ft. 10in. allowed them to negotiate very sharp curves, but precluded them from being used at speed on the main line, as they became unsteady. They will be be remembered for their duties in dealing with empty carriage stock at Paddington. Some members of the class were sold to the National Coal Board after withdrawal from British Railways, and No. 1501 was rescued for preservation from this source.

Plate 191 (below):   One of the three members of the class to receive the lined British Railways black livery was No. 1503. It is seen on 3rd October 1959, carrying out empty carriage stock duties at Westbourne Park, near Paddington.

R. C. Riley

The 1600 class 0-6-0 Pannier Tanks

This was another class of locomotive which was built too late by British Railways to have a useful working life. No. 1600 did not appear until 1949, and was the final design by Hawksworth. In spite of their late construction, seventy members of the class had been built by 1955. They were designed to be able to work all the lines, especially mineral branches, where the larger panniers were prohibited

Plate 192 (left): No. 1669, the last of the class to be built, in May 1955, was the last Great Western-designed locomotive to be built at Swindon, thus bringing to an end many Swindon traditions. After this date only BR Standard designs were constructed. It is pictured on 9th September 1962 at Whitland.

Gavin Morrison

The Absorbed Companies
The Barry Railway

Plate 193 (below): The Barry Railway Company came into existence in 1884, and started operation in 1888. The prime traffic, as with nearly all South Wales lines, was coal, and in 1913 it carried no less than eleven million tons. There were 65 route miles and 148 locomotives which were absorbed into the GWR in 1922. Most were 0-6-2 tank locomotives, but there were ten 0-6-4Ts, seven 0-8-2Ts and four 0-8-0s, which were definitely non standard for the GWR. In this scene, photographed on 5th June 1938, a Hosgood Class B1 0-6-2T, built by Sharp, Stewart & Co., in the 1890s, stands at Radyr Junction.

J. G. Dewing

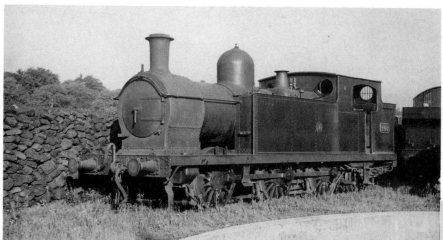

The Cambrian Railways

Plate 194 (below): A separate section is devoted to the Cambrian Railways Company in *Plates 214 to 229.* One of the 107 locomotives taken over by the GWR in 1922 was 0-6-0 No. 880. The class was built between 1894 and 1899, the locomotives being supplied by Neilson & Co., and Vulcan Foundry. No. 880 is pictured at Oswestry Depot on 14th September 1937.

J. G Dewing

The Alexandra (Newport & South Wales) Docks Railway

Plate 195 (below): The company was founded in 1865. A wide variety of locomotives, 39 in all, were absorbed by the GWR, one of which was this one, No. 680, which survived until 1948, outliving its sister engine by 22 years. It is seen on 14th September 1937 at Oswestry Shed.

J. G. Dewing

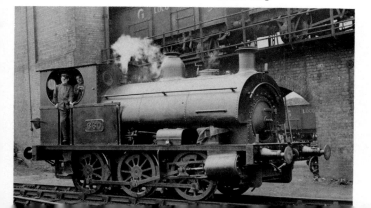

Plate 196 (below): Another class to last well into nationalisation from the Alexandra (Newport & South Wales) Docks Railway was the Hawthorn Leslie-built 2-6-2T. Only two locomotives were constructed in 1920, and No. 1205 is seen here at Cardiff (Canton) Shed on 23rd July 1955. It appears to be out of use and was in fact officially withdrawn the following year.

F. J. Bullock

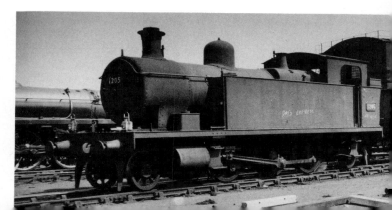

Plates 197 & 198: This was originally the Bute Docks Railway Company, which started as early as 1839 and was owned by the Second Marquis of Bute. It changed its name in 1897 to the Cardiff Railway Company. The GWR took over 36 locomotives in 1922. Most locomotives were either 0-6-0Ts or 0-6-2Ts, one of which was No. 681, an 0-6-0T, built in 1920 by Hudswell Clarke, which is pictured at Swindon on 24th April 1955. The railway also owned two Kitson-built 0-4-0 saddle tanks, Nos. 1338 and 1339. Constructed in 1898, No. 1338, shown here, is at Swansea East Dock on 9th September 1962, and lasted until 1963 when it was bought for preservation.

B. Morrison and Gavin Morrison

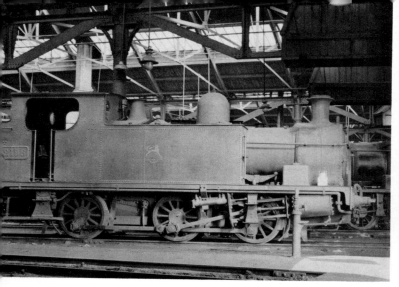

Plate 199 (above): No. 2198 was built in 1910 by Hudswell Clarke, and was in fact the only member of the class, although it was very similar to another 0-6-0T, built by the same company in 1909. Surprisingly, it lasted until 1959, and it is seen on 13th May 1956, inside Llanelly Shed.

B. Morrison

Plate 200 (above): No. 2176 was an Avonside saddle tank, constructed in 1907, and again was the only member of the class. It was originally named *Pembrey* but the nameplate was removed in 1927. In this picture it is out of use at Swindon Works dump, on 24th April 1955.

B. Morrison

The Burry Port & Gwendraeth Valley Railway

Plate 201 (right): The BP&GVR was only a small company which passed over fifteen locomotives to the GWR, all of which were 0-6-0Ts. The railway originated in 1865, being a development of a canal, harbour and tramway system, dating back as far as 1765. It was not until 1909 that the line handled any passenger traffic. Locomotive No. 2194, built by Avonside in 1903, is seen during her spell of duty with sister locomotive No. 2195 at Weymouth Docks, shunting coaches on 1st July 1935, a very wet day.

J. G. Dewing

Plate 202 (right): On 21st June 1955, lying outside Swindon Works cutting-up shop, is Hudswell Clarke 0-6-0T No. 2166. The class was built between 1909 and 1919. Seven of these locomotives were built, the first being withdrawn in 1929 and the last in 1956.

B. Morrison

Plate 220 (above): 'Dukedog' No. 3202 (later No. 9002) when less than three years old, is seen carrying out one of the duties for which the class was specifically built, namely passenger traffic on the Cambrian lines. It was photographed on 10th April 1939, climbing to Talerddig Summit with a local passenger train.

J. G. Dewing

Plate 221 (below): An Aberystwyth to Whitchurch train, with some vintage rolling stock, leaves Carno on 18th July 1938, headed by 'Dukedog' No. 3211 (later No. 9011).

J. G. Dewing

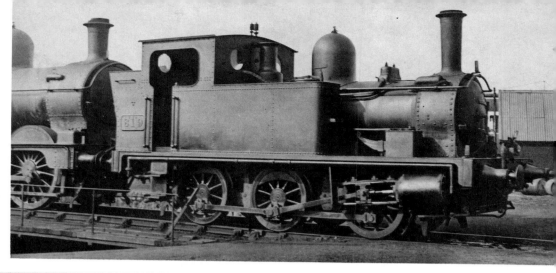

Plate 222 (right): This little Hunslet Engine Co. 0-6-0T, No. 819, built in 1903, had an interesting life. It was absorbed by the Cambrian Railways in 1904 from the Lambourne Valley Railway, and then into GWR stock in 1922. It was originally named *Eadweade*. The original Hunslet chimney was replaced by Swindon in 1938, and the locomotive is seen on 10th April 1939 at Moat Lane Junction. It was the only member of the class and was withdrawn in 1946.

J. G. Dewing

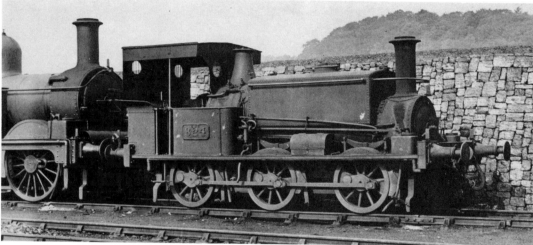

Plate 223 (left): On 14th September 1937, Oswestry Depot had Manning Wardle 0-6-0ST No. 824 on shed. This locomotive, built in 1865 and acquired by the Cambrian Railways from the Mawddwy Railway in 1911, survived until 1940.

J. G. Dewing

Plate 224 (below): This delightful little 2-4-0T tank engine, No. 1308 *Lady Margaret,* was built in 1902 and survived until 1948. This scene was photographed on 14th September 1937, at Oswestry Station.

J. G. Dewing

Plate 226 (right): Three of these Sharp, Stewart 2-4-0Ts were built for the Cambrian Railways in 1866. They were all rebuilt at Swindon in 1922, and in 1927, No. 1192 went to the Hemyock branch and was scrapped in 1929. The other two lasted until 1948 at Oswestry, and both achieved a remarkable million miles in service. No. 1196 is pictured at Oswestry on the Tanat Valley Light Railway train to Llangynog on 11th September 1935.

J. G. Dewing

Plate 227 (below): A 'Dukedog' and 'Duke' are pictured double-heading near Commins Coch on 18th July 1938, with the 1p.m. Aberystwyth to Paddington express. 'Dukedog' No. 3204 (later No. 9004) is piloting 'Duke' No. 3268 *Chough* (note the variation in chimneys).

J. G. Dewing

Plate 228 (right): The 2.05p.m. Whitchurch to Aberystwyth train is seen near Carno headed by 'Dukedog' No. 3213 (later No. 9013) on 18th July 1938. These rather old-fashioned looking locomotives do not look as if they were built as late as 1936 to 1939. They were extremely successful and operated over the Cambrian lines for over twenty years. Happily, No. 9017 is preserved.

J. G. Dewing

Plate 229 (below): A train for Shrewsbury is pictured shortly after leaving Welshpool, on 19th July 1938. It is headed by one of the 156 'Bulldog' class locomotives, No. 3437, which was one of the few members of the class never to carry a name. Parts from 29 of these locomotives were used in the construction of the 'Dukedogs'.

J. G. Dewing

The Dean Designs after the Grouping

Plate 230 (left):   One of the 156 3300 'Bulldog' class double-framed locomotives, No. 3405 *Empire of India*, waits at Wolverhampton (Low Level) on 2nd June 1936. Many members of the class had their names removed in the 1920s and early 1930s. They were built between 1889 and 1910, the last one being withdrawn in 1951.

J. P. Wilson

Plate 231 (right):   Another member of the 'Bulldog' class, No. 3378 *River Tawe*, is pictured at Bristol on 5th June 1938. The name was removed in 1939.

J. P. Wilson

Plate 232 (left):   On 11th July 1925, No. 3715 *City of Hereford*, a member of the famous 3700 'City' class, passes Chipping Campden with an 'up' Worcester to Paddington express. There were twenty locomotives in the class, and No. 3717 *City of Truro* was preserved, after withdrawal in 1931, after its historic run down Wellington Bank in 1904, when a speed of 102.3m.p.h. was claimed.

H. G. W. Household

Plate 233 (right):   A 3252 'Duke of Cornwall' class locomotive, No. 3290 *Severn* is seen, on 7th April 1936, at Oswestry. Sixty of these fine locomotives were built between 1895 and 1899, the last to be withdrawn being as late as 1951.

J. G. Dewing

Plate 234 (right): A 4120 'Atbara' class locomotive, No. 4133 *Roberts*, hauls a Cardiff to Gloucester slow passenger train in October 1924. The class consisted of thirty locomotives, all being withdrawn by 1931 after only twenty years of service.

H. G. W. Household

Plate 235 (left): No. 4161 *Hyacianth* hauls a Wolverhampton to Weston-super-Mare train near Hatherley Junction, Cheltenham, on 9th July 1924. At one time the name carried an 'E' at the end (*Hyacianthe*).

H. G. W. Household

Plate 236 (right): The Dean 3521 class had an interesting career. No. 3525, seen in this view, started as an 0-4-2T in 1887, was converted to an 0-4-4T in 1892, and was rebuilt to a 4-4-0 in March 1901. The locomotive, looking rather dirty for the period, is seen near Charlton Kings, Cheltenham, on 5th July 1924, with through coaches from Paddington, which it had hauled from Kingham.

H. G. W. Household

Plate 237 (left): No. 3204, one of the 'Stella' 3201 class 2-4-0s, simmers at Wellington Shed on 28th April 1922. The last of these Dean 2-4-0s was withdrawn in October 1933.

H. G. W. Household

Plate 238 (right): One of the eighty one 2600 class 2-6-0 'Aberdares', No. 2629, heads a freight from Bordesley near Hatherley Junction, Cheltenham, on 24th September 1924.

H. G. W. Household

Plate 239 (below): Two hundred and sixty of the 2301 class 'Dean Goods' 0-6-0s were built between 1883 and 1899. No less than 54 passed into British Railways' ownership, the last one being withdrawn in 1957. Many saw service overseas in both world wars. Most returned from World War I, but many were lost during World War II in France. No. 2566 is seen leaving Didcot on 10th June 1939, with a train for the Didcot, Newbury & Southampton line.

J. G. Dewing

Plate 240 (right): No. 2104, one of the 140 class 2021 0-6-0PTs, is seen on 5th August 1947 at Tyseley Shed, Birmingham. Note the bell fitted above the boiler; this was a feature of the locomotives allocated to Birkenhead for working in the docks. The locomotive was originally built with a domeless boiler, but No. 2104 had since acquired a standard domed version.
J. P. Wilson

Plate 241 (left): A class 455 'Metropolitan' tank, No. 3585, was on Oxford Depot on 17th June 1938. One hundred and forty were built between 1869 and 1899. This locomotive, at this date, was not fitted with condensing apparatus. The last one to be withdrawn was in 1949, which was, in fact, 51 years after the first withdrawal.
J. G. Dewing

Plate 242 (right): An 850 class saddle tank, No. 1925, stands on Didcot Depot on 28th September 1936. It was built in 1883, the class consisting of 170 locomotives, 43 passing into British Railways' ownership, and most being altered to pannier tanks during their careers.
J. G. Dewing

Plate 243 (below): A pannier conversion of the 850 class seen in *Plate 242.* No. 1902, converted in December 1927, is ready to leave Cirencester Town on 19th September 1937. The locomotive was withdrawn in 1943.
J. G. Dewing

Titled Trains

Plate 244 (left): An immaculate Worcester-based 'Castle', No. 7013 *Bristol Castle*, restarts the 'up' 'Cathedrals Express' from an out of course signal check at Port Meadow, on the approach to Oxford, on 6th July 1962. This locomotive was, in fact, the original No. 4082 *Windsor Castle* (see Plate 62).

R. Leslie

Plate 245 (below): Storm clouds seem to be brewing around the coast at Teignmouth as 'Castle' No. 5071 *Spitfire* blows off just at the right moment for the photographer, as it heads the 'down' 'Cornishman' along the sea wall on 19th July 1956. This locomotive was originally named *Clifford Castle* but altered in September 1940. The name *Clifford Castle* was ultimately carried by 'Castle' No. 5098.

R. C. Riley

Plate 246 (right): Nearly at its journey's end is the 'down' 'Devonian', seen leaving Teignmouth on 17th July 1958, headed by Newton Abbot 'Castle' No. 4083 *Abbotsbury Castle*. This train, often loaded to fourteen or fifteen coaches, started at Bradford (Forster Square) and travelled via Leeds, Birmingham (New Street), and Bristol (Temple Meads) to its destination at Paignton.

R. C. Riley

Plate 247 (below): The little girl on platform 3 at Paddington seems totally absorbed by the magnificent spectacle of immaculate Old Oak Common 'Castle' No. 7024 *Powis Castle*, ready to leave on the last steam-hauled 'down' 'Bristolian' on the morning of 12th June 1959.

J. D. Edwards

Plate 248 (right): The driver of single-sleeved chimney 'King', No. 6003 *King George IV*, appears to be rather anxious about something, after its arrival at Wolverhampton (Low Level) with the 'down' 'Inter-City' on 21st July 1954. The train was the 9a.m. from Paddington.

B. Morrison

Plate 249 (below): On 28th March 1959, the Pwllheli portion of the 'up' 'Cambrian Coast Express' runs along the banks of the Dovey Estuary, between Aberdovey and Dovey Junction, where it will be attached to the portion from Aberystwyth before heading for Shrewsbury with a 'Manor' class locomotive. Machynlleth Shed kept locomotives well groomed for this working, as is evident from the condition of 2-6-2T No. 5541 in the fully lined green livery.

Gavin Morrison

Plate 250 (right): The 'down' 'Torbay Express' heads rapidly along the level track as it approaches Twyford on 5th July 1951. The locomotive is Newton Abbot-based 'Castle' No. 5011 *Tintagel Castle.*

B. Morrison

Plate 251 (below): The 'up' 'Cambrian Coast Express', headed by an immaculate 'King', No. 6002 *King William IV*, approaches King's Sutton, just north of Aynho Junction, on 23rd June 1961.

R. Leslie

Focus on Paddington

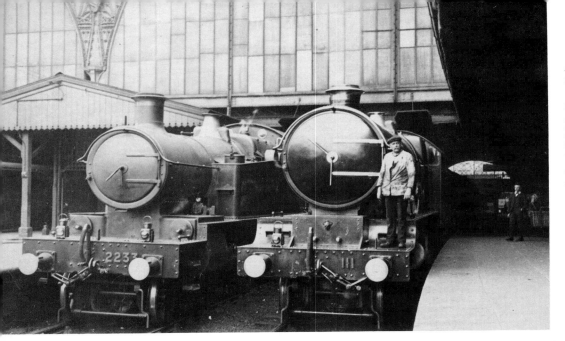

Plate 252 (left): The driver of the famous Great Western Pacific No. 111 *The Great Bear* poses on the running plate before leaving with an express for Bristol, whilst on the left, 'County' tank No. 2233 is ready to depart with a train from Paddington for the outer suburbs, a duty for which they were specifically designed.

OPC Collection

Plate 253 (below left): The name-board of the 'Cheltenham Spa Express' lies on the running plate of 'Castle' No. 7000 *Viscount Portal*, after its arrival at platform 9, Paddington, whilst on platform 10, double chimney 'Castle' No. 5061 *Earl of Birkenhead* has arrived with the 'up' 'Capitals United Express', in April 1961.

J. B. Snell

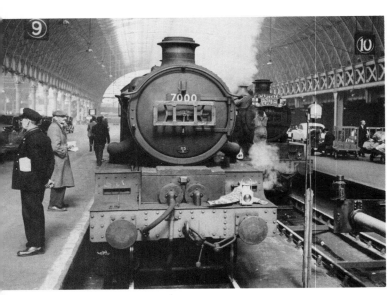

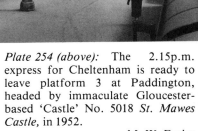

Plate 254 (above): The 2.15p.m. express for Cheltenham is ready to leave platform 3 at Paddington, headed by immaculate Gloucester-based 'Castle' No. 5018 *St. Mawes Castle,* in 1952.

M. W. Earley

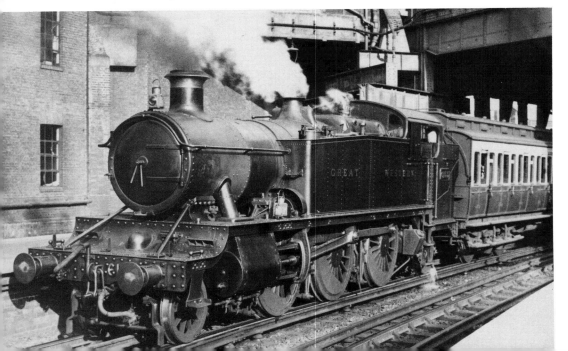

Plate 255 (left): The 6100 class 2-6-2Ts were specifically built in the early 1930s for the London suburban services, and continued on these duties until ousted by diesel multiple units in the 1960s. A member of the class awaits departure from Paddington in October 1933.

J. G. Dewing

Plate 256 (right): One of the eleven condensing 0-6-0 pannier tanks, No. 9703, performs empty carriage shunting duties at Paddington on 4th July 1959. These locomotives were always shedded at Old Oak Common Depot for their duties on the Metropolitan lines.

C. R. L. Coles

Plate 257 (below): A fine picture of No. 1027 *County of Stafford*, making a spirited departure from Paddington with a 'down' express for Bristol (Temple Meads) on 27th August 1960. The locomotive is fitted with the ugly double chimney and new double blastpipe, which did little for the appearance but gave an improvement in performance and efficiency.

R. C. Riley

Focus on Bristol

Plate 258 (left): A bird's-eye view of No. 6832 *Brockton Grange* leaving Bristol (Temple Meads) on 2nd June 1962, with a train for Weston-super-Mare.

John Whiteley

Plate 259 (below): An immaculate 'Castle' has been turned out for the last steam-hauled 'up' 'Bristolian' on 12th June 1959. No. 5085 *Evesham Abbey* had been given the honour, and judging by the number of people on the platform, it looks like being a full train.

J. D. Edwards

Plate 260 (above): A 'Castle' class locomotive, No. 5071 *Spit-fire*, fitted with a double chimney, pulls into Bristol (Temple Meads) at the head of an 'up' Liverpool to Plymouth express on 2nd June 1963.

John Whiteley

Plate 261 (below): An interesting view showing a train to Portishead passing beneath Clifton Suspension Bridge over the Avon Gorge, headed by a Class 4500 2-6-2T on 5th June 1938.

J. P. Wilson

Plate 262 (above): On 13th May 1952, two immaculate Cardiff (Canton) 'Castles', Nos. 5007 *Rougemont Castle* and 4094 *Dynevor Castle*, prepare to change over on the 'up' 'Red Dragon' express to Paddington, at Cardiff (General) Station. Note the two different types of chimneys fitted to the locomotives.

R. C. Riley

Plate 263 (below): A picture which was typical of the Welsh Valleys for many years shows a Cameron Taff Vale Railway A class 0-6-2T, No. 312, which was rebuilt with a Swindon taper boiler in 1928, entering Pontypridd on 13th May 1952, with 'British Railways' painted on the tank sides.

R. C. Riley

Plate 264 (right): No. 7828 *Odney Manor* was only seventeen months old when this picture was taken on 15th May 1952. It is on an 'up' freight passing Cardiff (Canton) Depot. The locomotive is in the lined black British Railways livery, and had been parted from the normal standard Churchward 3,500 gallon tender, and connected to an 'intermediate' 3,500 gallon type with long side fenders.

R. C. Riley

Plate 265 (left): A recently ex-works 2-8-2T No. 7240, heads a rake of empty coal wagons from Radyr on 12th May 1952, and is pictured passing Penrhos Junction on its journey up the valley.

R. C. Riley

Plate 266 (right): Ex-Rhymney Railway Hurry Riches A class 0-6-2T No. 59, built in 1909, is seen shortly after an overhaul at Caerphilly Works, working a freight near Heath Junction, north of Cardiff on the Rhymney line, in 1952.

R. C. Riley

Freight around the Great Western Lines

Plate 267 (above): One of the 260 Dean 2301 class locomotives, No. 2395, is seen on 4th May 1940, heading an 'up' goods near Gerrards Cross on the Great Western & Great Central Joint line. Note the immaculate state of the cutting sides, compared with the 1980s.

J. G. Dewing

Plate 268 (below): One of the Class 3000 Robinson (Great Central Railway) 2-8-0s, purchased by the GWR from the Railway Operating Division of the Royal Engineers (ROD), is seen in British Railways livery passing Kennington Junction, Oxford, with an 'up' freight, on 30th August 1953. Eighty two of these locomotives were purchased by the GWR, the last one working until 1958.

L. Elsey

Plate 269 (above): Most 4200 class 2-8-0Ts were based in South Wales, but a few were allocated to St. Blazey Shed in Cornwall for the china clay traffic. No. 4247 heads empty china clay wagons near Par on 8th July 1955.

R. C. Riley

Plate 270 (below): The wartime dirt is well and truly encrusted on 'Saint' class locomotive No. 2906 *Lady of Lynn*, as it heads a train of milk empties past Reading (West) Junction in 1943. Note the ARP curtain over the cab roof, and the signals which are positively black with grime.

M. W. Earley

Plate 271 (left): Ex-Swansea Harbour Trust 0-4-0ST No. 1142 (see Plate 205) shunts at Clee Hill Summit before leaving for Bitterly with chippings from Titterstone Quarry on 15th August 1958.

B. Morrison

Plate 272 (below): It was an unusual sight, in 1955, to see a Class 6100 2-6-2T on freight. No. 6101 is seen on a 'down' goods from Slough to Reading (West) Junction, in Sonning Cutting, in April 1955.

M. W. Earley

Plate 273 (right): No. 5818, which was one of the twenty locomotives of the 4800 class 0-4-2Ts built without auto-train gear and ATC apparatus, shunts at Abingdon on 28th July 1959. The locomotive was built in 1933, which is much later than its appearance would suggest.

J. D. Edwards

Plate 274 (below): No. 2894 was one of the 2-8-0s of the 2800 class fitted with side window cabs. It is on an 'H' class freight crossing over from the goods lines behind Reading Station to the 'up' main line at East Main box in 1949. This batch of the class was usually known as the 2884s.

M. W. Earley

Plate 275 (above): Displaced from passenger duties by diesel multiple units, 6100 class 2-6-2T No. 6136 of Slough leaves Hinksey Yard, south of Oxford, with an 'up' freight on 4th March 1960.

J. D. Edwards

Plate 276 (above): An Oxford-based 7200 class, No. 7218, leaves Hinksey Yard, Oxford, with a freight from Morris Cowley on 4th March 1960. This locomotive was a rebuild of 4200 class 2-8-0T No. 5293, which was one of the batch of twenty which was stored when originally built in October 1930 until being rebuilt in November 1934.

J. D. Edwards

Plate 277 (right): A 4300 class Mogul, No. 6326, passes Kennington Junction, Oxford, with a special train of BMC products for the Scottish Motor Show on 6th November 1959.

J. D. Edwards

Plate 278 (below): A recent ex-works 2-8-0 of the 2884 class, built as late as 1939, is seen at Hinksey South with a 'down' freight for Oxford on 15th August 1959.

J. D. Edwards

Double-Heading around the Great Western

Plate 279 (right): Llangollen Station is the setting for this picture of 0-6-0PT No. 9669, helping out an unidentified 'Manor' on a summer Saturdays only train from Butlin's, on the Cambrian Coast, for Manchester. It was photographed in August 1954, before most of the 'Manor' class had been given the improved draughting.

J. B. Snell

Plate 280 (below): On the last day of service on the Cardigan branch, an unusual double-heading occurred using two Class 4500 2-6-2Ts, Nos. 4569 and 4557, pictured leaving Boncath on 8th September 1962.

Gavin Morrison

Plate 281 (left): One of the early batch of 'Halls', No. 4915 *Condover Hall*, pilots No. 1012 *County of Denbigh* away from Newton Abbot, past Aller Junction, prior to the formidable climb to Dainton Summit on 16th July 1955. Both locomotives are running in the British Railways lined black livery.

L. Elsey

Plate 282 (right): Assistance is given to 'Castle' class locomotive No. 5049 *Earl of Plymouth* by 'Grange' No. 6873 *Caradoc Grange* up Wrangaton Bank, west of Brent, on 21st June 1958.

L. Elsey

Plate 283 (below): A summer Saturdays only train from Ilfracombe to Wolverhampton climbs Wilmcote Bank, on 22nd August 1964, headed by an unidentified 'Hall' and Mogul No. 6364. The Mogul would have been attached at Stratford-upon-Avon.

J. R. P. Hunt

Plate 284 (right): Power at the head of this 'down' express on Rattery Bank is being provided by No. 6907 *Davenham Hall* and No. 6003 *King George IV* on 20th August 1949. Note the absence of the crest on the tender of No. 6907, which is in lined black livery.

J. G. Dewing

Plate 285 (left): On 20th August 1949, No. 6907 *Davenham Hall* was rostered for piloting duties over the South Devon banks. It is pictured assisting No. 6022 *King Edward III* with an 'up' express on Hemerdon Bank.

J. G. Dewing

Plate 286 (right): A 4300 class Mogul, No. 7310, pilots 2251 class 0-6-0 No. 2209 away from Ruabon with a 'down' Barmouth express on 9th August 1956.

B. Morrison

Plate 287 (above): On 6th July 1957, a heavy 'up' summer Saturdays extra needs double-heading on the easier gradients, east of Exeter. No. 5999 *Wollaton Hall* is giving assistance to No. 6830 *Buckenhill Grange* as the train passes Stoke Cannon, which was the junction for the Exe Valley line to Tiverton. *R. C. Riley*

Plate 288 (below): The external state of these locomotives is not what one would have expected for such a prestigious train as the 'down' 'Cornish Riviera Express'. On summer Saturdays, in the mid-1950s, the 'King' class locomotive was detached at Newton Abbot as the train ran fast to Truro and 'Kings' were banned west of Plymouth. No. 6855 *Saighton Grange* and 'Modified Hall' No. 6988 *Swithland Hall* blast their way past Stoneycombe Quarry, on the 1 in 46 section of the climb to Dainton Summit, on 19th July 1958. *R. C. Riley*

Plate 289 (above): The Great Western introduced diesel railcars in 1934. There were two basic designs as shown on this page. Nos. 1-16 were like No. 4, seen here at Swindon on 18th March 1960. This railcar, together with Nos. 2 and 3, had buffet facilities, and was used between Birmingham and Cardiff. Happily No. 4 has been preserved; the bodywork was by Park Royal Ltd. and the builder was AEC.

J. D. Edwards

Plate 290 (below): On 19th April 1958, No. W21W waits in the bay platform at Slough with the Windsor branch service. It was one of the batch of twenty built between 1940 and 1942. These units had AEC engines and were constructed at Swindon. They were fitted with standard buffers and drawgear for hauling up to 60 tons. A speed of 40m.p.h. was the maximum for No. W21W. No. 17 and 34 were parcels cars and Nos. 35 to 38 were twin units.

J. D. Edwards

Plate 291 (above): One of the two 2ft. 6in. gauge Beyer Peacock 0-6-0Ts, built in 1902, is No. 822 *The Earl*, seen without its nameplate. It has just arrived at Welshpool with a freight on 10th August 1956, which was the year that the line was closed by British Railways.

B. Morrison

Plate 292 (above): The other locomotive on the line was numbered 823 by the GWR, and named *Countess*. It is pictured resplendent in its GWR livery on 12th September 1935.

J. G. Dewing

The Narrow Gauge

The Welshpool & Llanfair Railway

Plate 293 (left): The line opened in 1903 and passenger services lasted until 1931, but the freight operation continued until 1956. This delightful photograph shows No. 822 with its nameplate *The Earl* in place, on a freight near Welshpool in March 1941.

J. G. Dewing

Plate 294 (right): The end came for the line in 1956, and the future for the locomotives looked bleak. Instead of being cut up they were stored in Oswestry Works until 1961/2, when they were sold to The Welshpool & Llanfair Light Railway Preservation Society. The two locomotives are pictured inside the works on 21st June 1958.

Gavin Morrison

Plate 295 (right): On 30th May 1964, the Vale of Rheidol Railway had a busy day, as the Gainsborough Model Railway Society arrived with a nine coach special at Aberystwyth for a trip on the line. Locomotives No. 8 *Llywelyn* and No. 9 *Prince of Wales* were rostered, both, at this time, running in the smart lined Brunswick green livery of British Railways. Note the 6F shed plate on No. 8, showing that the line was now under the control of the Midland Region of British Railways.

Gavin Morrison

The Vale of Rheidol Railway

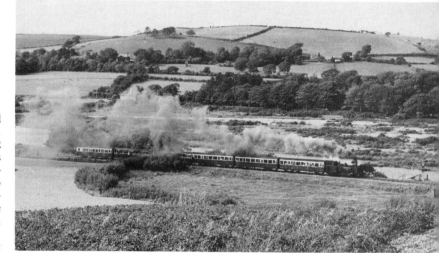

Plate 296 (right): The line was opened in 1902 and Davies & Metcalf built two 2-6-2Ts of 1ft. 11½in. gauge, these being numbered 1 and 2, becoming 1212 and 1213. It is sometimes overlooked that the line has had four locomotives built for it, the two already mentioned plus two more built by Swindon in 1923. No 1212 was withdrawn in 1932, but No. 1213, which became No. 9 in 1946, is seen here, bearing the name *Prince of Wales*, en route to Devil's Bridge on 8th September 1962.

Gavin Morrison

Plate 297 (right): No. 9 *Prince of Wales* is seen again on 8th September 1962, running round the coaching stock at Devil's Bridge. Happily, British Railways have continued to run this spectacular line, but the liveries of locomotives and stock have seen many changes. Other major changes to the line have been the alteration of the departure point, bringing it into Aberystwyth's BR station, and the closing of the old shed. The locomotives now use the former standard gauge depot.

G. W. Morrison

LEAMINGTON

Plate 303 (above): The train arrangements board at Leamington, on 9th May 1965, captures the atmosphere of the steam shed signing-on area.   *J. R. P. Hunt*

Plate 304 (above): A 2-6-2T, No. 4178, simmers gently on Leamington Shed, on 29th March 1964, while Nos. 4133 and 4151 appear to be not in steam.   *J. R. P. Hunt*

Plate 305 (below): On a Sunday in September 1962, two of Carmarthen's 'Castles' are seen on the depot waiting to be steamed for the following week's duties. They are No. 4081 *Warwick Castle* and No. 5087 *Tintern Abbey*.

Gavin Morrison

CARMARTHEN

WORCESTER WORKS

Plate 306 (right): An interesting picture, taken in Worcester Works on 18th April 1964. The locomotives from the rear are No. 5054 *Earl of Ducie*, No. 4920 *Dumbleton Hall*, now preserved on the Dart Valley Railway and undergoing restoration, and No. 6873 *Caradoc Grange*. By this time, it is doubtful if some of the locomotives ever re-entered traffic.

J. R. P. Hunt

Plate 307 (below): Lined up at Cardiff (Canton) Depot on 2nd June 1962, are No. 4080 *Powderham Castle*, No. 6010 *King Charles I*, being prepared for a train to Shrewsbury, No. 7913 *Little Wyrley Hall* and 2-8-0 No. 3860. Only a few 'Kings' were allocated to Cardiff (Canton) and then only for a short time around 1961/2. No. 6010, and others, were withdrawn during June 1962.

Gavin Morrison

CARDIFF (CANTON)

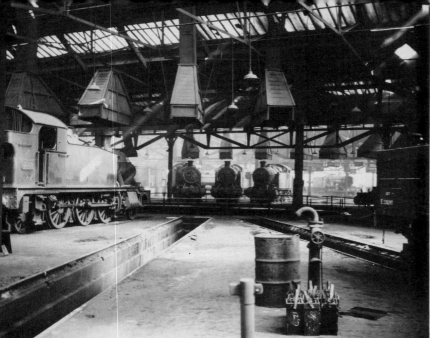

LLANELLY

Plate 308 (left): On 12th August 1963, Llanelly Depot does not seem to be very full. Present on this occasion are a 'Castle' in the background, a group of 2-8-0Ts, and one of the small 2-6-2Ts of the 4575 class, No. 5554.

J. R. P. Hunt

SWINDON

Plate 309 (below): Some of the finest roundhouse sheds in the country were to be found on the Great Western, with Swindon being one of the most impressive, as it could be relied upon to produce fine line-ups. On 2nd September 1956, an unidentified 'Modified Hall' was present with No. 5000 *Launceston Castle*, No. 5009 *Shrewsbury Castle*, No. 6023 *King Edward II*, not long before being fitted with the double chimney, and 2-8-0 No. 3836.

Gavin Morrison

Great Western Miscellany

Plate 310 (right): No. 102 *La France* was the first of the three 'De Glehn' Compound Atlantic locomotives, which G. J. Churchward ordered from the Société Alsacienne des Constructions Méchaniques in 1903. The locomotive was assembled at Swindon, and it was an impressive machine. It was rebuilt with a Swindon taper boiler in 1916, and remained in traffic until 1926.

OPC Collection

Plate 311 (left): No. 1364 was one of the five Churchward-built 0-6-0Ts of the 1361 class built in 1910. It is pictured in ex-works condition at Plymouth Docks on 12th July 1955. The very short wheelbase allowed the class to operate the sharp curves around the docks. They were, in fact, of a non-standard GWR design by Holcroft.

R. C. Riley

Plate 312 (right): One of the nine Midland & South Western Junction Railway Tyrrell 4-4-0s, No. 1126, built between 1905 and 1914, is seen at Worcester about 1937. This locomotive was rebuilt, along with five others in the class, with Swindon taper boilers, during the period from 1924 to 1929.

J. G. Dewing

Plate 313 (above): Looking very smart in the British Railways lined green livery is 5100 class 2-6-2T No. 4111, lined up at the coaling stage at Tyseley on 16th June 1957.

Gavin Morrison

Plate 314 (above): A 'Saint' class 4-6-0, No. 2933 *Bibury Court*, performs mundane duties whilst working out its last few months. It prepares to leave Shrewsbury with the 4.50p.m. train to Gobowen on 28th August 1952.

B. Morrison

Plate 315 (left): 'Modified Hall' No. 7924 *Thornycroft Hall* stands on Westbury Depot on 25th February 1962. The locomotive was built as late as September 1950.

Gavin Morrison

Plate 316 (below): The first of the 1923 batch of the 4200 class 2-8-0Ts was No. 5205, photographed on Gloucester Shed on 20th August 1964. This was the first locomotive of the class to be built with outside steam pipes and the increased cylinder diameter of 19in.

Gavin Morrison

Plate 317 (below): Seen taking water at its home depot of Old Oak Common on 5th May 1956, is 'King' No. 6028 *King George VI*. This locomotive was originaly named *King Henry II* until January 1937. Built in July 1930, and withdrawn November 1962, No. 6028 covered 1,663,271 miles.

R. C. Riley

Plate 318 (right): Together at Southall Shed, on 14th October 1962, are No. 7923 *Speke Hall* and 6100 class 2-6-2T No. 6133. Both locomotives look quite well-kept considering steam was rapidly being run down in this area at the time.

Gavin Morrison

Plate 319 (left): 'Grange' class locomotive, No. 6824 *Ashley Grange*, makes a fine sight as it pulls away from Oxford on 13th July 1963, with the 'down' 5.15p.m. Paddington to Worcester express. This train was formerly the 'down' 'Cathedrals Express'.

R. Leslie

Plate 320 (right): The end has come for 'County' Class No. 1014 *County of Glamorgan*, as it lies cold and lifeless at the back of Swindon waiting to be cut up. Note the wooden numberplates and, presumably, the nameplate as well, as it was the only locomotive to have the name left on it in the dump on 26th April 1964.

Gavin Morrison

Plate 322 (below): Carmarthen-based 'Castle' No. 5054 *Earl of Ducie* has just returned from its last overhaul at Swindon, and is seen at its home depot on 9th September 1962, looking immaculate and well-loaded with coal. This locomotive worked the Bristol to Paddington leg of the famous high speed railtour to Plymouth on 9th May 1964, achieving a speed well into the upper nineties.
Gavin Morrison